CREATIVE CARING:

THE VITA-LIVING STORY

RENÉE WALLACE

Order this book online at www.trafford.com
or email orders@trafford.com

Most Trafford titles are also available at major online book retailers.

Note for Librarians: A cataloguing record for this book is available from Library
and Archives Canada at www.collectionscanada.ca/amicus/index-e.html

Printed in Victoria, BC, Canada.

ISBN: 978-1-4269-2729-4 (sc)
ISBN: 978-1-4269-2363-0 (dj)

Library of Congress Control Number: 2010901387

*Our mission is to efficiently provide the world's finest, most comprehensive
book publishing service, enabling every author to experience success.
To find out how to publish your book, your way, and have it available
worldwide, visit us online at www.trafford.com*

Trafford rev. 1/29/2010

 www.trafford.com

North America & international
toll-free: 1 888 232 4444 (USA & Canada)
phone: 250 383 6864 ♦ fax: 812 355 4082

DEDICATION

To Ricky, even though he will never read these words, it
is my love for him that started me down this path.

And to the memory of Stan whose unfailing love and belief
in me sustained me during the writing of this book.

FOREWORD

T HE STORY of our family's journey from Ricky's birth until the 20th anniversary of Vita-Living parallels the movement of mental retardation services. As I wrote this book I was aware of how far we have come in recognizing the humanity in all of us and how far we still have to go.

There have been some notable accomplishments that have improved the lives of people diagnosed with Intellectual and Developmental Disabilities (IDD). One is the passage by Congress of the Individuals with Disability and Education Act in 1975 requiring school districts to provide public education to all children regardless of their disabilities. Another is the Supreme Court decision in 1985 that permitted six people living together with staff in a single home to be considered a family thereby meeting deed restriction requirements allowing small group homes to be operated in local communities. Additionally, at a later date the federal government created a program which permitted federal money to be used to assist people living at home with their families or living on their own but in need of some help. In many parts of the country people with IDD now have the opportunity to make choices as to where they will live and work. All of these changes were the result of much work on the part of organizations like the Arc and leaders like Senator Ted Kennedy .

Yet there is still much to be done. Many people with IDD are still living in large state institutions waiting for the chance to live more independently in the community.

All names have been changed to protect the privacy of the people in the book unless I received permission to use their correct name.

The glossary defines some of the diagnoses mentioned in the book. It is not meant to be all-inclusive.

TABLE OF CONTENTS

ACKNOWLEDGMENTS

First I want to thank my daughter Melanie for her suggestion that I write this memoir and thank my sons Andy and Lee for their support during this lengthy process. While attending a workshop on how to do it, I had the good fortune to meet author Nan Mooney. She agreed to help me as I attempted to describe how Vita-Living came to be. Without her, I don't know if I would have been able to persevere. She helped me tremendously forcing me to dig deep into my soul to relive the feelings of despair and anguish that I experienced when I first learned of my son's handicap.

I also want to thank Dr. Jesse David Wood, Dr. Carolyn Callahan and Geri Hooks who were kind enough to read the early chapters and encouraged me to continue.

Thanks to proofreader extraordinaire, Nini Boch, who was most helpful as I moved towards completion.

Most important are my thanks to all of the staff who worked with me (some going back to the earliest days in 1982) to provide the best care possible to our clients. And thanks to the clients and their families who moved into my life when they needed our specialized care. I think of all of them as extensions to my family and recognize that Vita-Living would not be the success it is without their contributions.

My acknowledgments would not be complete without thanking the board members of both the Vita-Living, Inc board and the Vita-Living Foundation board. Without their support there would not be a Vita-Living agency today.

PREFACE

T HE SMELLS and sights of Thanksgiving permeated the air. The house gleamed with polish on the mahogany tables and chairs, and all of the glass sparkled. The vacuumed Persian rugs lay like gems of ruby, emerald, and sapphires scattered on the terrazzo floors.

The turkey was roasting, mashed sweet potatoes, topped with snow-white marshmallows, were tanning and the green bean casserole smothered with onions was sitting in the warming oven.

Doorbells rang and horns honked, as the family gathered for the 1981 annual Thanksgiving get-together, but this year was different from the last 18. My son, Ricky, was here. At 23, Ricky was 5' 8" of restless energy. Eyes wandering, he ran up to everyone with a laugh, unable to speak and say how happy he was to see them, but letting all know through gestures and hand signs his joy at being back with his family. Ricky's only words are "Ma. Ma." Using gestures he told and retold one favorite story. His arms first stretched, as if he were waking up, then rubbed his eyes, and suggested he was washing his face and body and brushing his teeth. He waited for his listeners' smiles and smiled when he thought that they understood how great he was.

Ricky has been away at a school in New Jersey specializing in edu-cating children with intellectual and developmental disabilities (in his case, mental retardation). The family received Ricky with affection but also with some anxiety and apprehension. They had heard much about him while he attended the school but, other than his brothers and sister, had not seen him since he had left home.

I announced that dinner was served and everyone started toward the dining room except Ricky. He shook his head from side to side to indicate "no," made the sign for "eat," and pointed to the television. Stan, his father, told him that the TV would be turned off and he was to come to the table. In a flash Ricky threw himself down kicking and screaming, knocked over a table, and threw a chair. Stan and Ricky's brother, Andy, immediately moved to subdue him and managed to restrain him. Ricky sobbed convulsively, his shoulders shook, and tears cascaded down his bearded face until he was released. He ran to me and I embraced him, my tears mixing with his.

As he started to calm down, I thought back to the time when he was five, and because no public school or day program in Detroit would have him, we had found a residential school in New Jersey where we hoped he would receive the education he could not when living at home. Leaving my darling little boy with strangers and hearing him call "Ma, Ma, Ma, Ma" as he ran after our car felt as though something was tearing at my soul. I truly understand what people mean when they talk about a broken heart. The pain may dull but it never ends, even after 18 years.

As Ricky returned to the TV, the rest of the family who seemed to have lost their appetites, ate some of the dinner, and then turned to card playing, watching the ball game, or conversation. Ricky's sister, Melanie, motioned me to follow her into my bedroom. We faced each other on the bed. "We are all worried about what will happen if Dad and you can no longer care for Ricky," she said.

My immediate reaction was to deny that anything would happen to us for a long time, but on seeing the look in her eyes, I apologized and recognized her legitimate concern. "You and your brothers will decide where he will go and how he will be cared for," I told her.

"STOP," she shouted. "We don't know what you want for him. You have over 20 years of experience working with people like Ricky. What about you starting something that will provide care for him and other people like him?" she asked.

My skin paled and I had trouble catching my breath. "You have no idea what you are asking," I said.

"Mom, I know exactly what I'm asking," Melanie said. "Think about it and talk to Dad."

It was a clear, starlit night as Stan and I sat at our kitchen table after everyone had left and Ricky was asleep. I told him of my conversation with Melanie. At first he stared at me as if I had just landed from

Mars. "Of course, you told her that it would be impossible, didn't you? he asked.

"No, I told her I would talk to you about it." I said softly.

"I know you. You are considering it," he said.

"Well I have the money Aunt Mina left me, and I have been working with people like Ricky for 20 years," I said.

"Are you willing to use your inheritance in such a risky venture?" He asked. "We're not kids anymore. You are 57, you know."

I could feel my anger rising. "Yes, I think it could work, and don't remind me of my age again. Please be with me on this. At least we will have tried and if it fails, we will have done the best we could. I've been thinking of ways to help Ricky for so many years and have always been afraid to take the big step. Now we have been forced into it by the abuse at Ricky's school and the need to remove him from that environment."

"You'll work crazy hours and never be home," Stan argued. His voice was beginning to escalate.

"Probably, in the beginning," I agreed. "But I never questioned you and your working hours. This is our chance to try to help our son," I said.

"What do you really want to accomplish?" he asked. He sounded as if he might be coming around to my way of thinking.

"I want Ricky to have a vital life in the community near you and me, not away in an institution," I said.

Stan said nothing for about five minutes and then his eyes lit up, with a smile, "I think we can use that for a name," he said.

"What?"

"Vita-Living"

I was excited and so grateful. I ran to him and gave him a hug. We were on our way to opening the first small community home licensed in Texas to serve people with severe intellectual disabilities. I had no idea of what lay ahead for us, but I didn't fool myself that it would be easy. I believed in Ralph Waldo Emerson's words: "America is a country of new beginnings, of projects, of vast designs, and expectations."

CHAPTER I

THE BEGINNING OF THE JOURNEY

T HAT NIGHT as I lay in bed next to my husband of 33 years I thought back to the time we met, fell in love, and married. As a favor to my best friend I agreed to go out with her boyfriend's buddy from Detroit, Stan Wallace. The doorbell rang and as I was descending the staircase I heard my father moving to the door. When I reached the landing, I looked up to see a man whose appearance made my heart race. That never changed in all of the years we were together.

"Hello," he said in a booming voice, "I'm Stan Wallace your date for the evening."

"Hello to you," I said with a smile in my voice, "I'm Renée. Where are Margie and Phil?"

"They are waiting in the car," he said. "Let's go." As he was helping me on with my coat, I moved toward the door, waved to my folks, and left before my father could start talking about the Detroit Tigers and the Cleveland Indians.

In my eyes Stan was a big man in many ways. He was handsome, six feet tall with a great physique, an exhaustive vocabulary, and an impressive intellect. In spite of the fact that he had nystagmus, an inherited condition characterized by involuntary eye movement that may reduce vision, he became a very good reporter and rewrite man for the *Detroit Times*, a job his eye doctor told him he could not perform.

I loved to dance and we did just that until the early hours of the morning. We moved from the two-step, to the fox trot and the waltz. I know that Margie and Phil were with us but, honestly, I remember little about them. I was so impressed with Stan that, on my return to Cornell, I told my roommate I had found the man I was going to marry.

The long-distance romance lasted three years. We wrote to each other and talked on the phone at least weekly. Stan told me about the stories he wrote for the *Detroit Times,* and I thought that being a reporter was so glamorous and exciting. He sent me a picture of himself with Bob Hope during an interview he conducted when Mr. Hope was in Detroit for a show.

I had to do an internship to complete my studies for a position in dietetics. I was offered three opportunities and I chose the one at the University of Michigan in Ann Arbor about an hour away from Detroit and Stan. Stan was my date for the Senior Prom at Cornell, and I was his date for many parties at his fraternity house at the University of Michigan. Stan didn't drive because of his impaired vision, but he always managed to create a caravan for our dates. He had many friends who drove us on the activities he organized and led. I did not like sharing him with a large group every time we went out in Detroit but realized that this was his way to get around without a car. My first exposure to egg rolls was when I visited Stan in Detroit and accompanied him, his two brothers, and parents on their Sunday ritual: eating at their favorite Chinese restaurant.

It was on his trips to Cleveland, usually over a weekend, that we really learned about each other. I drove and always arranged for just the two of us to go out. Dancing was our favorite activity, and we had a favorite place in the Statler Hotel with a live band on the weekends. We sat at small tables lit with candles surrounding a large dance floor. Stan requested our favorites, "If I loved you" and "Saturday Night (is the loneliest night of the week)." We danced into the wee hours of the morning. Then we returned to my house and to the basement where we listened to the music of the Big Bands like Benny Goodman, Jimmy Dorsey, and Artie Shaw. More than our physical attraction, which was very strong, was our respect for each other and our trust in each other. In those days a woman's success was judged by the success of her husband and her children. I knew that Stan would be a success in whatever area he chose. My parents insisted that I have a profession, but I was only to use it if my husband died or became incapacitated.

I was short with dark hair and eyes and not sure of myself in large groups of people. I always wore 3"-to-4" heels to make my 5' 3" frame appear taller. I had survived polio when I was five and pneumonia, scarlet fever, and strep throat during my growing years when those diseases were life threatening. I was always rushing, talking fast, moving fast, eating fast, and trying to prove my mother wrong when she said, "You aren't strong; don't do too much."

I remember Stan and I making plans for our wedding that took place in the ballroom of the Cleveland Hotel followed by a honeymoon in Bermuda. We talked about starting a family upon our return to Detroit.

"I want a large family of at least six children," I told him. Because I was an only child, I really thought that a large family would be wonderful. Stan agreed but not as enthusiastically as I.

Our first child, our daughter Melanie, was born in 1951. My mother-in-law had to drive me to the hospital because Stan still did not drive. Melanie was a beautiful baby who cried constantly until we discovered she had many allergies. One was to milk so we substituted soymilk for cow's milk. The other allergy was life-threatening since she could not tolerate the three-in-one shots that she was given at three months. She spiked a temperature of 105 and was rushed to the hospital with seizures and possible brain damage. After we brought her home, her progress put any possibility of brain damage out of mind. Ironically, this was not the last time we would hear about brain damage in one of our children.

I told Stan that his brothers, who had the same eye condition, were driving and I thought he should try now that our family was getting larger. He was nervous about driving but he did take the test and passed.

Thirty months later our second child and first son, Lee David, was born. This time Stan drove me to the hospital. Lee appeared to be a healthy, happy baby, and we were on our way to our planned six children. We felt blessed indeed.

Lee was six months old when Stan came home one night, sat me down across from him and said, "I just met a wonderful woman who is running for Congress and I'd like to help her. What do you think?"

"Tell me about her," I said.

"Marta Grand is a lawyer who has been active in local politics for many years and married a lawyer who also was involved in local politics. If she won, she'd be the first woman from Michigan to go to Congress."

"I'd love to help also," I said. "I can pass out leaflets and knock on doors if I can bring the children with me."

Marta Grand lost the first campaign but ran again and won as the first Congresswoman from Michigan. She asked Stan to become her administrative assistant. That meant that we would have to move to

Washington, D.C. with our two children. We could not afford to pay for two homes so we would have to rent the one in Detroit, and then find a rental in our new location. We talked about whether to risk Stan's leaving the paper for a job that might last only two years, but both of us loved challenges. The District of Columbia had just been desegregated, and there was much tension in the area about public accommodations and school desegregation. We felt stimulated at the thought of being in the middle of this important change in our country.

At the end of the second year, Stan and I talked about whether to continue this two-city life. The salary was so low and Melanie was turning five and ready for kindergarten. In addition, I was pregnant with our third child. "What about going back on the paper?" I asked.

"If we move back to Detroit I could go back into reporting at one of the papers," Stan said, "but I'm afraid that my poor vision would prevent me from getting the assignments I want. I think I need to strike out in a new field."

"How long can we function without an income?" I asked.

"We have enough money in the bank to last about three months once we move back to Detroit," Stan said.

While we were packing to return to Detroit, I noticed that I was bleeding. The doctor prescribed bed rest for three weeks. While I was in bed unable to do much, I thought about the child I was carrying. I didn't care if it was a boy or girl but hoped for a healthy baby who would grow into a strong, capable adult--maybe a doctor or lawyer, a professional or an artist. One of my uncles was an accomplished pianist, so maybe a musician. Since this was our third child, both Stan and I just assumed that this delivery would be as normal as the other deliveries and our child would be as healthy as Lee and Melanie.

I was more than a little worried about our lack of income with my being seven months pregnant, but I felt sure that Stan would find a job quickly. Looking back on that time, I don't know why I felt so confident except for my faith in Stan's ability. I trusted my life and my children's lives to him. I just knew he would succeed in whatever he tried. He never disappointed me in that regard. He gave notice and we packed up the car with our belongings and drove back to Detroit.

Stan said he was going to call one of his college friends, Clark, who had a job with a large public relations firm. He thought he might know of jobs that were available in public relations. On our return to Detroit, Clark told Stan of a possible position with his company. The firm was looking for a representative in Michigan for a large gas transmission company. My mother came to our rescue and stayed with the children so Stan and I could travel to New York to meet Clark and his firm.

I was excited because I love New York. My friends from Cornell met us and kept me company while Stan was interviewing. All of us went out to dinner that night. The maitre d' welcomed us to the large dining room with crystal chandeliers and walls of crimson velvet. Clark seemed to know him and all of the waiters tending our assigned table. I was impressed but thought the sniffing of the wine cork and the swirling of the wine "so it could breathe" a little much. The food was great and the company and conversation were stimulating, topped off with the news that Stan had been offered the job. He would represent the Panhandle Eastern Corporation in Michigan but be employed by the Tex McCrary Public Relations firm. It was his job to help Panhandle maneuver through the bureaucracy of the Michigan legislature. We were both so excited and relieved that Stan was starting a new career. I knew he would be successful. We talked about his new career coming at the same time as our new baby. How wonderful life was for us!

Melanie started kindergarten in September, and Stan started his new job the day Ricky was born, November 2nd, 1956. Stan's job required him to travel frequently to Lansing, the state capital, and New York City. I did not mind his travel since I had been brought up with the notion that wives were to support their husbands in whatever work they did.

When we first brought Ricky home from the hospital, we were impressed that he was moving all over his crib. He was never still and slept fitfully. At first we thought he was extremely gifted because he was moving so much and so quickly. When he was about three months old, we realized that, although he responded when we talked to him and he cried, we never heard him coo. Since Melanie and Lee had both cooed, we were surprised that Ricky didn't. When I took him to the doctor and asked about his lack of cooing, the doctor told me not to worry: " Many children talk later, it's nothing to worry about," he said. "Lee talked later than Melanie, so it's not surprising that Ricky may also talk later. He is doing everything that a child should be doing at this age other than the cooing."

"Lee cooed," I reminded the doctor. He did not respond but placed his hand on my shoulder, smiled, and left the room.

Lee and Melanie had been content to stay in their cribs playing with toys and investigating their toes and fingers. I do not recall Ricky ever doing that. He wanted out of his crib but once out, we realized that his constant movement was not a sign that he was extraordinarily bright but that he had extraordinary problems with his nervous system. He moved everything in his room. Lee and Melanie had never been so active so early in their lives. We removed all of the items in his room except for his bed and some large soft toys. We heard him moving around most of the night. He took 5-to-10 minute catnaps lying on the floor and then woke up full of energy as if he had had a full night's sleep. His brother slept through the night within a month of his birth, and his sister was sleeping through the night as soon as we solved her allergy problems. I thought Ricky might have allergies so we took him to the pediatrician, but he did not appear to have any.

When Ricky was 8 months old, I became pregnant with our fourth child. We were elated and looked forward to another addition to our family, moving us closer to our goal of six children.

I could not stay awake during the night, but Stan told me he heard Ricky moving about in his room when he awoke during the night. I did not know what to do and did not know who to go to for help. Our pediatrician did not seem concerned. I was concerned because I had not experienced this level of ceaseless activity with our other children. Ricky's motor ability was normal, but he was communicating with gestures only and never appeared to attempt vocalization. We took him to a speech therapist, but after chasing him all over the office, the therapist told me to take Ricky home and return when he was able to sit for more than two minutes. Once he started to crawl and move about, he was never still--and there was never a day without a crisis.

On a clear cold day in March, I was resting on our couch, feeling very large and uncomfortable, when suddenly I looked up to see that Ricky had pushed a chair over to the desk and was climbing to reach the indelible ink on the top shelf. As he was swallowing it, I tried to reach him but was unsuccessful. I called out to Lee as I put Ricky in the car and rushed off to the hospital. Ricky had to have his stomach pumped. He did not seem upset, and as soon as the procedure was over, he was moving around so fast that two attendants and I had to corral him to place him back in the car.

At a year, Ricky was walking with an odd gait. He "walked" at almost a run and bent over at the waist, looking as if he were about to fall forward, which he did frequently. One night, a noise in the kitchen awoke me at 2:00 A.M. As I entered the kitchen, I saw Ricky holding a large chopping knife. I screamed for Stan and at Ricky to put down the knife. As I grabbed for it, I cut my hand, and while wrapping it with a dishtowel, I guided Ricky back to his room. Stan stayed awake the rest of the night to be sure that Ricky did not leave his room. The next day he placed a slip lock on the outside of Ricky's room to prevent any more night wanderings.

We had no idea what was wrong with Ricky, so we started visiting different physicians, but no one seemed to know. The fact that Ricky responded to directions, was able to make himself understood with gestures, and seemed to relate to others gave us hope, but his lack of verbalization and his inability to tend to task for more than a second or two were major concerns. His mouth was always open and he drooled all of the time. He did not attempt to talk. He never stopped moving and only sat if he was watching TV. Otherwise he was moving and did not play with anything for more than a few minutes. People who met him for the first time commented on the "devil in his eyes" and joked that he must keep us hopping. He smiled most of the time and was very affectionate.

Finally an aunt of Stan's suggested we try a pediatric neurologist at the University of Michigan to get the best diagnosis. I set up an appointment for early May. We were lucky to be able to make the appointment as planned as our fourth child, Andy, had been born two weeks earlier on April 26th.

It was raining when we went into the clinic at the University Hospital pediatric neurological center. The lobby was a cheerful space with pictures of animals and nursery rhymes painted on the walls. There were toys and child-sized furniture for seating but the doctor's office had no toys, only a few chairs and his desk. Ricky, a hyperactive 17 month old, was running around inspecting the office while Stan, and I sat nervously on chairs waiting for the doctor who was to tell us what was wrong with our son. He finally entered and took Ricky into an examining area indicating he did not want us to follow.

Stan tried to read and I sat in the chair with my eyes closed thinking of the life threatening diseases our son might be facing. Neither of us looked directly at the other. I was sure we would be told that Ricky had not long to live. I was thinking of all we would do to help Ricky. My mind jumped from muscular dystrophy to some degenerative brain disease--all of them ended with Ricky dying at a very young age. I was already thinking of how we would tell our children and family and what we would do to change his room into a hospital room.

Finally the door opened and, with his white coat flapping, the doctor directed Ricky to a chair, which Ricky ignored as he ran back and forth between us. Peering over the rims of his glasses, the doctor said, "I'm sorry..."--I knew it. I thought. Ricky has only a short time to live-- "to inform you that your son has severe mental retardation," he continued in a matter-of-fact voice.

Neither of us said anything for a few minutes. We were stunned and surprised since that thought had never entered our minds. "What does that mean?" I asked.

The doctor gave me a puzzled look. "Your son will never mature intellectually or socially, but he is physically healthy and should live a normal life span."

"What can we do?" Stan finally said in a hoarse voice.

"You must take him home and care for him." The doctor said. "There is nothing you can do about this."

"Why did this happen? What caused it? I asked.

"I have no idea," he countered. "Did you have a normal delivery and pregnancy?"

"I spotted when I was three months pregnant, and bed rest was prescribed with some medication, but I don't remember the name of the medication," I told him.

"I don't know what to tell you," he said and waived us out of his office. We looked at each other, and I remember feeling as if we were moving in slow motion. I took Ricky's hand and Stan's hand and looked at both of them as we moved toward the door. Their faces appeared blurred to me. I turned back to look at the doctor, hoping he would tell me that it was all a mistake, but he already was leafing through papers on his desk.

"We have a son who will never have a bar mitzvah, will never go to college, who will never carry on our name," Stan said softly.

"What are you saying? I asked.

"Nothing," he replied. Neither of us said anything further, and as we walked through the doors to the parking lot, the rain mixed with our tears. We could not remember where we parked and walked up and down the rows until we found our car, oblivious of how wet we were getting.

On the ride home I remember the wipers moving back and forth as if chanting, "Not true, not true." Ricky loved riding in the car so he was laughing and smiling all of the way home while Stan and I were crying silently, listening to the wipers and watching the rain wash away our hopes for our son. Both of us were numb from the news. I thought about dying, and the way I was going to help Ricky through his critical illness, and I realized I was thinking of Ricky as if he had died. The boy I dreamed about when I was bed ridden during the pregnancy had definitely died. In his place was this boy sitting in the rear of the car. "Not true" was all I could think of as we drove home to the rest of our family. I learned later that I was in the first stage of acceptance, and that stage was denial.

As soon as we got home I ran into the room where my two-week-old son, Andy, was sleeping. I turned him over fearing that he might also be suffering from mental retardation and wondered how could I stand waiting to find out.

We did not know how to tell our other children, so we found a psychiatrist and took Ricky to see him. He talked to Ricky and when he was through he said he did not think Ricky had mental retardation but that he might be a little slow. Ricky understood everything said to him and so when he asked Ricky to hang up his coat or sit in a chair, Ricky could and did follow directions. We decided to tell our parents what the doctor in Ann Arbor and the psychiatrist said. I could tell from the way my mother talked that she did not believe the psychiatrist. I felt I could not deal with having a child that would not grow to an adult in everyway. I remembered the cabins with the gas heaters that we stayed in when we traveled with the children. I thought I could take Ricky and check into one of these motels, turn on the gas, go to sleep, and never wake up and face life, as it appeared it would be.

While I was doing the laundry and thinking of ways to get to the motel, my mother, who lived in Cleveland, Ohio, called to say she was coming for a visit. I couldn't wait to talk to my mother. I was anxious for her to legitimize my feelings. I hoped she would be able to make me feel better about what I wanted to do and anxiously awaited her arrival. When she arrived I told her I did not think I could live with a child who had to be cared for all of his life, a child who would never grow up to be a man. She looked me in the eye and holding my face in her hands, she said, "What choice do you have? You have three other children and a husband. Think long and hard about what you are saying."

A little later in the shower, I heard her voice saying, "What choice do you have?" As the water hit my body, I realized that I had no choice. I knew that Stan and I, for the foreseeable future, were bound together to care for the family we had. We would endure our life if not accepting it yet. There was no getting out of it no matter how much either of us wished we could. But I knew that our family was complete. The dream of six children was gone for good.

I received letters from relatives telling me about their feelings about our news. My Uncle Joe, a Catholic, had married my mother's sister, and since they had no children, they thought of my family and me as their children. The pamphlets he sent me from his church claimed that you were "chosen" because you could care for such a child. Judaism claims that supposedly we are the "chosen people." My immediate reaction was that I wished I would not be "chosen" for anything anymore.

We did not feel comfortable putting a newborn in with Ricky, so we decided Andy would sleep upstairs where Melanie and Lee had rooms. There was a door off the dining room that closed the upstairs from the rest of the house. Melanie and Lee were already placing all of their papers and personal items upstairs away from Ricky.

I heard about a group formed by a social worker from the state school for the mentally retarded, to talk about the feelings that arise when caring for a child with mental retardation. I thought it might help me accept my situation if I talked to other parents in a similar situation. The session was held in a public school classroom. I sat in one of the wooden desks along with about 20 other women in their late 20s and early 30s. At one point the facilitator asked if anyone wished that his or her child had died. I raised my hand. Looking around the room, I realized I was the only one. I picked up my purse and dashed out of the room never to return. Now I was convinced that I was wicked and a terrible mother.

I also read Pearl Buck's *The Child Who Never Grew,* published in 1950 and took great comfort in her story of raising a child with mental retardation.

When asked how to bear the sorrow of having such a child, she speaks of the endurance it requires as being "a harsh and bitter root in one's life, bearing poisonous and gloomy fruit, destroying lives. There must be acceptance and the knowledge that sorrow fully accepted brings its own gifts. For there is an alchemy in sorrow. It can be transmuted into wisdom, which, if it does not bring joy can yet bring happiness." Pearl Buck talks of feeling as though she "were bleeding inwardly and desperately" when she finally was told the truth about her daughter. She speaks of "the sorrows which can be assuaged are those which life can cover and heal. Those which cannot be assuaged are those which change life itself and in a way themselves make life. Sorrows that can die can be assuaged, but living sorrow is never assuaged. It is like a stone being thrown into the stream, as Browning put it, and the water must divide itself and accommodate itself, for it cannot remove the stone."

When I read the following I thanked whatever powers there were that someone else felt as I had.

"For, in addition to the practical problem of protecting the child's life, which may last beyond the parent's, there is the problem of one's own self in misery. All the rightness of life is gone, all the pride in parenthood. There is more than pride gone; there is an actual sense of one's life being cut in the child. The stream of the generations is stopped. Death would be far easier to bear, for death is final. What was, is no more. How often did I cry out in my heart that it would be better if my child died! I would have welcomed death for my child and would still welcome it, for then she would be finally safe."

I jumped up when I read those lines and thought that Buck spoke for me. I wondered how many others felt this way. I thought that what I had been feeling was normal and not disgusting.

I had moved from denial to anger that this should happen to me and then to depression and finally was beginning to accept my life and my son with mental retardation. I still believed that I must have done something or failed to do something that caused Ricky's brain damage. Stan and I just got through one day at a time. The days ran into weeks and the weeks into months and the months into years. I don't remember much of what we said to each other. I don't think I shared much of my desperation with my husband at this time. As I write this I can now see how I grew up sublimating my feelings. My father did not tolerate crying so I learned to "suck it up." Stan was dealing with his disappointment in his own way. He was away from home much of the time driving hours to the capital, Lansing. I felt he had so much to handle that I did not want to add to his load. Looking back, I wonder if we could have helped each other if we had talked about our feelings openly but at that time neither of us could.

I wore dark glasses most of the time to cover the grief that came in waves and the constant tearing. I requested some medication to help me get through the day from the doctor but after using it for a few days, I found I could not manage the house and care for my children while half asleep. It was difficult to be alert during the day. No baby sitter was willing to stay with Ricky so we never went out. Our social life was nonexistent unless my mother was visiting us from her home in Cleveland.

We took Ricky to many doctors and therapists hoping to hear something that would change our reality. The speech therapists could not work with him because of his inability to sit still. The doctors simply did not know what to do for someone like him. Somehow life went on. I worked at home, and Stan became very active in an organization called The National Association for Retarded Children (ARC) whose mission was to advocate for services for children with mental retardation. Started as early as the 1930's, it became a reality nationally in 1950. Founded that year, the Detroit chapter focused on improving the conditions at Michigan's state-run institutions. I resented Stan being away so many nights each week, but it was hard to argue with his working for such a good cause, so I never mentioned it. Stan left the Tex McCrary organization and started working directly for Panhandle Eastern Corporation, which gave us additional income and much-needed security.

Summer in Detroit was pleasant and always made me feel hopeful. This year was no different. One beautiful day, Lee was playing outside, our fourth child, two-month-old Andy, was asleep upstairs, and nineteen-month- old Ricky was watching TV. The house was quiet for a change, so I decided to clean the oven. I placed the oven cleaner on a high shelf that I thought was safe. In a flash Ricky was out of his chair, found the top of the cleaner jar, and licked it. Immediately I dropped everything and yelled for Lee as I ran upstairs to grab Andy from his crib. Ricky stood still for a change looking totally shocked. I pulled Ricky by the arm as I ran to the car with Andy in my other arm. Lee came running when he saw me and got into the car. I placed Andy on his lap and put Ricky in the front seat next to me. Ricky started to cry and pointed to his tongue as the car careened into the parking space at the emergency room. It appeared that he might lose his tongue. Ricky looked so puzzled by his pain and obviously did not connect his licking the jar top with his pain. The doctors treated his tongue and told me how lucky I was that Ricky could still use his tongue.

I finally realized that I could only use cleaning supplies at night when Ricky was safely in his room. I had to do most of my house cleaning after everyone was in bed since Ricky had to be watched every minute he was out of his room. Because of my inability to do anything but watch Ricky, I looked for help and was fortunate to find a wonderful woman, Lorry Reed, to help me one day a week. She loved Ricky and held him on her lap while she ate. One day I saw him tap her on the shoulder, and when she turned to look, he grabbed her food. We thought he was a big tease and laughed at his antics, but in spite of these moments of normalcy, we realized that something was not right with him. I wanted to believe that Ricky was just different--not "bad" different but just "different." He marched to his own beat but he would march and become a man. Stan and I wavered between talking about Ricky's future to talking about Ricky without much of a future.

One summer evening, when I was outside playing with the children, Ricky and I came in for a minute to check on dinner. When my back was turned, Ricky grabbed an apple from the table and ran back outside. I followed him and was talking to our neighbors when I heard Lee, who was four and half shout, "Mom, come quick. Ricky is choking."

Ricky was trying to swallow a large chunk of the apple, but he never took the time to chew. The apple had lodged in his throat, and he was turning blue. With Lee holding the baby on his lap in the car, we rushed Ricky to the emergency room. While we were racing through the streets the car hit a big rut in the road and jarred the apple loose. It flew out of Ricky's mouth. He laughed as though this were a game. I pulled over, took a few deep breaths, and turned around for home.

A few days later while I was placing Andy in his high chair I heard Lee again call to me, "Mom come quick, Ricky is bleeding." I picked up the baby and rushed outside to the back yard to find blood gushing from Ricky's face. One eye was almost shut and already turning black and blue. Again Lee held Andy in the car as we drove to the emergency room. They knew us by now. It took a few stitches to close the cut so near to Ricky's eye. At home again, Andy finally got his dinner and Ricky ran happily around the house and sat quietly for a while when I turned on the TV.

Ricky had a high threshold for pain so was not always aware that he was hurt. We noticed it only if there was a bleed or swelling or if someone saw Ricky get hurt. He fell often and put everything into his mouth. The emergency room became a familiar spot since we seemed to make weekly visits there. Not surprisingly, Ricky's accidents happened primarily during the day when Stan was at work, and in a strange way I completely accepted and understood "ambulance driver" to be my role.

Lee started kindergarten in 1958 and that left me at home with 5 month-old Andy and 22-month-old Ricky. When Stan was home he helped get Ricky up and fed in the mornings and put him to bed in the evening. Frequently Stan was away on business, so on those days Ricky had to wait in his room behind a locked door. I prepared Melanie and Lee for school and while they were having breakfast, I awakened Andy, cleaned him and placed him in his high chair. After Melanie and Lee left for school, I fed Andy and placed him in his playpen while I got Ricky ready for the day. Since he had been awake for some time, he was happy and ready to be let out of his room. After I cleaned and dressed him, he sat in front of the TV while I prepared his breakfast. When he was eating, I had to watch him closely because he stuffed the food into his mouth and did not take the time to chew or swallow before he tried the next spoonful of food. After breakfast I placed Ricky in front of the TV set and cleaned up.

I played with Andy for about an hour while Ricky ran back and forth between the television and us. When Andy was napping, I took Ricky with me to make the beds and clean the rooms, closing the door of each, so Ricky could not leave and trying to entertain him so he would not destroy anything. It took a long time to finish cleaning. When it was time to get Andy up from his nap, Ricky came with me. I screamed a lot at Ricky not to touch or break anything. Ricky did not always respond unless I raised my voice.

Melanie and Lee always walked home for a quick, 15-minute lunch before returning to school, and Ricky and I usually joined them. Many of their friends were driven to school but I felt strongly that walking was healthier. Again I placed Ricky in front of the TV while I cleaned up.   Thank goodness for TV and thank goodness that Ricky was mesmerized by it and sat for as long as an hour watching it and actually seemed to follow the action on the screen. Howdy Doody became a good friend, as well as the Mousketeers.

After school, Melanie and Lee, watched Ricky while I prepared dinner with Andy in his highchair watching me. There was nothing routine about our daily activities. If Stan was coming home we waited for him, but otherwise we ate as soon as it was ready. Ricky always ate so fast that I had to leave the table to chase him while the other children completed their meal.

Melanie and Lee had many friends and spent much of their time out of the house either playing outside or visiting at friend's homes. Many of their friends visited our home and seemed to accept Ricky's level of activity. One day Lee's friend Mark was watching Ricky running aimlessly around the house with me in pursuit. With a smile on his lips Mark said, "One day, Ricky, your mother and father will tell you how you acted when you were little and you will be so surprised."

Feeling desperate for some help to calm Ricky, I took him to the family doctor and asked if there was any medication, to help slow him down. The doctor prescribed Thorazine, which changes the actions of chemicals in the brain. Thorazine's use was fairly new in the 1950's. I was thankful that it worked to reduce Ricky's constant motion. It enabled Ricky to sit and play with Andy for longer periods of time and during this period Ricky even started to say some words. One day I was folding clothes when I heard "Ma Ma" coming from the other room. I went to see who was calling me and was amazed to find that it was Ricky. He wanted to show me something on TV. When Melanie came home Ricky ran to her and said "Meyanie" and gave her a book to read to him saying "boo" when he handed it to her. We were all so excited. One night when I was getting Ricky ready for bed, I noticed a red rash on his arms and back that he had been scratching so severely that it had started to bleed. The doctor told me that the Thorazine had caused Ricky to become sun-sensitive and that he had to stop taking the medicine. I said that I could not stop the drug because Ricky was doing so well on it. After a few days, however, I noticed that the rash had spread. Heartbroken, we had to stop using the medication. Within a week of stopping the Thorazine, Ricky was back to constant movement and no language except "Ma Ma." How unfair this was! How could I see Ricky improve only to have my hopes shattered? I wanted to strike out but I did not know whom to strike.

The world famous Detroit zoo was within walking distance of our home and frequently I went with our children. It was a happy place to go. One day when I was watching the monkeys ride bikes and jump through hoops I wondered how they were trained. I thought if people could train animals then surely I could train Ricky. This was my first exposure to the building blocks of a training method that I would use throughout my professional life.

I could not have cared less about current events or politics. For our family and me it was one day at a time. As fall rolled around and Ricky was almost five, I took him to the local elementary school to register him for kindergarten. The office clerk looked at me as if I were crazy and bluntly said: "We do not teach people like him in our school. He can't come to this school."

"What do you mean people like him?" I asked. "His brother and sister attend this school. Maybe I could wait a year, and he could start next year because he will not be five for two months." I said hopefully.

"He could not start in this school if he were ten years old. He is all over the place," she snapped. "A child has to be able to sit at a table or desk for more than one minute."

"You need to learn how to talk to people," I screamed at her. I took

Ricky by the hand and ran out of the office and into the car where I hugged him and said, "You will get an education. I will find a place for you, I promise".

I felt as though a hard blow had knocked all of the air out of my chest. I had no idea what to do. Desperate, I thought that our friends at The National Association for Retarded Children might have some ideas, so I called the chapter's president, Ruth Glass. "What do you do with your children when they turn five and the school will not take them?" I asked her.

"My daughter is at Lapeer State School. There are no day programs for children like ours;" she responded. When I asked her if she could arrange for me to see where a child like Ricky might be placed at Lapeer, she offered, "Of course, I will tell them to show you where children live who are hyperactive."

I wanted desperately to talk to Stan but he was out of town and not home until the next day. I had to wait to tell him what I discovered and we would decide together. Two hours away from Detroit, Lapeer was the oldest state school in Michigan serving people with mental retardation. I knew nothing about it or any other state school but it was the school that Ricky would have to attend if we decided to place him.

Stan arrived home to find me an emotional wreck. The thought of Ricky not receiving an education was something I could not conceive, but the thought of him leaving our home was something I could not tolerate. We talked into the night and decided that I should at least check out the state school.

When Ruth contacted me with a time, date, and the name of the social worker to see, I was ready to make the day trip to the school. I arranged for Lorry to come to the house and stay with the children and drove along a winding road to reach the four-story-high, dirty, redbrick buildings, that appeared menacing from the outside. The first thing that struck me was the small, barred windows; then I noticed the high iron fence with locked gates that surrounded the buildings. Overhead and on the ground were splashes of orange, yellow, and red from large trees that were losing their leaves. There were no toys on the grounds but there were a few benches and picnic tables. I entered a lobby with a cracked linoleum floor, and a few straight-back chairs lining the hall with a wood table in between. A woman behind a window asked what I wanted. I gave her my name and asked for the social worker. She told me to wait. After a few minutes a middle-aged woman, Miss Greene, welcomed me and asked me to follow her.

"I have a little, five-year-old boy who is very hyperactive. I would appreciate it if you could show me where children like him live and go to school." I said.

"I will be happy to show you where he will sleep and where he will spend his days, but there is no school for children here." she responded.

I should have known that but I kept hoping. At last we reached a corridor with a locked door. As she opened the door the whiff of urine combined with the odor of disinfectant almost knocked me out. I wondered if I could continue but swallowed and smiled. She took me to the day room where I saw young boys and girls around Ricky's age running around aimlessly or sitting in the corner blank-eyed. There was a TV attached high on the wall, some broken toys on the floor, and two attendants with keys hanging from their belts standing around trying to keep track of the children. Many of the children were dressed, but there were a number who were only partially dressed. Some wore diapers and more were defecating on the floors. I felt light-headed and wanted to run away. I steeled myself and asked to see where the children slept and the bathing areas.

The dormitory was a large, narrow room with beds lined up on each side and one table with drawers between each bed. Forget privacy, I thought. I asked about those children who did not sleep through the night. She advised me that many were strapped into bed "for their own good."

Nausea enveloped me. I thought I would be sick. "Can I please have some water?" I mumbled. She took me to a fountain in the hall with some paper cups near the nursing station. I drank a little but it didn't help. Then she took me to the communal shower room where some of the residents were being hosed down. The water ran down a big drain in the middle of the room. I wanted to run out but forced myself to continue to the dining room.

The children, who were able, lined up in a row and went through a cafeteria line. The others came in a group, sat at a table, and were served by other older children with mild mental retardation. I asked what they did for children who eat so fast that they were in danger of choking. She said they would be served mashed food or baby food. I could not wait to get out. I thanked Miss Greene and told her I would get back in touch with her.

Walking as fast as I could, I managed to get to my car. My head was spinning, and I had to pull over so I could vomit. Drenched in perspiration, my head felt as though it were in a vise. One thing was clear, there was no way I would put my son in such a place, no matter what.

When I arrived home I prepared statements for all of the family to sign. They were never to place Ricky in a state school. Stan took my word on the situation. We had many talks about what we were going to do to help our son learn and grow into a man. I did not feel that I had enough knowledge to teach him. My training was in nutrition services and as a dietitian. We decided we needed to find a private school where he could learn.

President Kennedy's sister was in a school called St Coletta. I wrote to them about placing Ricky there, but they said they could not serve someone like him. We found that most of the private schools were on the east coast. There was one in Texas, but at that time we thought Texas was too far. We discovered a family on our street that sent their handicapped child to a private school in upstate New York. Stan and I met with Melanie, Lee, and Andy and told them that Michigan had no schools for people like Ricky, so we were going to look for a school outside of Michigan. When we found one, Ricky would have to live there for a while.

There was a look of relief on Lee and Melanie's faces but a totally perplexed look on Andy's face. He had no idea that his brother was handicapped. He understood that Ricky was "bad" and always in trouble because he was "bad". When I tried to explain that Ricky was sick and needed special training, he walked away. He yelled over his shoulder that Ricky was not sick, just "bad". Ricky had just turned five, and the thought of sending him away from our family made me sick.

My mother came to Detroit to care for the children while we searched for a school. We saw many schools in New York, Pennsylvania, New Jersey, and Rhode Island. All of the schools were expensive and most of them required the children dress up and have social activities such as dances and dinner parties. I looked at my son and knew that this was not in his repertoire. We were totally dejected and thought we would never find a place for our boy. Finally we came to Vineland Training School in Vineland, New Jersey, which had cottages with foster parents to care for the young children. Vineland had many acres of land where residents grew their own food. It had a homey feel to it and I thought Ricky could be loved in that environment. In addition, the school was accredited by the State of New Jersey, and we hoped it could work for Ricky. I remembered that this was the school Pearl Buck had chosen to care for her daughter and thought that if it was good for Pearl Buck, it must be good for Stan and Renée.

The cost was as much annually as we had to live on for our entire family. Stan and I talked about how to handle the cost and still care for our other children. The only alternative was for me to return to the work force. This was the early 1960s, and none of our peers had a wife that worked outside of the home. It was particularly difficult for Stan to admit that he could not care for the family without his wife working. I rather looked forward to it. My only concern was that, since Andy was only three and a half, I be home when the children returned from school.

After days of tears and inner turmoil for both of us, we made the hard decision to place Ricky at Vineland. I had never seen Stan cry before. Seeing him break down made me sadder and weakened my resolve. Every time I thought about my son living with strangers, I felt ill. At the end of the week, however, we looked at each other and admitted that, for Ricky's sake, we needed to help him get an education. We told our children and family of our decision. My mother returned to Detroit when we flew to Philadelphia to rent a car and drive to Vineland with Ricky. There was no way to explain to him what was happening and why. We did try but we could see that Ricky could not understand what we were talking about.

The day we left him the staff told us we could not talk to him or see him for a month. We were both aghast and said we had to see him. He would not understand what happened. They were certain that a clean separation was the best way to help Ricky adjust, so we drove off with our son running after the car crying yelling, "Mama, Mama, Mama". I wanted to die. We stayed at a motel near the school that night. Neither of us slept, and in the morning I said we had to go back to bring him home. Stan said, "OK, but you know we will have to do this again. How is he ever going to learn anything staying at home?"

I reluctantly agreed, and knew that neither of us was capable of going through leaving him another time. Little did I know that over the years we were going to go through this wrenching ordeal of leaving our little boy over and over again.

As we drove away from the training school on our way to the airport, neither of us said anything, perhaps because we didn't know what to say or how to describe the despair and loneliness we felt. As the plane was taxiing down the runway, I felt as if I were screaming, "Let me out. I need to get my son." but no sound came. I clamped my lips shut and swallowed the tears. I looked at Stan and saw him wiping his eyes under his glasses. The two of us held hands but said little all of the way to Detroit. Once in the car on our way home we talked about what a good thing this school was for Ricky and how happy we were to find such a good school. I don't think either of us convinced the other, but we tried.

CHAPTER II

ONE GONE BUT NOT FORGOTTEN

Iᴛ ᴡᴀs 1961. The Soviets built the Berlin Wall. Yuri Gagarin was the first man in space. The Bay of Pigs Disaster occurred. Again I could not have cared less. We just had to get through one day at a time. Our lives had been patterned around Ricky's needs and now he was gone. We had no idea how his absence would affect us.

We opened the door to our home as if we were entering a strange place. Ricky was not running up to us. There was no yelling, no loud voices calling out his name. Melanie and Lee seemed subdued and talked quietly, waiting to take their cues from us. Andy refused to even look at us. We had not gone out for dinner as a family for so long that we thought we might try the night we arrived home. Eating out was so different from what we did when Ricky was home that all of us felt a little guilty enjoying the outing.

That first night we all went to bed a little sadder but trying to figure out what our life would be like now that we were five at home. We kept Ricky's room ready for him to visit, and Andy remained upstairs with Melanie and Lee. Everyday when I saw Ricky's empty room, it reminded me of my son away, at a distant school.

I knew I had to find a job and daycare for Andy. I first looked for a good situation for Andy. When I found the River School, I was hopeful he would like it. I took Andy to the school and as I left, there was a very angry three-year-old glaring back at me. I went food shopping and arrived home to hear the phone ringing. The teacher at the school relayed to me that Andy had told her that his mother was not "dumping him like she dumped his brother." She thought we should know. Andy's message was coming in loud and clear.

That night Stan and I talked about what to do. We agreed Andy would be happier if he could stay home with me but if he did, how could we pay for Ricky's school? We brainstormed into the night about where to find the money for Ricky's school expenses. We had no collateral so going to a bank was not plausible. Stan and I were proud of the way we had managed to care for our family up until now but agreed that we might possibly need some financial help from our respective families for the next two years--at least until Andy started kindergarten. We had to swallow our pride. Neither Stan's nor my parents were wealthy. They were comfortable financially, but what we were asking would not be easy for either family. We did not want to burden them, but we saw no other way.

We went together to speak to Stan's parents. Stan told about Andy's anger and his refusal to go to the day program and our concerns about forcing him to go at this time. We laid out our financial needs and promised to pay them back as soon as we could but admitted that it might take awhile since I could not go to work until Andy started kindergarten. Dad Wallace nodded his head when he said, "We will help all we can. How much do you think you will need each month?"

"We'll pay what we can every month and then we'll divide the rest between you and my parents," I said. "We will keep a record of what you have loaned us and will set a schedule of repayment when I start to work." We had not yet asked my parents but I was sure they would help. Dad and Mom Wallace gave each of us a hug and told us not to worry, that everything would work out. We were so grateful that they made the asking so easy.

Because I could not afford to wait until we visited, I called my folks in Cleveland and asked them over the phone for the same help as we had of Mom and Dad Wallace. Their response was the same. Stan and I looked at each other and both said how lucky we were that we could get such help. Stan prepared the loan agreement that we delivered to our parents, and our life for the next two years was pretty much set in stone.

We also examined ways we could cut our living expenses. We told Lorry, my stalwart helper and friend, who was so loving to Ricky, that we could no longer afford her services. I became exceedingly careful with our food costs and found more ways to use ground beef, beans, and eggs than I thought possible. I had learned many ways to cut food costs during World War II and was able to incorporate those ideas into our daily diet. The children walked to school. I had the use of our car since Stan was given a company car.

When Ricky had been home, Stan and I could not go out because we could not find a sitter. Now we could not go out because we did not want to spend the money. We spent our evenings reading and talking about Stan's work and how great it would be when I could go to work and help with the expenses. Often we spoke about what was going on with The National Association for Retarded Children (ARC). Stan was still very involved with their activities. One meeting, in particular, stands out in my mind. A parent talked about the government's responsibility to help with the cost of caring for our children. I felt that since these were our children, it was our responsibility to care for them. My attitude changed dramatically once I started to work in the field.

My way of handling stress was to be physically active. I took pride in my home and became the Mrs. Clean of our neighborhood. I told my children that "Cleanliness is next to godliness" so many times that I think they could chime in as soon as I said "clean". You could eat off the floor and I ironed all of our clothing--even the underwear. I was up most nights keeping busy cleaning, ironing, and cooking.

Andy and I spent our days together, but he was still angry about Ricky's absence and always let me know how he felt. One day he was playing train on the stairs and was going to visit Ricky. I said, "Wait. I want to go, too"

"No you can't go," he shouted as I settled on the stairs.

"Why not? I want to see Ricky, too."

"You are a bad mother and a bad birther," he said loudly looking right at me.

I ran down the stairs and never spoke to Andy or anyone else about our conversation. I did not know what to say to him other than what I had said before. We played games and Andy loved me to read to him, but whenever there was a mention of Ricky, he let me know he was angry that Ricky was not home to play with him.

On top of all the work at Panhandle and his commitments to the ARC, Stan believed knowledge of the law would be helpful in his work, so he enrolled in Detroit School of Law. Although his job involved public relations and advertising, he worked closely with the lawyers in the company and could see that it would make his job easier if he better understood the law as it applied to the oil and gas business. Now he was gone every evening and the children and I saw him mostly on weekends. Stan tried hard to develop his relationship with the kids. When he was home, he participated in sports with Lee and took Andy to the park and other activities they both enjoyed.

Finally Ricky's first month at Vineland was over and we were permitted to visit him. Everyone piled excitedly into the car. We left on Friday afternoon driving through Cleveland to spend the night with my folks. Early on Saturday we set off to visit Ricky. Our plan was to arrive on Saturday and leave late Sunday afternoon.

We arrived in Vineland around noon and went directly to Ricky's cottage. We never told the staff we were coming because we did not want Ricky to be disappointed if something should happen to prevent or delay our arrival. He recognized us immediately and ran up to all of us for hugs and kisses. Andy pulled back, not joining in the hugs and kisses.

Ricky was clean and well dressed but his shirt was wet due to his constant drooling. He ran from one to the other of us until Stan picked him up and held him. He was making hand gestures, but none of us knew what he was trying to tell us. After much guessing on our part we decided he was telling us about his school and his housemates. Melanie and Lee took Ricky and Andy to the playground so we could talk to the house parents in private. Ricky was not sleeping through the night so they placed him on medication. I reminded them of the reaction Ricky had to Thorazine, and they told us the medicine was in the same family but had different side effects. He was tolerating it well but his sleeping had not improved yet. He was going to the school every day and they hoped that the medication would allow him to sit longer and listen better to the teacher, but that had not happened yet either. At this point, Melanie interrupted us, saying it was hard to keep track of Ricky and she needed help.

We heard there was one movie theater in town and since Ricky loved to go to the movies we headed to the theater. Unfortunately you could not reach the movie screen without passing the candy counter. The stimulation was too much for Ricky. He wanted all of the candy and popcorn. We stationed one of us on either side of him and insisted that he have one candy, one box of popcorn, and one drink. Of course the other children also wanted their treats so it became a juggling act. Once in the movie, loaded down with snacks, Ricky was mesmerized by the big screen. Sitting quietly through a movie was most unusual for someone with his poor attention span, yet he sat quietly until the movie was over. Over the years I have tried to understand his fascination with the small and big screens coupled with his inability to attend to any other task in other situations, but no one has been able to explain it. All I know is that I was grateful to find an activity that he could sit quietly and enjoy.

Walking out of the movie, we tried to pass the food counter quickly to avoid another battle over candy. The counter was closed since there was only one afternoon matinee, but a closed candy counter made no sense to Ricky. He threw himself down on the floor and screamed. The exiting crowd walked around him, and his brothers and sister walked as far away as they could. Stan and I tried to coax him to his feet, but finally Stan just picked him up and carried him out of the theatre crying and screaming. Once outside he laughed as if he wanted his father to pick him up and was happy to be in his arms.

We headed to the motel for a swim, which turned out to be the most relaxing part of the trip. Stan supported Ricky while he kicked his feet and flailed his arms. He loved it and laughed the entire time in the pool. After the swim we changed and headed for dinner at one of the few restaurants in the town. Thank goodness no one in the restaurant seemed upset by the wild actions of a child from Vineland Training School. I was embarrassed by Ricky's behavior at the table, but Stan was so cool about it. He acted as though he never noticed Ricky's grabbing food from his siblings' plates, stuffing his mouth, or dropping the food all over himself and the floor. Ricky ate so fast that I had to take him outside when he was done so the rest of the family could finish their meal in peace. He was happy to walk around with me until they finished. We tried to have him sleep at the motel with us, but we were all up the entire night because he still couldn't sleep through the night. We learned to take him back to his cottage for sleep and pick him up in the morning. The next day we had breakfast together and then a quick swim in the pool before we left for home.

Leaving was torture. Again Ricky ran after the car crying and calling "Ma Ma". All of us were upset as we slowly drove off the grounds. We made certain that Ricky had a visit at least once a month from someone in the family the entire time he lived at Vineland, but the act of leaving was always emotionally difficult. We tried to bring Ricky home for holidays but the change in his routine was too traumatic for him.

I remember Ricky's first home visit the Christmas after he was placed. Stan flew to Vineland to pick him up and flew home with him. He was excited to be home, but he was without his routine. He was extremely hyperactive, not knowing what to do and where to go. We tried to establish a new routine for him with his brother Andy as his playmate. I remember one night Lee came downstairs looking very disturbed. Stan and I asked him what was troubling him.

"I can't sleep. I feel so sorry for Ricky and so sorry for me." He whispered. We tried to assure him that we understood and that it was natural he might feel this way. We told him that Ricky was not aware of the stares people gave him or of the way other people reacted to him. Lee on the other hand was extremely sensitive to the reactions of others. We told him that he was an individual separate from his brother and, although we always wanted him to love and care about Ricky, the way Ricky acted was not a reflection of Lee's behavior. He could be proud of being Lee. I asked our doctor for something to give Lee to help him sleep and the doctor gave me some medication to relax him. Lee began to sleep better after he took the medicine.

I felt terrible that Lee was so troubled. Balancing the needs of all of my children weighed heavily on my mind. Frequently I felt that I was caring for one of my children at the expense of the other. I was angry that I had to make such choices, but I didn't see many options.

During the vacation our home was open to all of the children in the neighborhood. I liked to bake and made cookie houses at Christmas and dozens of holiday cookies to give to all of our children's friends. By the time the holiday was over and Ricky returned to Vineland, I was totally wiped out. Stan took him back to the school and then made a detour to New York for business before he returned home. Whenever Stan traveled to New York on a business trip, he added another day to see Ricky. That saved us the cost of the trips for everyone. Andy always asked for his birthday present to be a trip to see his brother, and we met his wish for all of the years we lived in Michigan.

Stan was an extremely gifted man and was able to talk about most subjects with great knowledge and expertise. Although his vision was poor, he read constantly, often using clip-on glasses over his regular prescription as well as a magnifying glass. I was always impressed by his determination and intelligence. One of the main projects Stan undertook for the ARC was to create the first sheltered workshop, New Horizons, to provide jobs for people with mental retardation in Oakland County. For the first time, I saw how much time and effort it took to successfully start and finish something that no one had attempted before. I think that one of the reasons I felt able to do whatever I did was because I had seen what Stan could do.

Stan and I were both committed to our marriage and to our children, including Ricky. We had many disagreements about little things, but there was never disagreement about the important things in our lives such as our children and our drive to succeed in finding the American dream. One of our close friends referred us to other families who were facing similar problems with their children. Some of them were not able to tolerate the pressure of providing for private care and often placed their children in state-run institutions and then gradually stopped visiting them because it was so difficult to see them in that environment. In addition, I saw many families break apart over the stress of caring for a handicapped child.

There was tremendous relief in knowing that my husband and I were in total agreement over how to care for Ricky and the necessity to do whatever was required. I remember a conversation with a mother who had placed her son in a private school in New York and then reluctantly transferred him to a state institution because of the high cost. She asked about Ricky. I said we had just placed him at Vineland Training School. She said she was surprised I would put that kind of pressure on my husband. I did not know what to say but was filled with gratitude that I did not yet have to face what she had had to do. I wondered how long we could pay for Ricky's care. We could not go back to our families. Stan simply had to earn more money, and I had to find a job.

Andy started school in September of 1963, and I immediately found a job as a dietitian in a school cafeteria. My duties were to plan menus, order food, and monitor preparation and cleanliness as well as the food served to the students. After a year I wanted to earn more money and looked into a graduate degree I could pursue in the evenings. I enrolled at Wayne State University in Detroit to study food service administration in large institutions. Sometimes Stan was at home and other times I hired a sitter.

Later that year our friends at the ARC asked me to interview for the job of dietitian at a new state school opening in Plymouth, Michigan. It was close to home, but I had some serious misgivings about the character of the place. I knew I could not work in the same environment I had seen at Lapeer. I went for an interview with the new director, Dr. Jacob Ravitz, and was very impressed with him.

He told me he wanted to improve the residents' care. The facility was new so buildings and grounds were in good repair. Large patches of green lawn with flowerbeds of riotous colors surrounded the one-story building. There were children's swings and benches and tables on the lawn. There were no foul odors present yet. Dr. Ravitz spoke knowledgeably about the fiscal problems facing an administrator in a large state school and the limited remedies available. He said he wanted to hire innovative staff that would be willing to try new ways to serve his residents. I said, "You have to hire me because I am good at thinking out of the box. I will improve the care of the residents without it costing a lot."

Actually I had no idea what I could or would do, but I wanted to work with this man. He smiled and told me he wanted to see what I could do. Then I told him that I needed to be home by 3:30 in the afternoons and that I could not work on school holidays. He frowned but agreed to my terms.

About this time we received an emergency call from Vineland informing us that Ricky had been taken to a Philadelphia hospital. Swallowing a tack had collapsed one of his lungs, and he was scheduled for surgery the next day. Stan and I flew to Philadelphia. During the flight I prayed and hoped for Ricky's recovery. I realized that I desperately wanted him to live and thought back to the time when I had thought it best if both Ricky and I had died. Obviously I had come a long way. We arrived at the hospital to learn that Ricky was already in surgery. We waited for a few hours and then heard someone call, "Where is the Wallace family?" I looked up and saw Ricky sitting up on the stretcher very much awake. The attendants said they had a hard time keeping Ricky anaesthetized during the surgery. Ricky never slept in the hospital bed. I held him on my lap and we watched television all night. Actually television went off at midnight so we spent much of the night staring at a blank screen. Stan went to a motel room and came in the morning to relieve me while I went to the motel for a nap. Ricky was released the next day and we drove him back to Vineland.

I returned to my job in the kitchen of Plymouth State School but actually shied away from the wards that housed the children with hyperactivity. I felt guilty that these children, so similar to Ricky, were living a life that I would not tolerate for my child. At this time I had no idea how to improve their lot so seeing them every day would have been very difficult for me.

The kitchen was of excellent design and outfitted with the latest-model equipment. I was impressed until I noticed that the cooks were grinding the meat, starches, vegetables and salad together in one pot. It was a gooey mess. "Whom are you cooking that for?" I asked. The head cook informed me that he was told he had to prepare the food that way for the residents in the "back wards" or they could not eat.

The back wards housed children and adults with profound mental retardation and cerebral palsy. Their bodies were twisted and contorted. I got so many complaints about the food from those floors that one day I went to observe a feeding.

These wards were called the punishment wards for staff that had performed in an unsatisfactory manner in other locations at the school. Feeding time was not pleasant to watch. The attendants held the children on their laps, many with their heads hanging down, and force fed them with s spoon while the children gagged and choked the food down.

It was obvious that there were several big problems. I thought that input from an occupational therapist would be important, but there were no therapists assigned to the back wards. Without input from the therapists who could have helped with the feeding of the residents, the staff did the best they could. There was one nurse on the floor and many direct care workers who fed and bathed residents and changed their diapers. Except for feeding and bathing, the residents spent the entire day in their cribs.

The night after seeing the feeding in those wards, I went home and tried to imagine what it would be like to be fed that way. I asked Stan to feed me some applesauce while I was lying in bed. I could not swallow and started coughing. If I could not swallow in that position, how could the residents who were so much more physically limited, get any food down? The next day at work I went to the record room and asked to see the statistics on the deaths of those living in these back wards. What I saw astounded me. There was a high incidence of deaths due to pneumonia caused by residents aspirating food into their lungs.

I decided we had to change the way we prepared and served food. I informed the cooks that they were to follow the recipes as written and each food was to be ground separately. I had to add liquid to some recipes and thickener to others, but we managed to get the food to the proper consistency for swallowing. I also noticed that cooks were smoking cigarettes while stirring the food and ashes dropped into the food. I informed them that smoking while they were on the job was to stop immediately. "How would you like to eat this food mixed with ashes?" I asked.

The head cook informed me: "We are not like these people."

"What do you mean, not like those people?" I countered.

"You know what I mean," he said.

"No, I don't," I said angrily. "You could have an accident and suffer brain damage and end up much like the residents you seem to think so little of." I was furious and informed him and all the other cooks that they were never to talk about the residents in that manner. There would be absolutely no smoking while working. All food was to be ground separately and served separately to the residents.

The next day the head of nursing called me into her office. "I hear you are changing the way the food is served on the back wards. Is that true?"

"Yes," I replied eagerly. "I think the residents will be able to swallow their food more easily."

"You might have talked to me first," she scolded.

"I thought you would be happy. It is certainly more appealing even for the nursing staff," I said patiently.

"Did it ever occur to you that by separating the foods, it takes longer for nursing to feed the residents and that they'll just mix it altogether on the plate anyway?" she said.

"I'm sorry that I did not think about talking to you about it," I apologized. "I won't make that mistake again. However our cooks are not going to mix everything together and will not serve it that way," I stated firmly.

Then I requested a meeting with Dr. Ravitz, the director, and told him of my concerns about the residents dying of pneumonia. At the same time I told him of my conversation with the head nurse and the changes I had made in the kitchen.

"Wow! You know you have really stirred things up," he told me. "The union called me, the kitchen staff complained about the smoking restrictions, and I have heard from nursing about the way the food is being served." I expected to be told that I was fired but instead he said, "I agree with everything you did. Go ahead, and I will deal with the union and nursing."

I was relieved and pushed my luck further by asking, "Why are there no auxiliary therapies being used on those floors such as occupational, physical or even recreational therapy? Since many of these residents are children, education might make a presence sometime during the day."

He said, "There are not enough therapists to serve those residents who have mild mental retardation, so there are none available to go to the back wards. The State made no provision for education for such residents."

Of course I had already experienced that, so I was not surprised. I asked, "Could I try some therapy with those residents? I think we might be able to position them so they can swallow their food better."

He wished me luck and asked to be kept informed.

I met with the occupational, physical, and speech therapists to ask them to help. They were wonderful about sharing their knowledge with a young dietitian. In most cases the occupational therapist had the job of helping residents eat. Usually the dietitian did not concern herself with the positioning of residents or with teaching residents how to chew and swallow. I had read that the same muscles in the mouth used for speaking are used for eating so I asked the speech therapist for help. She told me of a school in Kansas that specialized in speech. I wrote to the Institute of Logopedics and asked for help. They sent reams of material, which showed me ways to stimulate the face and mouth muscles to assist chewing and swallowing. There were diagrams showing how to position fingers around the mouth for massage and how to use the broad handle of a spoon to "walk the tongue" (using the spoon handle to apply pressure as it moves slowly from the front to the back of the tongue). I studied the information and then developed a plan for positioning the residents so they could eat more comfortably and safely.

This was really exciting. Finally I was going to develop a new way to feed the people who have been ignored for so long and make a difference in their lives. It was a "high" for me. If I figured out a way to improve the lives of other people's children, then maybe someone else would improve life for my son at Vineland. I know this was wishful thinking, but it helped me to rationalize why I was working here and not with Ricky.

Since positioning was so important when eating, I needed to find proper seating for the residents. I met with the head of the carpentry department to ask him if we could modify chairs so the residents could be positioned better for eating. I wanted to provide more support for the residents in a more upright posture. I love challenges, and this was a challenge that I was sure I could meet.

As busy as they were, the carpenters were not happy to hear of my plans, but Dr. Ravitz contacted the head carpenter and told him that modifying the chairs for the residents in the back wards was important to him. That did it! The head carpenter and I worked closely together. We came up with the idea of attaching plastic-coated foam cushions in different shapes onto the wheelchairs with Velcro. This provided support for the residents where they needed it so they could sit in a more upright posture. At first the carpentry department resisted because of the cost, but in the end I prevailed and Velcro was the magic that kept the cushions fastened to the wheelchair. We also made lapboards and foot supports that attached to the wheelchairs. The chairs looked like something from a monster movie, but they served the purpose. The resident was supported in an upright position ready to learn to swallow.

I showed my plan for a feeding program to both the director at Plymouth State School and to my advisor at Wayne State University. I requested that I write my master's thesis about the development of a feeding program for the residents of a large state school. Both the director and my advisor agreed that I pursue this project. This was the start of my total immersion into all aspects of the lives of people with mental retardation. In 1964, I was referred to one ward to start my feeding program. Ricky was eight years old, and I was starting on a big experiment.

Since there were no activities offered to the residents of the back wards, Dr. Ravitz was happy to have someone develop a program that stimulated the residents, who, except for bathing and feeding, spent their days lying in cribs. Today there would be no opportunity for a dietitian to get so involved in all the daily activities, but in 1964 and 1965 there were no activities for these residents. I was at the right place at the right time. I felt so lucky to be involved because it opened up an entire new world to me where I was a success.

When we got started, one of the most important things I told the staff was that they had to talk to the residents using their given names. It was difficult to talk to people who did not respond. I kept reminding them how important it was to speak to the residents throughout all of the activities.

I wrote a program to be followed by all staff detailing a new schedule for the 24-hour life of a resident with profound cerebral palsy and mental retardation. At the start of the day, staff awoke and fed the residents, followed with personal hygiene activities such as bathing and brushing teeth. After bathing residents, staff placed them on mats in a large room where there were activities to stimulate the senses. Staff moved between the residents lying on mats, rubbing their arms and legs with cloths of different textures, wafting vials of different odors under their noses, and making different noises from soft to harsh sounds. At mealtimes they were fed a variety of textures and tastes. Breakfast, lunch, dinner, and three snacks took up a large part of the day for these residents. All wore diapers, and staff was instructed to change the diapers when necessary so residents did not lie in their own waste. There was no attempt to toilet train or regulate their bowels.

Positioning was important, and the carpenter shop was successful in making the adaptations necessary. The footrests with straps helped stabilize residents' feet. If staff could not position the resident in the chair, the caretaker held him/her in as near to an upright position as possible on their lap. Often this was difficult because the pull of the muscles was so strong that the caretaker could not maintain them in an upright position for long. After residents ate and rested upright, staff returned them to the mats.

Staff had to turn the residents on schedule to reduce the chance of sores forming at the pressure points on their bodies. I attached a large 24-hour schedule to the walls in the day room and in the dormitory. Every resident had his/her own 24-hour schedule. I directed the activities to be sure that they were followed and was able to show an increase in weight gain, and alertness as well as a reduction in aspirational pneumonia before I left this job.

I remember a supervisor asking me to go to a different ward with similar residents to see one particular man. After I recommended a program for him, I asked the referring doctor about all of the other people in this ward. He said that this man's family was the only one demanding the service. This was a good lesson for me. The old adage that the squeaky wheel gets recognized is so true.

I felt so much better about myself once I saw how much the program helped the residents. It was great to talk to Stan and the children about my work. When I asked, "What did you do today?" no longer did I get the pat answer "Nothing". My stories elicited stories from my family and encouraged us to exchange information about our lives in school and at work. I think my enthusiasm was catchy.

My thesis was the story of creating a life out of the crib for this population. I wrote of the value of the program by documenting the improvement in the resident's weight, alertness, and responsiveness. I showed a reduction in cases of pneumonia and death from aspirated food.

I presented this program at a national convention of the American Association of Dietetics. Mrs. Katrina Frank, then the Director of Food Service in New York State Department of Mental Health and Mental Retardation, asked if I would send her a copy of the program. She wanted to institute it in New York State. I was flattered and happy to share my findings with anyone interested.

At home, however, the atmosphere was completely different. Stan often came home late when he was in town because of law school and his meetings with the ARC. If the house was not straightened and all of the toys put away he complained, "What a mess! You could at least pick up the stuff."

I was angry and hurt but said nothing. Inside I was fuming because I had worked all day, gone to school, made dinner for the children, helped everyone go to bed and, for the first time I was sitting relaxing. On one hand, I was feeling successful in my work and in school, but I continued to feel unsuccessful in my role as mother and wife. Looking back, I realize I should have shared my feelings with Stan, but we did not talk about our feelings good or bad.

Lee was experiencing some problems in school in the 6th grade. He was refusing to write required compositions or hand in homework. Talking to him or threatening to withhold privileges was not working. We were advised to seek help from a social psychologist by the name of Dr. Zion. Andy was still angry with me, and now Lee was having problems. I blamed myself for his problems, too. Dr. Zion insisted on seeing all members of the family. At first Stan and I met with him together, and then he requested that we meet separately. He had picked up on our inability to really talk to each other about our deep feelings. It was through his counseling efforts that Stan and I managed to communicate better. Stan said he had no idea I was angry or why I was angry. The improved communication brought us closer than ever. I noticed that I was not feeling as though I had the weight of world on my shoulders. I felt lighter and better about myself as a mother and a wife. Lee seemed to be helped by his meetings with Dr. Zion. Things on the home front were definitely getting better.

Suddenly Stan was asked to pick up his family and transfer to New York city. He was already spending every week in New York, coming home on the weekends. We met with all of the children to give them the news. After the meeting, Andy looked at me and asked, "Which one of us is going to be left behind?" Melanie answered before I had a chance and said, "Why would you think that anyone would be left behind?" Andy did not answer.

"We are all moving together," I said loud and clear.

Ricky had been gone from our home for five years. Happily we were moving closer to him and soon would be able to visit more frequently than once a month, but our visits with Ricky were not very satisfying. He was getting bigger, more anxious, and even aggressive. He could force himself to vomit and would do so when he thought we were leaving. Many times I left Vineland with his unhappiness on my clothes. I continued to talk to the staff about his problems but always came away thinking that there was nothing we or they could do to change Ricky's behavior. The school made a big staffing change, replacing the couples that served as foster parents in the group home with shift staff. The administration could not find couples that wanted this kind of work. I was looking forward to keeping a closer eye on his program after the move.

For Melanie, the move to New York gave her a chance to reconnect with a camp friend. Andy showed no feelings after he was assured that he would come but stayed very close to me whenever we left the house. Lee asked how he was going to have his bar mitzvah in November if we moved. We talked about it and all of us decided to have the ceremony in Detroit followed by a lunch. We would return to New York on Sunday. We were also concerned that Lee might suffer from leaving Dr. Zion's counseling and asked him to recommend a doctor in New York. He said he didn't know one to recommend. I hoped that Lee would make the transition successfully. We decided that if he had trouble we would simply have to find a doctor where we settled.

My roommate and many of my friends from Cornell lived in the New York area and the thought of being closer to them was exciting for me. I was worried about finding another job but felt good about myself professionally, confident that I could find work that I liked. I remembered Ms. Frank from the New York Department of Mental Health and Mental Retardation and intended to contact her as soon as we were settled in our new home. Stan had concerns about mixing with all of the top executives who worked out of New York, so he had some professional anxiety but knew that moving was necessary for career advancement.

Stan and I treated the trip to New York to find a home as a second honeymoon. We decided to settle in Roslyn, Long Island on the north shore. This was close to Melanie's and my friends. Stan joined the commuters on the Long Island Railroad everyday and enjoyed the quiet time to read the paper and prepare for his day.

It was a bit strange for me. We were moving to a new home in a new city that Ricky might never know. We insisted that Andy's room be large enough for both boys, always hoping that one day we could bring Ricky home. I felt confident that as a family we would do well in this new environment and looked forward to a big slice of the Big Apple.

CHAPTER III

THE BIG APPLE

In 1966 Ronald Reagan became governor of California, the Supreme Court ruled poll taxes unconstitutional, New York City made 5th avenue and Madison Avenue one-way streets and we arrived at our new home on Long Island.

Amid much laughter and some apprehension, the five Wallaces opened the door of their new home at Birch Drive in East Hills. The house was on three levels built into a hill, so while every one investigated the floor plan and decided on a bedroom, Stan and I unpacked the boxes. The telephone started ringing as soon as it was connected. It didn't take long for teenagers to let other teenagers know that they were available. Neighbors knocked on the door welcoming us to the neighborhood.

The next weekend the drive to visit Ricky was so short that we were able to return the same day. What a relief that we didn't have to fly or stay in a hotel to see our boy. Melanie and Lee chose not to join us, but Andy wanted to visit his brother. After the hugs and kisses, Ricky was running around aimlessly, and while there was no danger of him being hurt on this large campus, it was not easy running after him. He ran to the car expecting us to leave immediately.

There was no time to talk to any of the staff once Ricky spotted us. Ricky seemed to know we were coming even though we never contacted the school in advance. He sat in front of the window with his coat on, refusing to go to school or other activities. I was told that happened frequently when I visited but not as frequently when his father came. His "strike" occurred often enough to make me believe that a strong tie existed between Ricky and me that miles apart never severed.

After five years away at school, we were disappointed that Ricky had not developed more self-control. He still ran aimlessly, had no vocabulary, did not know sign language, and other than in size, had not matured beyond that of a two-or three-year old. He reacted impulsively and unpredictably to any stimulus.

Taking him to a restaurant was a daunting experience. He pointed to all the food on the menu and demanded instant service by yelling or hitting the table with the silverware. He wanted to eat everything on the menu, and it was difficult to get him to sit and wait for the food to arrive once ordered. We finally found a cafeteria where he could point to what he wanted and we could place it on his tray immediately, but that didn't work. He screamed when he could not have everything. We abandoned the cafeteria and found a restaurant like a Denny's that had pictures of the food on the menu. One solution that seemed to help was offering Ricky raisins or small bits of cereal one piece at a time until the food was actually delivered to the table. I carried treats in my pockets whenever I was with Ricky, since this was the only way we were able to help him wait. His constant movement kept him thin so weight gain was never a problem. The treats were a reward for his self-control and for delaying his satisfaction. Without my being aware of it, this was the beginning of my work with behavior modification.

I was grateful that going to the movies continued to be the one activity Ricky loved, but I dreaded the constant fight over candy and other treats from the food concession. We hoped the school would help him with his wanting everything. We met with staff to learn about their behavior modification treatment plans. The response we always received from staff was that there was nothing more they could do to help Ricky control his impulsivity except more drugs. He was on so much medication at that time that his hands shook constantly. He continued to drool because he never closed his mouth, and if you do not close your mouth you drool. It disgusted me to see my 10-year-old drool like a baby. We requested that the staff remind Ricky to close his mouth and swallow.

Stan and I shared the school-related issues. I was the one who spoke with the school about programs while Stan dealt with the finances. At this time I felt that I was not doing a very good job of helping Ricky. Seeing him more frequently made me more aware that although he was growing bigger, he certainly was not maturing either socially or intellectually, which is exactly what the Michigan doctor had told us and I had refused to believe.

Ricky's abilities were confusing to me. He had an amazingly good sense of direction, and no matter where we drove, when we turned the car to return to the school, he screamed and shook his head from side to side. One time while I sat next to him in the back seat, he spat at me and struck me with his open hand as he kicked the front seat and attempted to kick the windows. "You have to go back to the school. They are waiting for you, and we have to go back home," I yelled.

He shook his head and kept screaming and kicking. Finally Stan pulled the car over to the side of the road, got out, grabbed Ricky by the shoulders, and shook him while telling him in a loud voice he had to return to the school. I became frustrated, turned my back on Ricky, and got back into the car while Stan guided him firmly into the seat next to me. Ricky continued to shake his head, and as soon as Stan started the car he started his screaming and kicking again. "Do something", Stan yelled.

"I don't know what to do. Just keep driving and pretend you are not hearing what you are hearing," I yelled back. We put up with Ricky's screaming and kicking until we reached the school. Stan walked around the car to the back door and opened it. He called to staff standing in the front of Ricky's cottage asking for help to forcibly remove him from the car. I moved to the front passenger seat quickly to avoid the spray of vomit that Ricky directed at me. Stan was not so lucky and had Ricky's anger all over his shirt. I was prepared with paper towels and cleaning supplies to help us handle the drive home.

It was hard to keep going back when Ricky was so unhappy, and we had no idea how to make him happy about staying at Vineland, but we visited as often as we could. I was frustrated because I didn't know what to do and didn't know where to go to get the information that might help. All of the work I had done with the clients who were so profoundly retarded and physically disabled at Plymouth State School did not prepare me to help my son.

I remembered our trips to the zoo and thought about behavior modification. I went to the library and read all I could on the operant conditioning experiments psychologist Dr. Skinner was conducting. Skinner developed the behavior modification or operant conditioning theory of changing behaviors that centered on rewarding positive behaviors instead of punishing negative behaviors. I became excited and hopeful that this might work with Ricky, but how could I find the behaviors I could reward? Maybe when he sat still if even for a minute. After reading about Skinner's successful experiments with rats and other animals, I felt that we should be able to successfully implement some of these practices with Ricky. I felt guilty comparing my son to the animals Dr. Skinner used in his experiments, but I was desperate. For a moment I felt hopeful that Skinnerian concepts could work and that I could convince the school to work with me on implementing them.

On my next trip to Vineland, I talked to the head of programming about my concerns and Ricky's inability to tolerate any delayed satisfaction. I asked them about the use of behavior modification; they reassured me that medication was the answer. They maintained that Ricky was too severely retarded to benefit from behavior modification and told me not to worry. I also asked staff to teach Ricky some sign language because I thought that if he could communicate better, it would reduce some of his frustration. He was very interested in communicating and used gestures all of the time. They stated that Ricky had such poor eye-hand coordination that he could not use signs. "How do you know if you do not try," I asked. Ricky was ten years old and I wanted us to get a handle on these difficult behaviors before adolescence, but I was unsure of myself in this area, so with reluctance agreed to let the school continue to handle Ricky's training or lack there of. I was not giving up on behavior modification, but I had to do more reading and talking to other professionals before I was ready to try it on Ricky.

Right now I had to find a job. We still had the expense of Vineland and Stan's salary alone could not cover our living costs and Ricky's, even with his salary increase. I contacted Mrs. Frank, the Director of Nutrition Services for New York State Department of Mental Health and Mental Retardation and reminded her of my presentation at the convention. I was surprised that she remembered me and wanted to hire me. She said she had no money to employ me at a state school serving people with mental retardation, but if I was interested in the meantime in working at an institution serving people with mental illness, she could find the money for me to work at a state school in about six months. I accepted and started working at a state hospital for patients with mental illness. This work was completely different from caring for people with profound mental retardation, cerebral palsy, and autism. The meal preparation process was the same as in any of the large institutions where I had previously worked, but these patients had definite ideas about what they liked and did not like, and they let you know.

One instance stands out in my mind. I put baco chips and meat on the menu for a Friday night dinner. When I came to my office on Monday, a rabbi and a priest were waiting for me. I asked if there was a problem, and the rabbi told me that the Jewish patients were upset because there was bacon on the menu. I informed him that the baco chips were not bacon but soy. He looked me in the eye and said, "The patients do not know they are soy"

The priest said that the Catholic patients were upset because there was meat on the menu Friday. I said that the Pope had issued a directive that it was all right to eat meat on Friday. The Priest looked me in the eye and said, "The patients do not know the Pope has allowed meat on Friday."

I was embarrassed by my mistakes and vowed to be more aware of the isolation of the people living in institutions. Within six months Mrs. Frank called to advise me she had found the money and wanted me to consult at a school for people with mental retardation, Suffolk State School on Long Island. I was delighted and surprised, "How did you know you could obtain the money needed to hire me? I asked.

"Renée, there is always money in a large bureaucracy like the State of New York if you know where it is and whom you need to ask to get it," she replied. Excited, I looked forward to getting back into nutrition and the feeding program that I had developed in Michigan. On my first day I met the head dietitian who had no idea what I was doing there, since dietitians typically had nothing to do with actually feeding the residents. She couldn't understand why I was hired. No dietitian ever moved out of the kitchen to advise about anything but nutrition and menus. She was not alone in her disbelief.

The nursing department and all of the allied therapies also did not know what I was doing there. I realized that unless I made believers out of the nursing staff, I was not going to be able to do my work. They were the ones who worked most closely with the residents on a day-to-day basis. I also had to relieve the anxiety of the dietary staff that I required nothing more from them than their current duties. I requested a meeting with the nursing staff and invited the dietary staff also. We sat around a large conference table. I explained what I had done in Michigan and got a "so what?" response. I said, "Let me feed the resident who is the most difficult for you to feed in this entire institution. If I do not convince you that I have something to offer to you, I will tell Albany that I can do nothing here."

The head nurse looked at me and said that I should come prepared the next day at 11:00 A.M. to meet a young boy, James. He had a condition called opisthotonus, which caused him to regurgitate the food he ate so he needed to be tube-fed because he was unable to ingest food by mouth. I thanked them and left. I rushed to a medical library to look up the word "opisthotonus". It is a condition in which severe spasticity pulls the head back toward the heels of the afflicted individual. Not a good position for eating, I thought.

The feeding program I designed, with the help this time from the Cerebral Palsy Association, required the feeder to be a bit of a contortionist. My bag of tricks included a pillow to go under my arm, a plastic hose made of fish tank tubing, a hair-dye bottle found in a drugstore, three special spoons coated with latex, a special dish that kept the food warm for a long period, and a vibrator.

The method I was going to use to feed James I developed during my years in Michigan. At that time I read all I could and talked to many therapists and tried many different approaches to feeding. It was a trial-and-error methodology for sure. I had found that using a metal spoon injured the gums, teeth, and jaw when the resident clamped his or her mouth shut as soon as any object was placed on the tongue. The coated spoon for infants turned out to be an answer for that problem.

I needed to squeeze liquid into James's mouth so I tried many plastic bottles. The easiest and cheapest was the hair-dye bottle. Regular straws didn't work because they collapsed when the residents firmly closed their teeth on them. One day when I was placing the tubing into my son's fish tank, I realized that it was very firm. I boiled it to sterilize it, cut a large hole in the top of the dye bottle so the tubing could pass through, and then tried pushing liquid up through it from the plastic bottle. It worked.

Keeping the food warm during the lengthy feeding process was also important. The texture of the food changed when it cooled and there was the danger of bacteria growing when protein dishes sat at room temperature. I looked through catalogues and at an infant's store found a plate with the section underneath for warm water.

I had the tools needed to get the food into James's mouth, now I had to figure out how to help get the food into his body. According to what I had read from the Institute of Logopedics, stimulating the muscles around his mouth and cheeks was important. I needed something stronger than my fingers and thought of a vibrator, but the only place I could find one was in a shop dedicated to "sex" toys. Embarrassed and looking furtively over my shoulder to be sure that no one I knew saw me, I quickly entered a shop at a local mall, purchased the vibrator, and exited. My tool kit was complete.

I knew the process of feeding could last several hours, but I felt prepared. I arrived with confidence and high hopes at the appointed time, dressed in a silk dress with high heels and silk stockings, ready to convince the nurses that I knew what I was doing. There was an armchair for me with a table next to it to hold all of my paraphernalia. One of the attendants brought me a large sheet to cover my dress but I refused the offer. Either I was going to make a big impression or I was on my way to look for another job. I needed this job badly, so I was highly motivated.

The staff brought James to me, and when I saw how badly he was bent backwards, my confidence began to fade. I propped my arm on the chair arm, had the pillow placed under my arm, and cradled his head in my arm. The spasm pulling his head back was so strong that it felt as though someone had placed a concrete block on my arm.

I started talking to him in a quiet singsong voice, using his name and smiling. I used the vibrator around his mouth and on his cheeks, all the while speaking to him. The staff brought the food to me, and I requested they place the food in the dish I brought and the drink in the plastic bottle that I had already prepared with the tubing straw. Slowly I presented the food to James with the special spoons. One fell to the floor but I had an extra so that was not a problem. After a bit, I stopped the food, picked up the bottle and placed the tubing in his mouth with my right hand while pressing his lips over the tubing with my left hand. At the same time I pressed the sides of the bottle with my right hand, pushing the liquid into his mouth. I waited until he had swallowed before serving any more food or liquid. If he had difficulty swallowing, I stroked his throat in an upward motion with my right hand.

It actually took over two hours, but I fed James, and kept him on my lap for a while so the food would remain down. The nursing staff could not believe what they saw, and the word quickly got around that there was a lady who might be able to help them do their job better. They treated me as an important person on their team. The most amazing part of the entire process was that James didn't regurgitate any food, and he showed no distress from eating more food than he had in a long time.

I received great support from the main office in Albany as well as all of the staff at Suffolk State School. My next big challenge was finding a chair the residents could use to position them properly to eat. In 1967 there was nothing available for purchase so Mrs. Frank made a connection for me with a furniture manufacturer. He and I designed a chair to my specifications for use with our residents. I called it the Suffolk Chair. It was on wheels, with a high back that had cushions attached, a foot support with straps to position the feet, a lapboard, and a strong head support. "How can we attach the cushions and straps?" I asked.

"Thank goodness for Velcro," the manufacturer said. "It's a wonderful fastener for the cushions and the foot straps." I couldn't believe I had forgotten my experience in Michigan. The arms were adjustable, and the entire chair was covered in plastic cloth except for the foot supports and the tray. The Suffolk Chair was a big help in positioning those whose spasticity prevented them from sitting upright. Once it proved successful, I believe it was used throughout the New York system. Today, I am happy to say, many of the children born with severe cerebral palsy are given physical therapy at a young age so they don't have the awful body contortions that I saw in the 1960's.

There was another group of residents—those with hydrocephalous--who also needed help with positioning. The condition caused their heads to swell due to fluid accumulating in the brain cavity and made their heads so heavy they had to be supported so the weight wouldn't break their necks. These residents usually laid flat on mats during the day and needed at least two people to lift them. We used a physical support attached to the back of a wheelchair similar to the kind that beauty parlors use to support a customer's head during a hair wash. Once positioned correctly these residents had no trouble eating normally. Today most of the children born with what was then called "water on the brain" have shunts installed to drain off the excess fluid so today it is rare to find someone with an enlarged head.

I traveled frequently to Albany to meet with the nutrition staff and wrote detailed descriptions of what was going on at Suffolk State School including the improvements in the residents, the reaction of the staff, and the wide scope of the program. I don't know why I was so careful to document everything that was happening, but it seemed the correct thing to do at the time.

We continued to see Ricky two or three times a month and it was no easier leaving him or controlling him. He was growing taller and stronger as he entered his teen years. I continued to read about behavior modification, always thinking of ways we could use it to help Ricky but, still, was not sure of myself. I talked to Vineland staff about offering him small pieces of food such as raisins or cereal when he complied with a directive. It worked when we were in restaurants and he had to wait for his food. I suggested rewarding him with TV time when he was doing what staff asked and again mentioned possibly teaching Ricky sign language to help him communicate, but the staff at

Vineland were not interested; more medication and restraints continued to be their only answers to his problems.

In April of 1968, Stan arrived home from work with an anxious look
on his face. "I have good news and bad news to tell you," he said as he
sat in his favorite chair.

"Give me the bad news first," I said worriedly. I thought he might
have lost his job. My children always accuse me of thinking of the
worst possible events that could happen.

"We're being transferred to Houston, Texas." Absolute silence on my
part. I could not believe what I heard.

"We have just settled in, and the children have settled in, and we are
close to Ricky. No way are we going to move. Absolutely not," I said
with determination. "What is the good news?"

"I'll receive an increase in salary and a good possibility of a move to
vice president after we arrive in Houston," Stan replied.

"Let's talk about ways we can stay here,' I said. 'Are they closing the
office in New York?"

"There will only be a secretary in a small office here," Stan said. "If I
stay with the company we have to move."

"Could you get a job in public relations in New York? I asked. "I
think it is a great place to perform your job. Maybe you could start your
own company," I said desperately.

"Renée, what are you sayng?" Stan countered. "We have Melanie
going to college in a year, and the expenses for Ricky won't go away.
With Panhandle Eastern, we have great insurance that helps with
Ricky's medical costs. How can we match that? My salary will be
larger, and I really think I have a good chance of being promoted to
vice- president."

"Let's think about it," I said. "Would you put out feelers with some
public relations firms? I don't want to think of moving further from
Ricky. I'm really not happy with his lack of progress and being so far
from him," I pleaded. Stan promised to explore other options as we
hugged each other, holding on tight.

We took out paper and pencil and started adding the pluses and
minuses of the move. On the positive side, working for the large corporation offered health benefits and financial assistance with Ricky's
care. In addition it meant a promotion for Stan with another increase
in salary. On the negative side, the whole family would have to leave a
favorite city and lose the ability to visit Ricky weekly with ease. I had
a great job and was uncertain whether I could find a comparable one

in Texas.

The next few days we did not talk about the proposed move, but by the end of the week I asked Stan what he had found about the chances of staying in New York. There were jobs available, he said, but not at the salary and benefits he was making. Besides, he confessed that he wasn't that happy with all the drinking and partying that were part of the public relations scene in New York. "I'm more conservative, and staying with this company is a good fit," he said.

We looked at the figures and talked and talked about not making the move and finally both looked at each other and had to admit that leaving the company and striking out on our own was too risky given our responsibilities. It felt good to us that we had been able to handle all of our expenses without debt once I started working and Stan received increases in his salary. We had paid back our parents for the two years they had assisted with the cost of Ricky's care. Reluctantly, we agreed to move to Houston but decided not to tell the children until absolutely necessary.

One day Stan told me I needed to meet him in Houston to find a house. I told the children that I had to go to Albany, the State capital, for a meeting with Mrs. Frank. Trips to Albany were common so nobody questioned my being gone for a few days. When the plane to Houston was taxiing for takeoff, we suddenly heard a big bang like a car backfiring, but louder. Everyone in the cabin looked up anxiously. The pilot advised us over the speaker that two tires had blown. He said not to worry because he had notified Houston, and they would be ready for us when we landed. I imagined something happening to me when we landed in Houston and my children finding out that I had lied. I was a nervous wreck. When we landed amid fire engines and ambulances, it appeared that all of Houston's news reporters and cameramen were present to document the event. I walked off the plane hiding my face behind my purse so I would not appear on the news in case my children were watching TV. I promised myself no more lies.

While in Houston we found a builder and planned the home we wanted, incorporating many ideas I had been thinking about but never really believed I would be able to have. We had to trust the builder because we were not going to be in Houston while the house was being built. This turned out to be a big mistake. I wasn't worried because we had been transferred every two years, so I really believed that we probably wouldn't be in Houston more than a few years. Some people might call that wishful thinking. I did not have to tell any more fibs about the move because all of the children were gone during the summer, the boys to camp and Melanie living in Chile as an exchange student. When they all returned from their summer trips it was August. Melanie was in her last year of high school, Lee was starting his first year in high school, Andy was in his last year of elementary school and Ricky was entering his teens.

When we told the children of the move all of them were unhappy. Melanie actually ran away to her friend's house and refused to talk to us for a few days. She asked that she spend her last year with her friend and her friend's family, but Stan and I felt strongly that our family needed to stay together as long as possible. I promised Melanie that if she moved with us for one year, she could go to whichever college she wished. My hope was that Melanie would meet Texans and like living in the southwest. The fact that one of our children had been separated from us made us very uneasy about any further separations until absolutely necessary. Lee and Andy were anxious about leaving their friends, and the thought of making new friends in a strange place was not easy for them either.

The packing completed, we spent our last night in New York City at the Marriott Hotel. We all walked the streets of Manhattan eating our dinner from a hot dog vendor with desert from an ice cream vendor. As a treat we shared two bags of hot chestnuts while "people watching". The sounds of the big city were music to our ears. Finally it was time to return to the hotel.

We gathered in our room and talked about what to expect when we arrived in Houston. The boys sat on the floor and Melanie sat on the bed while Stan and I took the available chairs. "It's August and we are moving when it is the hottest and most humid, Ugh!" Melanie grimaced.

"I hear there is air conditioning in every building and in all the cars," I told her.

"Do you think there will be cows on the streets of Houston?" Andy asked.

"Houston is a metropolitan city," Stan said. "There are wide streets with lots of cars and no cattle in the city. The ranches are outside of the cities in the country. Texas is very large you know. Houston is in east Texas and close to the coast. We can drive to Galveston in an hour and be on great beaches. You'll love that," he added hopefully.

"It will be exciting to be so close to the Space Center, and we can take a tour of it as soon as we settle into our home." I said as everyone returned to his or her rooms for the night. I fell asleep dreaming of beaches, oil wells, large ranches, and the Space Shuttle.

CHAPTER IV

GO WEST YOUNG MAN

1968 was the year that Senator Robert Kennedy entered the race for President of the United States and was assassinated, Martin Luther King was assassinated, Aristotle Onassis married Jacqueline Kennedy, and Astroworld opened in Houston.

As the plane circled the city, I was excited to see the skyline with all the buildings stretching upward, a mini version of the New York skyline. Houston was a rapidly growing city and we were going to be a part of that growth.

On our arrival, we rented a car and drove to our new home. What a surprise to find that our home wasn't ready. Our builder had neglected to inform us, so we spent the night in a motel and found a furnished apartment the next day. While searching for an apartment it became obvious that Houston had no zoning. It was not surprising to see strip clubs and triple-X stores next to condos and office buildings.

I had to drive the children to school because we didn't want them to have to start in one school and move again in a few months to another district. I had three children going to three different schools. There still was no public education for Ricky so no chance of moving him to Houston. Since Stan was totally immersed in getting to know his new job, I filled my time with driving the children and monitoring the progress on the house.

Finally our home was ready, and we all had to admit that it was a lovely place to live. There were five bedrooms, so each child had his or her own room with a room waiting for Ricky. Our small community held "Coffees' (small gatherings to introduce the newcomers), and, until I found work, I was happy to meet all of the new people. Houston had become a hot destination and every day new people were moving into the neighborhood. At one gathering there was talk about the way someone's roof was designed and I said, "Back in the States all of our roofs are pitched roofs." Dead silence followed that remark, and it took a few minutes before I realized what I had said. I apologized and made some excuse about how the heat had made me light-headed.

It felt as if we had moved to another country rather than to another part of the same country. Houston was so hot most of the time that I felt it was too hot to get stirred up about anything. Every day I had headaches, and it took most of a year before I could comfortably work and play in this climate. I was not used to air-conditioning in every room and car.

Stan and I talked about moving Ricky to a private school close to Houston. I visited the school and was not impressed with the program for people with mental retardation. The majority of the residents were children with emotional problems rather than intellectual problems. After talking to the staff, I realized that the program was no better than the one at Vineland. They, too, believed in controlling the residents with medication and restraints and thought that someone with Ricky's intellect could not benefit from counseling or behavior modification. They only used behavior modification and counseling on the children with emotional problems, not with those with mental retardation. The school actually cost more than Vineland, a factor we had to consider. Change is difficult for everyone but change for a person with brain damage such as Ricky's is even more difficult, and I wanted to be certain that if we put him through a move, it would be worth it. I did not feel the move would make up for the stress Ricky would have to handle.

Either Stan or I continued to return once a month to see our son. Fortunately, Stan's business required him to make monthly visits to New York, and he always included a side trip to Vineland. He reported that Ricky was getting bigger but not better. His drooling was still bad, and he still could not tolerate the separation from his parents. He continued to scream and cry and vomit when his Dad left. Each set of grandparents made a trip to Vineland and were so pleased that Ricky had not forgotten them. In spite of their joy at seeing him, they agreed that the separation was so difficult for Ricky and for them, that they doubted they could do it again. It hurt me to think of Ricky without family visits from his grandparents.

Richmond State School was the state school closest to our home so I sought a position there similar to the one I had had in New York. I met with the school administrator and tried to convince him that he needed me to improve the feeding of his residents. He informed me that he had occupational therapists to do that and saw no place for me in his school. I was disappointed but then I thought of the dietitian Mrs. Frank had recommended that I contact. She was in Austin and informed me that there were no positions for on-site dietitians in the state schools in Texas. The menus were completed in Austin and distributed to the kitchen managers in each locale. Again I was disappointed, but since I had needed a job, I decided to look into hospital work. I found a head dietitian position in a small private hospital in downtown Houston. It was not my favorite job. I had disagreements with the doctors and nursing staff, but I was able to reduce costs by reducing overtime so I became popular with the administrator. Nonetheless, I also met a wonderful woman by the name of Maria Barrara, who was the head clerk in the kitchen. We became good friends, and she and I worked together for many years in other settings.

Those three years at the hospital passed quickly, and I thought that my work with people with mental retardation might be over. In 1972 my mother became ill with what the doctor thought was a stroke. I quit my job and spent as much time as I could in Cleveland, Ohio, but in May the doctors determined that my mother had a malignant brain tumor and had not suffered a stroke. After the operation, we were told the tumor could not be totally removed so it would continue to grow and eventually kill her. I was stunned.

I could not imagine not having my mother to ask for advise and help. I knew I had to be with her, so we made arrangements for Andrew to go to summer camp, and I moved to Cleveland to care for my mother. Stan and Lee were living together in Houston, and Melanie was in London as part of her program at the University of Michigan. I watched sadly as my mother gradually lost her speech, her vision, her ability to walk, and her ability to perform any of the activities of daily living. I spent 8 to 10 hours a day with her and when I was not there, a private duty nurse was with her. The tumor had destroyed her appestat (the portion of the brain that controls the appetite), so she had no control over her appetite. The nurses began to feed her so much that she became grossly overweight. I finally took over the feeding so we could control her food intake. How ironic that I was monitoring feeding again, only this time it was for my mother.

While I was in Cleveland I received a surprise letter from the State of New York requesting that I come to Albany to meet with Nutrition Services. When Geraldo Rivera, a junior reporter, climbed through a window at Willowbrook State School on Staten Island and took pictures of the terrible living conditions, he triggered an expose of the New York state schools. The pictures were televised throughout the state, and viewers had responded by demanding better conditions. The governor's office required that each state department responsible for services send in a plan of improvement. As their suggested proposal for improvements, the Nutrition Services Department had sent the report of my project at the Suffolk State School. The governor's representative requested that Nutrition Services implement my program in all of the state schools. Mrs. Frank insisted that I be contacted to implement the program in New York. I was so excited and proud that Mrs. Frank thought my reports were good enough to send to the Governor. It was serendipity that I had documented my work so assiduously.

I spoke to Stan and we decided I propose my coming to help them in New York one week a month as a consultant. I flew to New York and advised Mrs. Frank and the other administrators that we were not moving back to New York, since Stan had just been promoted to Vice President of Public Relations and Advertising. I suggested consulting--that I come to New York one week a month to initiate the program and train the staff at all of the state schools. I called the endeavor the Living Program and assured them I would be in touch by phone with the staff between visits. The first comment after hearing the name I chose for the program was that all of the children already were in a "living program".

"No," I insisted, "they are existing but not really living." The interviewers said they would let me know and I returned to Cleveland and my mother. The third week in August Andy returned from camp, and I had to leave my mother to return home to Houston. I knew this would be my last good-bye. Within two weeks the word came, my mother was gone. The entire family except for Ricky went to Cleveland for her funeral.

On my return, I heard from New York: Nutrition Services wanted me on my terms. I was elated, yet I felt strongly I needed to try again to work with people with mental retardation in Houston. The pay from New York State was good but not enough without a second job, so I contacted Dr. Frank Borreca at the Harris County Center For the Mentally Retarded (the Center). Dr. Borreca was the Executive Director of the largest private non-profit agency in Houston serving people with mental retardation. I managed to convince him that he needed to hire me the three weeks I was in Houston each month.

Recently Congress had passed public law 94-142 (I.D.E.A.) requiring that school districts serve all children regardless of their handicaps. It was 10 years too late for Ricky, but just in time for me. The schools did not know how to handle the children with severe cerebral palsy and profound mental retardation, so the Center started a program for them, and the school districts were happy to contract with the Center. No one had experience feeding these children, but as part of their program they had to have lunch, so the program was in need of my skills.

Dr. Borreca hired me immediately to design the feeding program and run the kitchen at the Center. The three-week/one-week schedule was working out. I remember going to the Center building where the school age children spent their days. I took off my coat, rolled up my sleeves, and took all the tools I used out of my briefcase. The staff, including the program supervisor, watched me with a great deal of skepticism. There were 25 children in wheel chairs, all of them with severe cerebral palsy and mental retardation. The four staff had no idea how to feed them. Starting with the child closest to me, I sat on a stool on wheels and placed the dish, spoons, and bottle with tubing next to me. I used the vibrator around her mouth and on her cheeks. Then I placed the food into the warmer dish and used the coated spoon to start feeding as I talked softly using her name. It took over an hour, but she ate all the food and seemed comfortable. I then asked one staff person to pick a child to feed and helped as needed. When all the children had eaten, I met with the supervisor and gave her a list of the items she needed to buy for feeding. We scheduled time after the children had left for home for me to train the staff. For three weeks I met with staff daily and then continued to monitor and help them during feeding times. I also suggested that the occupational therapist be brought in to monitor what we were doing. She was surprised that the children were eating so well. It thrilled me that this part of my job was successful.

In addition to working on the feeding program, I also was in charge of the Center's kitchen. I contacted my friend, Maria, and asked her if she would work with me again. Happily she agreed. She and I ran the kitchen, and she was in charge when I was in New York. I developed recipes for the children's food using the knowledge I had gained from my experiences in New York and Michigan. The two aspects of my work life were complementing each other. Now I was doing what I wanted and did it well. The trips to New York were rewarding and

I did not have to prove myself since everyone had heard about what I had done at Suffolk.

I expanded my bag of tricks to include designing toys and environments for the clients. The residents in New York had not had any toys they were able to use, so I worked with the carpentry departments to make toys large enough for the residents to hold in their hands and to move them. The toys were painted bright colors with lead-free paint and made noise so they provided visual, tactile, and audio simulation when children played with them. I created smaller environments within the large institution that were decorated with colorful designs and filled with soft music. We planned programs to stimulate all of the residents' senses. We used cloths of different textures to rub their bodies and small fans to blow on their faces and keep feathers in the air. We passed small bottles with a variety of odors under the residents' noses and flashed lights to help them focus. Since many of the residents had seizures, however, we had to be careful with the use of the lights. We played classical, country, and jazz music throughout the day.

I noticed that there were a couple of residents who ruminated (brought up the food and chewed it again and again). This habit was dangerous for them and unpleasant for those around them. I had read that music with a strong beat---such as marching music--- might help the problem, so the next day I brought a record player and album of marching music into the dining room. We fed these two young men behind a screen in the dining room. While they were being fed the music played loudly. Amazingly the ruminating decreased and then stopped totally. We spread the word to the other schools.

Many patients made progress as I moved from school to school throughout New York State. Some actually learned to chew and others learned to feed themselves. All of them in the program increased their awareness and most of them gained weight. What I learned in New York I shared with the students in Houston and visa versa.

On one of my trips to a school in upper New York State, I noticed that the staff in another program nearby walked around with rods in their hands. When I questioned the floor supervisor, I was told that they were cattle prods. The school had received a grant to study the effects of using shocks to reduce self-injurious behaviors. The study included only those residents with the most severe self-injurious behaviors; such as poking out their eyes or biting themselves so severely that they permanently injured themselves or throwing themselves into walls and furniture. When one of the residents tried to hurt him/herself, he or she received a shock from the prod. Aside from the inhumanity of the practice, the concept of using electric shock was hard for me to understand and accept. Once the study was over, I thought these residents might return to their negative behaviors unless that behavior had been replaced with a positive one. Later I learned that what I feared did occur. Although the self-abuse diminished greatly while the cattle prods were in use, as soon as the program ended, the residents returned to their previous behaviors. Many years later I would remember the futility of using devices such as electric shock to change behaviors and instead chose programs that offered positive alternatives to the residents who were injuring themselves.

I always ended my trip with a day in New York City and a visit to Ricky in Vineland. Ricky was 17, 5'8" tall with no reduction in his hyperactivity. He continued to keep his mouth open so he drooled heavily. I was unhappy with his lack of progress. Once again I talked with the school's administrators and suggested using sign language to help Ricky communicate and a behavior modification program to help him keep his mouth closed and reduce his hyperactivity. They agreed when I was present but when I was gone did nothing. I didn't know what to do.

When I visited the state schools in New York, I inquired about the care of the residents who were hyperactive and similar to Ricky and asked the psychologists and the other therapists what I could do to help my son. They all gave me ideas but one psychologist was the most helpful. We discussed the expanding field of behavior modification. I continued to read about positive reinforcement and thought about how we could use Ricky's likes and dislikes to redirect his behavior. I had ideas I thought might work but was still unsure of myself and didn't see how to effect changes with him.

Once a year the Developmental Disability Council of Texas offered grants for proposals that might help the lives of people with mental retardation, and I entered a proposal to design equipment for positioning people with bodies twisted by cerebral palsy. My inspiration was a process for custom-fitting shoes designed and molded to fit people's feet. I thought about using that same process to help position people with cerebral palsy.

The idea was to place the person on a large plastic bag filled with small plastic pebbles and then deflate the bag with a vacuum. That deflated bag served as a model for a heat-molded replica of the shape. ABC plastic (a hard plastic sheet) was placed over the bag in the molding machine. When the machine was closed and the heat applied, it molded the plastic into the shape of the bag. After the plastic form had cooled, it was fastened to the frame of a wheelchair, and the person had a custom-designed seat.

I received the grant. With it, I paid for the heat-molding machine, all of the equipment and the salary for someone to run the machine. Dr. Borreca gave me room in the workshop to conduct the program. I traveled all over Harris County, and people from surrounding counties came to us to have the inserts made. The biggest problem for children was that they grew and their shape changed. For adults the inserts had a much longer life. It was exciting to see the impact these custom-designed seats had on their lives. All of the people in these custom designed seats were more comfortable, better able to eat and participate in their everyday activities.

Nothing is ever as it seems, at least not for me. In 1975 I was still working at the Center three weeks a month, but a new governor was elected in New York, and all contracts were cancelled. Dr. Borreca offered me the position of Director of Residential Services at the Hugh Roy and Lillie Cullen Residence Hall (Cullen). In 1973 the Center had opened the high-rise to serve people with mild and moderate mental retardation. The majority of people with mental retardation had mild forms, and most programs were geared to serve that population. This assignment would be totally different for me since I had not worked with this population previously. I talked to Stan and we decided I should try it.

CHAPTER V

THE CULLEN EXPERIENCE

IN 1975 Gerald Ford was president; John Mitchell, H.R. Haldeman, and John Erlichman went to jail; and the United Nations proclaimed this International Women's Year. It was definitely the year for this woman.

I opened the door to the Hugh Roy and Lillie Cullen Residence Hall (Cullen Hall), my new home away from home, and was greeted with the laughter and excited voices of men and women enjoying drinks and food in a snack bar off the lobby. The lobby was in a six-floor building designed to house 240 men and women with mental retardation. Some were lounging on the couches and chairs and others were playing cards and board games on the many tables placed strategically around the room. I greeted the woman behind the counter and introduced myself.

After standing for a moment enjoying the happy scene, I entered my office behind the front desk to find one of the parents waiting for me. She introduced herself and asked me about my background. When I told her my educational and professional background she challenged me, "You are a dietitian and you intend to manage this unit with over 200 residents."

"Yes, I do," I replied. "I have been in charge of over 50 staff in many different positions and I have 28 years of experience working and caring for a family of 6. My life experiences alone should prepare me for this position. I've also worked with people with mental retardation for over 15 years. Give me a chance to show you what I can do."

"We'll see," she scoffed as she walked out of the office. She became one of my biggest supporters even after I left Cullen. When I returned home that evening I talked with Stan about the challenges I faced caring for over 200 people with mental retardation and other developmental disabilities in a 24-hour home. I felt ready to meet those challenges. There would be no training period. I had to be ready to manage the day-to-day problems facing those people in my charge right from the start.

I realized that along with all of the scientific information available, common sense and respect played a big part in dealing with all people regardless of their I.Q.. In this residential program I could see there were the wheeler-dealers, the leaders, the socially conscious people-lovers, the scoundrels, the politicians, the society ladies, and the bag ladies.

Becoming fond of the residents was easy, and again I realized how much they were like the general population. I was able to work out problems most of the time because I thought about what I would want and what my young adult children wanted in their lives. I believed that the people at Cullen were more like us than they were different from us.

At that time there was no community or government funding for most of the people living at Cullen. Some of the residents were eligible for Supplemental Security Income (SSI) and received checks monthly, but the amount of the SSI check did not cover the cost of living at Cullen. When I started, there were 100 empty beds, and the board asked me to fill those beds. I had friends who had opened community homes and had received funding through a Medicaid program for licensed Intermediate Care Facilities for Mentally Retarded, known as ICF/MR to those of us in the field. Some of these were small homes for six people, but many were large and served over one hundred people. I suggested that we convert two of the six floors to the IC F/MR program and thereby become eligible to receive Medicaid dollars. This would fill the beds and remove the worry on the part of 86 residents for rent money.

The ICF/MR program provided per diem funding from Medicaid for people who had certain intellectual disabilities and met Medicaid (financial) guidelines. Most of the residents had no private income, were diagnosed with mental retardation, and qualified for the program. Once a person reached adult status their family income was not considered. It was my responsibility to obtain the license to receive the funding. I wrote to the state for the regulations and received 25 pages of standards required for licensure. We met each of the standards one at a time. It took about six months to complete the job.

In order to comply it was necessary to move the residents around so that all of those who met the intellectual requirements of the program were concentrated on the two floors. Surprisingly we managed the move with a minimum of difficulty for the residents, but there was one person who objected. Peter refused to move. He was a mild mannered man in his 30's who wore glasses and was always neatly dressed and well groomed. He worked in the sheltered workshop run by the Center during the day, and most of the time followed all of the rules. I was surprised that he did not want to move because his present roommate had severe mental retardation and had trouble with his personal care. The suggested new roommate was similar to Peter in intellect and interests. I asked that the staff invite Peter to visit with me. As soon as he entered the room I said seriously, "Hello, Peter. Thanks for visiting with me. Why don't you want to move?"

He responded equally seriously, "I don't want anyone to touch my TV and my roommate doesn't touch my TV."

"Is that all?" I asked.

"Yes," he replied.

I knew who his new roommate was and was pretty sure that he would not touch anything of Peter's without permission so I said, "I promise you that your new roommate will not touch your television without your permission so I am willing to replace your TV if anything happens to it. I'll put in writing that I will replace your television if your new roommate damages it. This is called a contract."

"You mean it?" he asked in a surprised tone.

"I'll write the contract right now, and both of us will sign it, " I told him. " I'll ask Paul, your staff, to introduce you to your new roommate and then come back to me. If it is OK with you to move, we'll place this contract in your personal file." His face lit up and we both signed the contract. He moved and never had a problem with his new roommate.

When the staff asked me what I had done. I responded that I had asked him "why?" If you respect someone, you must show that respect by finding out why they feel a certain way." I realized I needed to do more training. Most of my staff were in their 20's and did not have much life experience behind them. They were all either in college or recent college graduates but still needed training to understand how to work with people who looked like everyone else but because of intellectual limitations needed more support and assistance.

One of the challenges I faced was the need to establish my authority. The staff and residents had to know that I had the complete backing of the Center's Executive Director, Dr. Frank Borreca.

One resident, a young man named Miquel, had been severely abused by his father. He had a broken nose and cauliflower ears, and his face looked like a prizefighters. He had difficulty shaving and did not like anyone helping him, so he usually had some whiskers remaining after he shaved. Less than 5 feet tall with short brown hair, Miquel had a solid stocky body and always wore trousers that were too long for him, pulled up to his chest and held up with suspenders and a wide leather belt. He spoke mostly in monosyllables. One of the few residents who lived at Cullen with state funding, he was a favorite of Dr. Borreca and knew enough to understand his special position. He irritated and teased most of the other residents and no one was able to make him stop. Every evening when I was in my office I heard "Miquel, stop." "Miquel, Go away." "I hate you, Miquel," as he intruded into the residents' space. He laughed, ran away, and then returned again.

One morning he refused to leave his room. I sent the nurse to check on him, and she reported that he appeared to be in good health. I knew that I had to prove to him that he had to follow the rules. I went to his room and told him that if he did not go to the workshop, he could not remain at Cullen. He responded, "No place go."

"I will talk to Dr. Borreca and he will find a place for you to live until you can follow the rules," I said.

"No place go," again was his response. I knew that he didn't believe either that I would ask him to leave or that Dr. Borreca would find a place for him. I did not know how Dr. Borreca would receive my request, but I knew that Miquel had to recognize my authority or it would be bedlam every day. Dr. Borreca parked his car at the rear of Cullen and walked through the lobby on the way to his office every day. I waited for him and asked him to come into my office. "Miquel has created so much turmoil at the residence and does not listen to anyone because he thinks you will excuse everything he does," I said.

"What do you want me to do?" he asked.

"Miquel has refused to leave his room, and I've told him that he must follow the rules or else you would find another place for him to live," I said.

Dr. Borreca laughed, "I don't know of any place for him," he said in a surprised voice.

"I'm sure that you can find a safe place for him until he realizes that you mean for him to follow the rules, and you and I are in agreement," I said.

"I'm busy this morning. Maybe I can find someplace for him tomorrow," Dr. Borreca stalled.

"Either you help me establish order here, or you find another Director of Residential Services," I countered in a serious voice.

"All right," he capitulated. "Give me a few minutes and I'll get back to you."

"You have a few hours at the most," I told him. "Miquel will forget what I told him if he waits much longer, so please get back to me by 11:00 A.M." Dr. Borreca called me within an hour and said he had a friend who ran homes for recovering alcoholics and was willing to take Miquel. He returned to Cullen to talk to Miquel.

"Miquel, Mrs. Wallace has said that you refuse to follow the rules and do what she asks," he said as he sat across from him on Miquel's bed.

"No place go," Miquel repeated and smiled.

"I found a place for you to go with a friend of mine," Dr. Borreca told him. "Hy, (a staff member who works with Dr. Borreca) will drive you there now. Mrs. Wallace will help you pack."

"No place go," Miquel repeated but with some hesitation. I helped him pack, and Hy and I drove him to the home, a nice place out in the country. The men living there worked in the fields and accepted Miguel as you might a younger brother of five or six.

"Dr. Borreca and I will visit you next week," I told Miquel. "When you are ready to follow the rules you can return to Cullen," I said with a faint heart. It reminded me of leaving Ricky, and I was already weakening. I knew that I had to be firm, so I gave Miquel a hug and turned to leave.

"Ready," I heard him say as we drove away.

I checked on him every day, and Dr. Borreca and I visited with him in a week. I was told that he did what he was asked and that the other men treated him well.

Miquel stayed there for three weeks, and at the end of that time I felt he understood that there were rules and that Dr. Borreca and I were both in agreement on what he must do.

He returned to Cullen where the residents welcomed him back. He did a much better job of following staff's directions. Though he still behaved like a five-or-six-year old, he did understand that there were consequences when he refused to cooperate. This was a big change in his behavior and a breakthrough for my position at the helm.

Behaving in a consistent manner and establishing one's authority was important working with people like Miquel. Although I was not aware of it at the time, this practice would serve me well in my future endeavors.

In my second year at Cullen I was faced with a difficult decision dealing with a young woman with mild mental retardation. She was referred to Cullen by the local Mental Health Mental Retardation Authority. About 5′ 6″ tall and 170 pounds, Natalie had straight brown hair that she pulled back with bobby pins but often her hair pulled loose and hung on either side of her face. She wore dresses that hung below her knees and usually had a sweater around her shoulders. She lived on her Supplemental Security Income (SSI) check and the money she earned at her housekeeping job at Cullen. We had given her the job so she could have spending money as well as money for essentials. She was an excellent worker and was able to save money in the bank maintained by Cullen Residence Hall. Periodically she cashed out her money and went on a spree, picking up a stranger and spending the weekend with him at a motel. At the end of the weekend she called for assistance to get home. Frequently she had been physically and sexually abused and needed at least first aid in the infirmary. There were times when she needed more serious care and then was taken to the emergency room. Our social worker and psychologist counseled her, but it didn't seem to make a difference. After her fourth spree, I requested that she speak with me. "Why do you take all of your money that you work so hard to get and give it to some strange man you meet on the street?" I asked her.

"I don't know. The men are nithe (nice) to me," she said.

"Do you want to move to another place?" I asked.

"No," she replied.

I told her that I was concerned for three reasons. "First and most important, is that you might get hurt on these trips into town and, second, you need to have enough money to care for yourself. The third reason is that the Center that owns Cullen Residence Hall is responsible for you when you live here. If something should happen to you, the Center and I would be held responsible. Do you know what a sexually transmitted disease is?" I asked.

"No" she said.

"Have you heard of syphilis in your sex education class?" I went on.

"Yeth", Natalie said "I know that you can get thick from having thex," she said with certainty.

"Do you have sex with the men you meet?" I asked.

"Yeth," she admitted.

"Aren't you worried about getting sick?" I asked.

"I don't know," she responded haltingly.

Finally I realized that she did not see any cause and effect in what she was doing so I told her, "The next time you leave Cullen and spend a few days in motels and are hurt, you will not be able to return to Cullen. I really want to help you, so when you feel as though you need to get out, come talk to me and we can arrange for you to do something other than hurting yourself and losing all of your money."

"OK," she answered. I repeated what I said and asked her to talk to her floor staff when she was upset or come to see me so we could help her to avoid getting hurt and also being asked to leave Cullen. She agreed and all went well for about two months, and then I learned that she had again cashed out her savings and been gone for two days and nights. The next day I received a call from her asking us to pick her up because she was hurt and out of money. I sent staff to take her to the emergency room and then to bring her back to pick up her clothes and personal items and take her wherever she wanted to go. I hated to do it, but I knew that she would continue to hurt herself, and no matter how many times she had been counseled and how many times she had been hurt, she couldn't put two and two together and see the cause. She had no guardian or family, and we had no authority to stop her from doing what she pleased. All we could do was talk to her and make suggestions. She really wanted to live without conditions and so she did. The last I heard she was living on and off the street, with different men. She gave them her SSI checks, and when that did not work out she changed the men. She managed to obtain medical care and dental care. Actually she was very resourceful.

Telling Natalie she must leave was extremely difficult for me--- perhaps more difficult for me than for her. She did not seem to mind because she could not foresee the problems she would face. I knew that I had a responsibility to the Center to maintain it's reputation, and I also had a responsibility to the people we served at Cullen. This proved to be a dilemma for me during my time at Cullen and in my future work.

I learned that not everyone with mental retardation wanted to be in a sheltered environment. Some wanted to take chances much as we all do, and we needed to respect that. Most people with mental retardation require some level of support, but we cannot force that support on them if they do not want it. This was another example of a young adult who did not act responsibly and endured the natural consequences.

In another case, helping a resident with mild mental retardation make a decision that affected his future worked out better for both of us. The mother of a 25-year-old man, Nathan, living at Cullen called to complain that her son wanted to take driving lessons, but she did not think he was responsible enough to drive. I asked her to come to a meeting with Nathan and me so we could talk about it. The last thing I wanted to do was throw cold water on his hopes. Nathan was an attractive, clean-shaven young man who looked as though he could be on any college campus. He wore neatly ironed jeans with his shirt tucked in. Keeping a job was difficult for him because he walked off when his boss asked him to do something he didn't want to do. There was little incentive for him to keep a job since his parents paid for his room and board as well as his clothing and recreation.

We met in the conference room where I asked Nathan what he wanted most. He said he wanted to get a driver's license and a car. I asked him if he had a car or could use someone else's car if he had a license. He said no. I asked his mother and she stated emphatically that there were no cars available for him in their family. I then asked him if we could agree that he could take the driving and written test required to get a driving license when he had saved enough to purchase a safe car. The car had to be approved by his father as a safe car to drive. He agreed. Later, I assured his mother that it would take a long time for him to save enough to purchase a car and if his desire to drive gave him the motivation to stay on a job and be more responsible, it would be good for him. He did put some of his salary away weekly for about six months and then he lost interest in saving. He continued to talk about driving and was enrolled in classes to pass the written test. Until he had enough money to buy a car, however, his talk about driving was just talk. He still felt that his feelings and ambitions had been respected, and his mother stopped worrying about his driving.

In my third year at Cullen, an event happened that strongly influenced my future plans. Terri was a good-looking 20-year-old man still attending school. He had total hearing loss and poor impulse control. Most of the staff could communicate with him in sign language but they were not as proficient as he was, so it often was difficult for staff to understand what he needed and wanted. When Terri could not do something he wanted, he often struck out or threw furniture in frustration. One night he threw a chair through a window on the fourth flour. Cullen had strict rules against property destruction and aggression to others. Those behaviors were not tolerated, so I was directed to help him pack and drive him home. I was uncomfortable carrying out the order but did it anyway. After previous instances of property destruction and aggression, his mother had been warned that he would be asked to leave. When his mother opened the door, I wanted to run but I told her what I was directed to do and wished her luck. I felt terrible and swore that I would never do anything like that if I had my own program. Of course I had no plans at that time to start my own program, but what happened with Terri stuck in my mind.

Another event that later helped me work with my son, Ricky, and others like him occurred in my fourth year with a young man named Sam, who had severe mental retardation, no speech, and poor impulse control. He moved into Cullen when he was 18, after his father had died suddenly and his family had difficulty caring for him at home. His behavior reminded me of Ricky's, and I was particularly interested in how to help him live in this busy environment. When he was frustrated and did not get what he wanted, he became aggressive, screamed, and struck out at anyone in his space. Normally someone with his needs did not stay at Cullen, but his parents had been big supporters of the Center so we had to do what was necessary to keep him and others safe. Cullen had a store in the lobby with glass display cases, and I remember one day when Sam entered and wanted something he did not have enough money to buy. I could see he did not understand the abstract concept of money and was starting to become agitated. A room full of glass cases was not a good place for him. I tried to direct him out of the store. He refused to leave." Sam, relax," I said. "Let's count one, two three, take a deep breath, another deep breath, four, five six, take a deep breath, another deep breath."

I kept this up for what seemed like hours but was only about 15 minutes when he actually began to show less anxiety and distress. We continued until he was able to handle the fact that he did not have enough money, and for the first time I saw him cry. The tears rolled down his cheeks, and after he finished crying he relaxed and returned to watch TV in his room. I put my arm around his shoulders and complimented him on his control. When he became upset, we stressed his getting control and he was successful that day. Eventually he left us and went to a state school. Then he returned to the community to a six-bed group home. Cullen was much too big with too much stimulation for someone like Sam.

After four years of challenges and pleasure serving as Director of Residential Services at Cullen my career there became tenuous when I read a story of abuse occurring at the second-oldest school serving people with mental retardation in the United States. Actually Dr. Borreca called my attention to the story in our morning paper. As soon as I read it, I knew the article was referring to Vineland. I panicked and called Stan immediately to ask him to meet with me and then called Dr. Borreca to advise him I was leaving for home. This was no small feat since we were in the middle of a state review that could determine if our funding continued and our license was renewed. At that moment, however, all I could think about was my son with all of his behaviors being in an abusive environment. I knew he had to come home with me, and as I drove home I knew what we were facing was going to be really hard. On the way home I took a detour to the art museum because looking at art always helped me think straight and soothed my troubled mind. When I left the museum, I had pretty well determined that Ricky must come home but, of course, I had to convince Stan that it was best for everyone.

When I walked in the door Stan met me with a worried look and told me he had been calling all over looking for me. He said he called Dr. Borreca who thought I was going directly home and so both of them were concerned that I might have had an accident. "What happened?" Stan asked.

"I went to the art museum to clear my mind. I'm really sorry. Please forgive me," I said contritely.

"Of course, but let's talk. Did you call Vineland to find out how Ricky is?" Stan said as he took my arm and we walked to the couch.

"No, I'm sure they would tell me he is fine", I said bitterly. "We have to bring him home. All of the other kids are gone. Life is good for both of us. I won't be able to continue my life, as it is knowing that Ricky is in danger. This is the time to bring him home. I believe I know how to care for him and to help him. He's not being helped and has not been helped for many years," I pleaded.

Stan shook his head and said, "Wait! Let's think about this. Our life will change drastically. We will be totally tied down and have no free time to do anything but care for Ricky. He is unmanageable, so how are we going to manage him?"

I began to feel real panic that I had not experienced before. I was certain that bringing Ricky home was the right thing to do. I felt that I had the ability to change Ricky's behavior, but I thought that I couldn't do it alone. If Stan refused, I didn't know what I would do. I insisted, "I don't think he is unmanageable. He needs structure and a consistent program that he can depend on. I think we can create a life for him at home with us that will work. I've learned a lot from working in all of these different places over the past 20 years."

"You need to talk to Dr. Borreca," Stan said hopefully. "Maybe he'll have some ideas of another place we can move Ricky that is better."

"I don't want to leave Ricky with strangers again. It broke my heart once, and I can't do it again," I said with as much strength in my voice as I could muster.

"Let's sleep on it," Stan said.

I thought I would never sleep again until Ricky was home with us, but I didn't say anything and agreed. The next day I returned to the Center and met with Dr. Borreca. I told him that I had to quit so I could care for Ricky. He asked, "Why not try Ricky at Cullen?"

I was surprised to hear him say this because he knew as well as I that living at Cullen was not an option. If I had thought it would work, I would have moved Ricky to Cullen when I started as director. "Do you really think he could live at Cullen?" I asked with hope in my voice.

"I think it is worth a try," he said. I really knew that Ricky could not tolerate the stimulation and lack of structure at Cullen, but I didn't want to leave my job. I thought about it, talked with Stan again, and we decided to try it. My brain told me it wouldn't work, but I wanted to remain on my job so much that I listened to my heart instead of my brain, and so laid the groundwork for disaster.

I called Vineland and told them we were moving Ricky and set a date for us to pick him up. We flew to Philadelphia, rented a car, and drove to the place he had lived for 17 years. He knew nothing of our lives in New York or in Houston. He didn't know that his brothers and sister had all moved on with their lives to other cities and other interests. It was just the three of us. The flight was uneventful and we immediately drove to Cullen from the airport. Ricky was 22 years old, 5'8" tall and weighed about 160 pounds. His hands shook and he drooled constantly. His room at Cullen was like all the others, a double that he shared with another man of his age. He had a desk, dresser, single bed, comfortable chair, and television positioned so he could view it from the chair. Immediately I turned on the television, and he watched it happily as we unpacked his clothing and put his personal care items in the attached bathroom. Staff assisted us and got to know Ricky. We left after he was settled in his room.

As we drove home we both took out cigarettes and started to smoke. I looked at Stan inhaling the smoke deeply and realized I was doing the same thing. I thought about all I had heard about the danger of smoking and thought about Ricky whom we had uprooted from the place he considered as home. I knew then that I had to stop smoking.

"Stan," I said. "We have to stop smoking. It could lead to lung cancer and if we die, who will care for Ricky?" In 1979 smoking was common at all meetings and public places. I was always a social smoker of no more than 10 cigarettes a day at most. Stan, however, had smoked a pack and half daily most of his adult life. Stan said, "I don't know if I can stop. I'll try later"

"I'm stopping today," I told him. Please don't smoke in the house because it will be harder for me, and there's the danger of secondary smoke." I said with certainty. From that moment I never touched another cigarette.

"O.K," he said. "But smoking is the least of our problems."

The next year was difficult for all of us. The staff was anxious about caring for the son of the director. Ricky was not easy to care for, and he did as poorly as I feared. Every morning he refused to leave his room and was carried out of his room by two staff while he screamed and cried all the way to the sheltered workshop that was on the campus a few yards from Cullen. ICF/MR required that he had to go to a job or training every day away from his residence. There was no other workshop willing to take Ricky at that time. After he reached the workshop and realized that he was going to be there he calmed down. Sitting at a table for hours placing sugar packets into boxes was not his cup of tea no matter how much I wanted it. In the evening after dinner was also difficult. Ricky ran around the lobby with no direction in mind and no purpose to his movements. All you could hear was "Ricky, stop", "Ricky I hate you", "Ricky go away."

It was terrible and I felt terrible. I knew I had made a bad decision. Dr. Borreca tried to make it work, but I felt I could not stay on as director and thought that Ricky would be better if I was not there all of the time. I resigned after five years as residential director. I offered to perform any job that Dr. Borreca needed if Ricky could stay at Cullen. I provided job coaching for young men and women who were working in the community. The first job was in a bakery with two young men. I really enjoyed it, but it was not to last.

After six months, Ricky did no better even though I was not at the residence. Finally Stan and I agreed that Ricky needed to come home to live. In 1980 a new Director of Residential Services came to Cullen, and I left to return home with Ricky. Ricky was allowed to continue his work at the workshop.

Ricky and I left the Center to start a new and---I hoped---more successful life in the Memorial area of Houston. I was optimistic and felt confident that all that I had learned over the 20 years of work with people with mental retardation would hold me in good stead as I endeavored to create a life for Stan, Ricky and myself. I knew we could do it.

CHAPTER VI

THEN THERE WERE THREE

1980 was the year that Jimmy Carter lost the presidency to Ronald Reagan, that Gena Rowlands in *Gloria* lost the Oscar to Sissy Spacek in *Coal Miner's Daughter*, and, most important, that Post-It Notes were introduced nationwide. It was the year that Ricky finally returned home to live.

The three of us were Ricky, Stan and I. I was well aware of the turmoil that would occur as soon as Ricky had demands put on him and was concerned about his tantrums and physical assaults. Stan was strong, but he was 57 years old and I didn't know how much wrestling he could tolerate. We talked about calling Andy to help us since it was near the end of his term at the University of California in San Diego where he was completing his doctorate. Andy had been working out for many years and was in good physical shape. We talked every week and he knew we were considering bringing Ricky home. On our next weekly call, I said, "Andy, we need you to help with Ricky's return home. Could you take the summer off from your studies and help us, please?"

"I wondered how you and Dad planned on handling him," Andy commented.

"We need you to help," I repeated.

"OK," Andy agreed. "I'll be there as soon as this term is over, which is in a week."

Both Stan and I were elated. When we brought Ricky home, I told him in a serious and angry tone that he had to come home because he would not follow any rules at the Center. I watched as he looked at me with a serious look on his face and then he smiled a big happy smile.

It took a few minutes for him to realize what I was saying, but when he did, I realized that in his mind coming home to live was no punishment. He was so happy to be with us. The last time he had lived in our home we had to remove everything that he could break from the tables and walls. We had been collecting art for many years now and I did not want to live like that again, so I made it clear to Ricky that he was not to touch any of the pieces on the tables or walls.

I established a routine for Ricky to follow and we stuck to that routine. Every morning Stan got him up to go to his day program at the Center's workshop. They had breakfast in the morning together and then Stan drove him to the workshop. On the drive Ricky sat in the backseat and held the *New York Times* that Stan took to work in his hands in front of his face. If you did not look too closely he appeared to be a business- man driving to work with a co-worker. If you looked closely you saw that the paper was upside down. I worked around the house and then picked him up at 3:00 P.M.

Ricky sat in the back seat when we drove home, and periodically I checked on him in my rearview mirror. What I saw was a man with his mouth wide open drooling. This is it. I can't stand the drooling another day. I pulled the car over and asked Ricky to move to the front seat. When he was settled with his seat belt on, I reached into my pocket where I had stored my daily stash of candy. I told him to close his mouth and swallow, and when he did I gave him an M&M. For the remainder of the trip I gave him an M&M every time he closed his mouth and swallowed. This was the pattern we followed when we were together. Gradually I extended the time between the M&M's and, within a few weeks, Ricky had stopped drooling.

Every opportunity we could find we complimented Ricky on something he did. Even if it was sitting when we asked him to sit or coming to the table at mealtime when we asked him to join us for dinner, we told him, "Good sitting, Ricky" or "Good coming, Ricky".

When Ricky arrived home from the workshop, he had to play ball with me before he received a snack. He was not too happy about this rule, and about a week after Andy arrived, he went to a stand I had in the hall where I had placed a large piece of Eskimo stone sculpture. He shook the stand until the sculpture fell and broke into a hundred pieces. I tried to stop him but I couldn't move fast enough.

I knew we were in trouble and that I had to think quickly how to handle the situation. There had to be an immediate consequence. I reacted by shouting to Andy, "Come quickly. We have a problem."

When Andy reached Ricky, he found that Ricky had thrown himself on the floor and was crying. "What should I do?" he shouted.

"Take Ricky's shoes and throw them into the trash," I shouted back. Ricky can't tolerate to be without shoes, so I knew that he wouldn't like having to walk in his stocking feet. "You break my things, I break yours." I said loudly to Ricky. I repeated the sentence many times, and you could almost see the wheels turning in Ricky's head. I hoped he was getting the message. He didn't get those shoes back for a few weeks, and for the rest of the day he had to walk around the house in his stocking feet. He kept pointing to his feet, and I kept telling him that he broke my things and so I broke his things. I knew he "got it" and was definitely unhappy with the consequence of breaking the sculpture. Ever since that event Ricky, has not broken anything in our home. People who visit us cannot believe that Ricky can live here without demolishing our pieces of art since he has been described as a "bull in a china shop." I felt good about the way I handled that incident in spite of the fact that my sculpture was ruined.

I learned something from every incident, and this incident pointed out to me that immediate response to an action and being consistent with Ricky helped him to understand the rules. He needed to know what was expected of him. He had always received mixed messages, and rarely did the consequence consistently and immediately follow the action. When he did play ball with me, I said to him, "Good ball playing, Ricky," and he smiled. I knew that this pleased him. I tried to get Stan to talk to him in this fashion. Stan was a wordsmith so it was very strange for him to speak in three-and four word sentences, but he tried and eventually became good at it.

We also rewarded Ricky by taking him to the movies. If he was "good", he earned a movie. He could earn a movie Wednesdays and Saturdays. We placed a calendar on the wall so he could see when he could go to the movie even if he could not read. At the end of each day he had complied with our directives, he received a star, which he got to put on the calendar. The rewards of the movie and the stars excited and pleased him. If he refused to get up when we asked or brush his teeth or any of the other activities, we told him he lost his star for the day, and consistently made it clear why he had lost his star. I was not sure that any of these techniques would work but it appeared that his behavior was slowly changing.

Recounting our process with Ricky makes it sound as if everything was settled. *Not True.* Many an evening Stan or I told Ricky it was time to go to bed and he shook his head to indicate "no," and then if we persisted he threw himself down on the ground kicking and screaming. Stan had to wrestle with him until he gave in and went to bed. In the early days after Ricky moved back to the house, he fought us on every request we made of him, such as time to get up, time to go to bed, brush teeth, take a bath, shave, come to the table to eat (he wanted to eat in front of the television), go for a walk, go to work and so on. We picked our battles, so for instance, we did not push going for a walk, but Ricky had to comply with the other activities. I worried about Stan's ability to continue to physically make him perform some of the tasks. Stan was in pretty good shape for a 57-year old man but he was not accustomed to battling a young man of 25 whose adrenalin could be instantly elevated. Andy helped frequently, but he would be leaving at the end of the summer to return to school. The three of us had to learn how to live together. We knew that Ricky could not be left alone downstairs for even a few minutes.

Ricky tried to be helpful around the house, but much as a two-year-old needs to be watched, so did Ricky. One day I turned on the washing machine after filling it and adding the detergent. Fortunately I remained in the laundry room for a few minutes when I observed soap bubbles emanating from the top of the washer. I opened the lid to discover that Ricky had dumped most of a box of detergent into the machine before I had added the clothes. I had to dip out as much as I could and restart the machine. When I spoke to Ricky about this he gave me a big smile and made the sign of "help." He had no idea that his "help" had caused a problem.

Another day I was in the kitchen preparing dinner when I saw Ricky at the microwave and heard the click as he turned on the machine. I rushed over to discover that Ricky had put a wrapped package of microwave popcorn into the microwave without removing the wrapping. After showing Ricky how to remove the plastic wrapping, I had him put the package back into the machine and helped him set the timer.

I was not happy about the amount of medication Ricky was on. Working with the psychiatrist, we slowly removed some of the medications and reduced the amount he took of others. I wished Ricky was off all psychotic medication, but it didn't seem that we could safely do that. One Sunday I noticed that Ricky's medicine bottle was empty. I was sure that there had been at least ½ bottle of pills left. I asked Ricky if he had taken all the pills and with a big smile he indicated he had. He thought he had done a good thing.

We rushed him to a hospital and again, as when he was a little boy, he had his stomach pumped. The doctor told us not to give him any medications for the next three days. Ricky seemed so relaxed and so much brighter and responsive without his medications that I decided not to give him any even after the three-day period. I actually did know better. One should never stop psychiatric drugs suddenly, but taper them off gradually. Again my heart took over from my brain. I hated that Ricky was so dependent on so many drugs for behavior control and wanted desperately to have him off of drugs. I wanted him to be normal and not brain damaged. I wanted, I wanted, I wanted. He seemed so much easier to live with that I thought he was going to do well.

The next week the CEO of Stan's company invited Stan, me, and Ricky to fly to Nashville for a weekend with the other vice-presidents and their families. Ricky was doing so well we thought we could join the group. The trip on the company plane was exciting and Ricky behaved like a perfect gentleman. We looked forward to a few days of music and fun. When we arrived, we rented a car to go to the hotel. Once in the hotel we began to notice a change in Ricky. He ran up and down the halls knocking on the doors. We quickly left our luggage and went to the lobby where everybody was boarding busses to the fairgrounds.

Ricky had a great time on the rides, playing games, and eating ice cream and candy. When it was time to leave Ricky refused to board the bus. Finally we convinced him to get on and we sat in the far back. The bus arrived at the hotel and Ricky refused to get off of the bus. I left thinking he would follow me but to no avail. Stan tried to force him to get up, but he had no luck. Some of the other executives tried to help but they fared no better. Finally someone called the police and three big burly policemen dragged Ricky off. As he was being removed from the bus I called out to him to come with me for a ride. He got into the car we had rented and as we were leaving the parking lot, I shouted to Stan to arrange for us to fly out as soon as possible. We drove all night.

At 5:00 A.M. we returned to the hotel. Ricky and I went to the room where Stan was waiting for us. He informed me that the company plane was ready to fly us back to Houston. I felt terrible because I knew it was all my fault. I wanted so badly for Ricky to be all right without medications that I had allowed myself to act stupidly and that hurt my son and my husband's reputation in the company. Stan had to return to work on Monday and face all his peers who witnessed this debacle.

I knew that was not going to be easy for him. While on the plane I noticed that Ricky was twitching all over his body. He was going through drug withdrawal.

When we arrived home, we had to find a doctor immediately. Sunday was not a good day to get medical help except in an emergency room. I wanted the help of a neurologist, and Stan called some friends and was able to convince a neurologist to come to our home to look at Ricky. I do not know how he did it, but again I was so grateful that Stan was at my side. He never blamed me or said anything to me about the mess I had made.

The medication we tried was not a new medication but an old one that was used rarely, Thorazine. I told the doctor of Ricky's allergy. He told me that that was 22 years ago. It was worth a try. We started with a small dose and each day I increased it until the twitching stopped and Ricky was back to normal. The final amount was much less than he had been taking of his other medication.

Occasionally we brought a Center staff person from the workshop to sit with Ricky, but not too many of them were willing to stay with him. He had a bad reputation for difficult and dangerous behavior. If he had had no previous experience with a staff person, he would not listen and often would strike out at him or her. Only someone who had worked with him at the workshop and who had established a relationship with him could try to stay with him at our home and then we were never sure if Ricky would listen to his "sitter" in a different environment from the workshop.

We had totally renovated Ricky's bedroom. My thoughts were that we needed to remove as much ammunition from Ricky as we could. We took out his bed, dresser, chairs, mirror and nightstands and put all of the lighting in the ceiling. I found a furniture manufacturer who was willing to make a bed that resembled a waterbed without the water and with four drawers that could not be removed, under the mattress. Attached to the bed were two nightstands. Ricky's clothes were placed either in his closet or in the four drawers. The only decorations in the room were the posters we placed on the walls. There was nothing in his bedroom that Ricky could throw but his clothes and the posters.

I realized how effective this design was one morning when Stan was out of town and I went to wake Ricky. He refused to open his eyes. I brought the vacuum cleaner upstairs and started to vacuum the floor. He opened one eye and shook his head. I continued to make noise when he jumped out of bed and started toward me. I went downstairs with the vacuum cleaner and he threw his clothes at me. I was frightened and wondered how long his tantrum would last and what I would do if he decided to come downstairs. I picked up a broom and thought I would strike out at him with the handle if I had to protect myself. After emptying out his drawers and his closet, Ricky came to the top of the stairs and held out his arms and shrugged his shoulders with an expression of "what do I do now?" I breathed a sigh of relief and went back upstairs and said in a firm, steady voice, "You will pick up all of your clothes, and then we will get ready to go to work."

The two of us picked up his clothes and after breakfast we drove to the workshop. That was the last of the getting-up tantrums. There were times when he objected to getting up, but he never again threw a tantrum, and eventually he got up and went to work.

After a very rough nine months, we all learned to get along. Ricky realized that there were certain things he needed to do, and we realized that it was unwise to push him on things that would make us feel better but were not essential to his health and well being. Ricky did take his dishes to the sink after he ate and he did attempt to make his bed in the morning. He also dressed himself as best he could. He never was able to get his shoes on the right feet and frequently his underwear was on backwards but we were always with him and he was willing to change his shoes and underwear when asked. He did choose coordinating colors when he picked his clothes to wear. As long as I removed the out-of- season clothing he could pick what he wanted to wear. If there was a winter coat in his closet, however, he frequently chose to wear it on a day when the temperature was 95.degrees. He perspired and wiped his hand across his forehead to indicate he was hot, but he could not see cause and effect. Sometimes he put on shorts when the temperature was 35 degrees and then shivered. Unless we locked all the doors upstairs except for his bedroom and bathroom, he'd enter all of the bedrooms and toss the clothes during the night.

He did not sleep more than a few hours a night but he stayed upstairs and never came down until someone said he could. He stood at the top of the stairs and called "UH. UH, Ma, Ma" If it was too early to come down, we told him to go back to bed and he would return to his room. We never told him that he had to ask our permission to come downstairs, but somehow he determined that was what he should do and we never indicated otherwise.

We took Ricky to a delicatessen for lunch one day. He wanted everything he saw in the meat case and we had to drag him out of the deli. We said that we were never taking him out to eat again, but after six months things were going so much better that Stan and I decided to try Luby's cafeteria. Before we left, we sat him down opposite us and talked to him about going to a restaurant. He nodded and seemed to understand. We told him that if he grabbed at food other than his own and if he did not listen to us, he could not go out again to eat. We repeated this three or four times and each time he nodded and looked very serious. I had no idea if this approach would work but I did know that Ricky knew we meant what we said. We arrived at the cafeteria and I entered the line first, followed by Ricky, followed by Stan. I gave Ricky his tray and silverware and we approached the food. I told him he could have one salad, one meat, one potato, one vegetable, one roll, and one desert. He actually pointed to what he wanted and took one of each. He carried his own tray to the table I picked, and both Stan and I breathed a sigh of relief. Ricky still ate so fast that I left my food to follow him outside so Stan could finish, but we both considered the outing a great success. We praised Ricky and told him that he could come again next week. We showed him on the calendar when we would return to Luby's.

I felt really good about what I considered success in our handling of Ricky. I was excited that what I had read and heard about rewarding good behavior was actually working. Not seeing the drooling was so great. I was very happy that we had brought Ricky home. Even with all of the mistakes I had made, I knew that it had been the right thing to do for him and for us.

That is the way it was until Thanksgiving of 1981.

CHAPTER VII

GETTING IT READY

I N 1982 the Falkland Islands War broke out, AT&T broke up, and two of Ricky's. favorite movies were *Tootsie* and *Victor/Victoria*. It was also the beginning of an entirely new role for me in our family.

After the Thanksgiving holidays, everything returned to whatever passed as normal for the Wallace family with Ricky back home. Every morning Stan and Ricky ate breakfast together and then Stan drove Ricky to the Center workshop. As they drove off, I started my odyssey of getting Vita-Living off the ground.

I hoped to share the expense of opening and operating Vita-Living with other families who had children with similar needs. Many of these families I had met through my work at the Center. We invited the Hawlks, Cooks, and Greenbergs to our home one evening to share our ideas of this new venture with them. Stan and I greeted them warmly.

I started the discussion by asking them to read a business plan I passed out. The amount of money we needed was $80,000. That would be enough to purchase a home and convert it to meet licensing standards and to run the operation for six months until we receive government funding through Medicaid. This would require each family to come up with $26, 666.

Mr. Greenberg spoke up first, "I know the work you did when you were the director at Cullen Residence Hall. I respect your work, but we need our money for our son to be saved for an emergency. We are not interested in taking a chance with you on our son's future. Thanks for thinking of us, but we are not going to join with you on this venture."

The response from the Hawlks and the Cooks was pretty much the same, so we thanked them for coming and they went on their way. I was disappointed but definitely not ready to quit. Our goal remained the start of our agency. After they left Stan and I had one of our many "table talks." "What do you want to do now?" Stan asked.

"I think we will have to do it alone." I said. "Maybe we could start a profit-making business that would help support the nonprofit one. I always wanted to work with food, and we could make low-calorie gourmet food for take-out. I think that could really be successful. What do you think?" Stan gave me a look that made me realize I had gone too far. I said no more about the "profit-making business."

I told Stan I was thinking about a quote from George Bernard Shaw made famous by Robert Kennedy: " Some men see things as they are and say 'why'. I dream things that never were and say, 'why not.'" "I am saying 'why not'," I said. "Once we are licensed by the State we can bill for services, but we will have to underwrite the start-up and the first six months of operating cost. We need to become a non profit corporation so we can raise some money through donations," I said hopefully.

"And who is going to raise the money?" Stan asked. "I know you don't like to do that, so I suppose you will expect me to ask my friends and associates."

"You got it, but I will work at jobs during the day when Ricky is at the workshop and put that money into the Vita-Living fund started at the bank," was my quick reply.

"I hope you are patient because it's going to take some time. You are not the most patient person I know," Stan warned.

"I'll do what's necessary. I'm determined to see this through," I said firmly. We attended a workshop run by United Way on "How to Become a 501(c)(3)" and read "Establishing a Tax-Exempt Arts Organization in Texas". I knew that we were a far cry from an arts organization, but we were establishing a tax-exempt organization and I thought that the information would be relevant to what we wanted to do--and it was. We had to determine feasibility, so over the next few weeks we asked ourselves the following questions:

1. *Can we make a profit?*

There was no way we could make a profit. The income generated by serving six people in the group home was one half of projected cost. The state had never licensed a small group home in the community to serve people with severe mental retardation and behavior problems so the rate paid was based on costs in large institutions. Large institutions had efficiencies of scale so the rates were much lower than needed in a six-bed group home. We needed to raise the remainder of the money.

2. Will activities be exclusive to a specific group or community?

People with mental retardation are present in all groups and all cultures. They are not exclusive to any one community.

3. Is this idea the exclusive vision and effort of one individual?

This idea was exclusively ours. We know we will need to have a board of at least seven people and that we will need to share the management with them.

4. Are there any other organizations that provide the same services, programs or activities?

There were no other small group homes for six people in Texas serving people with severe mental retardation and behaviors in the community.

5. Is self-employment a goal?

I knew that I would have to work many years without a salary because we wouldn't bring in enough to pay me. Stan had a good position and we didn't need my salary to support us now that Ricky was living at home.

6. Is this nonprofit being created to facilitate a project with a definitive completion date?

There was no definitive completion date. Our goal was for Vita-Living to continue long after Stan and I were gone.

Following the guidelines laid out by these questions reinforced our belief that we were ready to form a nonprofit agency. Stan made an appointment for us to meet with Joe Gordon, a lawyer and friend. We explained what we wanted to do, and he offered to guide us through the process to obtain the nonprofit status for us pro bono. I was so grateful to hear that. The first thing was to develop our by-laws and articles of incorporation. I remember clearly that the State of Texas accepted our articles of incorporation on August 9th, 1982. In addition Joe helped me obtain the papers necessary to start a profit-making company, if I decided to go that route. The name of that company was a "Very Special Place." We had moved to the first rung of the ladder.

Next Joe said we had to apply for a certificate of occupancy from the city. We had to prove that the city needed this kind of service. I

researched what was available and with the help of our lawyer completed the forms required in two months. It took another three months
to get the certificate. We had moved to the second rung.

In addition to working on Vita-Living every day, I needed to find
time to do other things of interest to me. Kathy, my dear friend who I
mentored when we both worked at Cullen, introduced me to a young
woman, Karen, who worked as a medical technician in the medical center and loved to bake. Cooking and baking were hobbies of mine that
went back to my days at Cornell when I studied food chemistry and
was fascinated by the interactions of the different ingredients. Karen
had a body-builder boyfriend for whom she made whole grain breads
and special foods. She loved baking and trying new recipes. We hit it
off immediately. She and I met in my kitchen every Wednesday and
tested our new recipes. The food turned out so well I suggested we go
into business together to make food for take-out, thinking this would
be that profit-making business.

She was excited about the possibility of going into business with
me, and we actually developed a menu and tested the recipes. When
we thought we had enough tested recipes, we held a tasting party in
my home. We invited our friends and asked them to bring their friends
and handed out opinion cards to all of the "tasters". The response was
so positive that both of us felt that making healthy food for take out
was a great idea that would work. We planned our menu and looked
for a location. I was going to bankroll this operation. We found a store
that had been a small restaurant near the museum area, and we both
thought we could convert it to our use easily. Karen was going to quit
her job, and I would fund the start-up while she ran "Very Special
Place," the name we chose.

The day I went to sign the lease I realized just how big a monetary
commitment I was making and that fact made me hesitate. I had the
feeling that I should talk to Karen again to be sure that she was ready
to give her notice and make her commitment to start our venture. I told
the realtor that I wanted to meet my partner one more time before signing. I went home and tried to get in touch with Karen by phone. When
that was unsuccessful, I called Kathy and asked if she had heard from
her. We could not find her. At midnight I received a call that Karen had
been in a serious auto accident and was in a coma at the medical center.
She remained in a coma for three weeks and when she came out of the
coma, her family moved her back home to Buffalo, New York where she
recuperated. The last I heard she had married and had two children.

I believe that I must have had an angel on my shoulder looking out for me. I said to myself, "I get the message. I had better forget the Very Special Place and move on with my main objective, starting Vita-Living." It was clear to me that I needed to build up my bank account, so I contacted the Center looking for a job. They knew the quality of my work and fortunately, were willing to hire me for a variety of positions over the next three years. I worked as Director of the Prevocational Center, Coordinator of the Allied Health Services, and as a Coordinator of Supported Employment, from 8:00 A.M. to 4:00 P.M., the hours that Ricky was at the workshop. If I had to work additional hours, Ricky remained at the Center until I was ready to leave.

Every afternoon on arrival at home, Ricky and I followed a very structured routine. We played ball, took a walk, or participated in some physical activity. I believed this activity could help him release some of his energy, and I knew it made good sense for anyone to be active after sitting all day. Ricky had to participate before he received his snack. He wanted to eat as soon as he got home, but I wouldn't allow it. I wanted him to understand there were consequences for his actions, good and bad. After his snack Ricky watched television while I prepared supper. When Stan arrived we had dinner. It was a fight every night to get Ricky to sit at the table with us, but he was not allowed to watch TV after supper if he refused and so he did. When it was time for bed, again it was a fight to make him quit the television at 10:00 P.M. Finally we decided to allow him to watch television in his room for one hour after his shower if he showered and brushed his teeth. Watching TV was a useful reward. Ricky was refusing all requests to do anything other than eating and watching television unless we tied consequences to his refusals. Gradually this became the daily routine and the tension and arguments lessened as he came to understand what was expected of him.

After a year of this routine, Stan and I needed to get away for a few days. Stan loved Las Vegas and we asked Melanie and Andy to come home to "Ricky-sit" for us. They agreed so Stan and I could go on this trip with Stan's brother and his wife. While we were gone, Hurricane Alicia hit the Gulf coast. We worried about our three children being in Houston with no electricity, little gas, no television, no refrigeration, and no way to entertain Ricky. We tried every way to return to Houston. We thought about renting a car and driving but were warned not to try to drive to Houston. We waited anxiously to hear when we could return. Melanie and Andy took Ricky on drives as long as they had gas and somehow managed to entertain him until we arrived home three days late.

I bought gifts for everyone and one of the gifts was a plastic pencil case that looked and smelled like a Hershey bar, which I intended for my grandson. There was much excitement on our arrival, and after everyone left the three of us went to bed exhausted. In the middle of the night I heard noises coming from upstairs and went to see how Ricky was doing. I saw vomit on the floor in the bedroom and bathroom and Ricky indicating pain in his throat and inability to swallow. Ricky was unable to drink without spitting it out. We called 911 and when the EMT staff arrived, they told Ricky they were going to take him to the hospital. He shook his head from side to side, and they looked at me and said they couldn't take him. I couldn't believe what I heard. Stan and I both explained that he had severe mental retardation and did not understand that he needed to go to the hospital. They asked if I was his guardian, and we said we were his parents. Since Ricky was over 21 years of age and neither Stan nor I was his legal guardian and Ricky had communicated he did not want to go to the hospital, the EMTs said that they couldn't force him to go. They said they were leaving.

"What are we to do?" I asked desperately.

"Get guardianship," they shouted as they left.

We were frantic and tried everything to get Ricky to accompany us to the hospital, but he was too frightened and too big for Stan to carry. I was panicking and finally thought of getting help from Chris, a staff person from the day program, who seemed to have some influence with Ricky and called him. "Ricky is really sick and will not go with me or Stan to the hospital and the EMT people refuse to force him. I'm pleading with you to come to our house to help us get Ricky to the hospital. I'm afraid he'll die," I implored between tears.

Chris came immediately, and we finally got Ricky to the hospital at 4:00 in the morning. Stan called a surgeon friend of his, and Ricky was seen by 7:00 A.M. and operated on by 9:00 AM. The surgeon removed a large plastic mass from Ricky's throat. Nobody seemed to know what it was. Ricky's stay in the hospital required that he be physically restrained until the IV's were removed. Even though I sat with him all of the time, I was unable to prevent him from pulling out the needles. About a week later I asked our grandson if he liked the pencil case only to learn that he never took the case. A light bulb went on in my head, and I realized that Ricky had taken it, thought it was a Hershey bar, and tried to eat it. Again I realized how little Ricky understood the world he lived in and how important it was for us to "Ricky-proof" his environment.

As soon as Ricky returned home I obtained legal guardianship. That was a tough lesson to learn. I never dreamed that anyone would ignore Ricky's problem and listen to his wishes rather than to us, his parents. How ridiculous that the EMT people did not recognize the need to overlook Ricky's refusal for treatment. It was obvious to anyone that Ricky did not understand the consequences of his actions.

Now that Ricky's health crisis was over, I could focus again on my plans for Vita-Living. I thought about the changes that needed to be made to any home we might purchase. I remembered the design of the bedroom at our home that worked so well for Ricky and knew I had hit upon the technique I would use in designing the home. I had to remove whatever might be broken or destroyed. The changes we made to Ricky's bedroom were the beginning of the many environmental changes we made to the first home we established for our agency.

The residents had to be able to vent their anger and frustration in a socially acceptable way, and I had to come up with a way to allow them to do just that. When some of the clients that I had served previously were frustrated, they butted their heads into walls and doors. I wanted to design the house so it would be attractive yet livable for people who destroyed property when angry. We needed a place for them to hit and vent safely. Ricky threw things when he became frustrated so we had to remove all decorations that could be broken or be a danger to someone when thrown. I did not want a bare home but one that was pleasant to look at. We could paint designs on the wall or could put up pretty wallpaper, but the labor cost to paint or hang wallpaper was too much, so I had to come up with other ideas. Windows could be broken and dangerous, so we needed to find something other than glass.

Another problem to solve was shared bathroom use. Residents could not leave their personal items in the bathrooms. I had seen some caddies at Target used for carrying cleaning supplies. I thought they might work well to hold personal care items and would be kept in the individual bedrooms. The home had to be large enough to house six people in their own bedrooms with at least three bathrooms. At this point I had not figured out how we could do all that we needed without building our own home.

These concerns, however, had to take a back seat to the more immediate needs of getting the go-ahead from the State. We needed liability insurance, Director and Officer (D&O) board insurance, property insurance, and automotive insurance. Unfortunately we were not in any position to offer health insurance to our employees. Stan mentioned that we had an appointment to meet Irving Pozmantier, who would help us with our insurance needs. We decided to utilize the accounting services of our personal accountant who prepared our yearly income tax report. "I realize that I have no idea of the financial reporting that Uncle Sam requires. Is it so different from our personal obligations?" I asked Stan.

"Yes, it's very different and you need to talk to someone who understands the reporting obligations for a 501 (c) (3) corporation." Stan responded. The financial area was one where I had no previous experience. I had always worked in large companies that had specialized departments to handle all of the financial reporting obligations. I put the financial reporting requirements on the back burner for now.

I made many day trips to Austin and met with the deputy in charge of mental retardation services, Dr. McGraw, who referred me to a Ms Shirley Crow whom, he said, would tell me what I needed to do to open the first small group home to serve people with severe mental retardation in Texas.

"What did you learn?" Stan said when I returned from Austin.

" Ms. Crow told me that the State had never licensed a small group home in the community for people with severe mental retardation and behavior problems and didn't believe it could be done within the standards established." I learned that no one had ever tried to open such a home as I described. When I asked why, Ms Crow said that the rates paid to the provider were lower than the rates paid for services to people with mild and moderate mental retardation, and that people with severe handicapping conditions were better cared for in the large institutions that were run by the state or private providers. Many providers had turned nursing homes into Intermediate Care Facilities for the Mentally Retarded called ICF/MRs and served large numbers in these facilities. I insisted that she give me the standards required for opening a small six-bed home in the community. She offered to give me a large book of regulations, repeating again that these were the standards for *large* institutions. The State simply had no standards for small community group homes for the people I wanted to serve. Ms Crow gave me her telephone number as well as the phone number for Mr. Grupt, my contact in the Architectural requirements division.

Despite hearing that I would be opening the first small community residence for people like Ricky in the state, I was not discouraged. I was even more determined than before the meeting to succeed. "Are you ready to give up or have you decided to take the road less traveled? Stan asked. "Absolutely not giving up. I know we can do it. I just have to convince the powers that be in Austin that we can do it," I said in an edgy voice.

"I am with you but how are we going to do it?" Stan asked.

"I need to contact and meet personally with Mr. Grupt of the state's architectural section, and I also need to buy a computer and printer," I said. In 1982 computers were just starting to be commonplace.

"But you know nothing about computers and neither do I," Stan said.

"You have people in your company who know about computers; ask if they can help us," I countered. "Had my weekly talk with my Dad and he was in New York on business and saw *A Soldiers Story* by Charles Fuller and said it was very good. Do you think we'll ever be able to travel together to New York or anyplace else?" I asked wistfully.

"Can't you find someone from the Center to stay with Ricky?" Stan said.

"Sure, for an evening on occasion but no longer than that. If you mention Ricky Wallace to anyone except a few, they put up there hands as if shielding themselves from a missile and politely refuse to care for him."

Stan told me that his company's computer staff recommended that we get an IBM and that the store where it was purchased would train the purchaser. I got three lessons and placed the computer on our dining room table alongside the state standards in our dining-room-turned-office..

I had met with Mr. Grupt who advised me against trying to convert a small home into a home that meets the state standards. He said those standards were designed for large institutions that required commercial sprinklers and shut off valves for the air conditioning systems. But, I told Stan, "He was really nice and said he would help if he could."

"Well that's good. How sincere do you think he is?" Stan asked.

"I think he means it. He considers this a difficult task, a test," I said. One of the first challenges was the requirement for a commercial sprinkling system. Mr. Grupt said that while many states had accepted a residential sprinkling system, Texas had never approved one.

"Why not for heaven's sake?" Stan said in an exasperated tone.

"There had never been a need for it. The small homes previously opened were for people with mild mental retardation, and they can easily evacuate in case of a fire," I reminded him.

"This is a big liability," said Stan. "Do you think Ricky would evacuate if he heard a loud horn?"

"I think he could learn," I said. "When he was living at Vineland, he must have had to evacuate. I'll find out---and also find out more about the residential sprinkler system."

"I'm going to New York next week and got tickets to see *A Soldiers Play*, Stan said with a big smile.

I was happy for Stan. "Great," I said. "I am glad for you. One of us deserves to keep up with the good times."

While Stan was gone, I was determined to work with Ricky and figure out how to meet the fire requirements. I contacted two young women who had worked with me at Cullen to help me plan on ways to meet the standards using Ricky as the model. Kathy, the social worker and Kip, who had recently completed her masters in psychology, were my two co- conspirators.

I bought a loud horn to see if Ricky would evacuate after hearing the horn. I showed him what to do three or four times and picked a place in the yard for us to meet after I blew the horn. We practiced daily. I blew it louder and then longer, but nothing seemed to be working, Ricky lacked the proper motivation to make the connection between the horn blast and meeting me in the yard. Food, Ricky always responded to food. I took a small box of raisins and gave Ricky some before I blew the horn. Then I told him he could get the box when he met me in the yard. It worked! Suddenly I had solved another major problem, one of evacuation. I was making some headway. I felt as though I was wearing blinders and knew nothing about what was going on except in Houston and Harris County.

The earth was still spinning, the British succeeded in Falklands war, Israel invaded Lebanon, Princess Grace died when her car plunged off a mountain road, John Hinckley's insanity defense prevailed in the shooting of President Ronald Reagan, and John Belushi died of an overdose. The year 1982 was closing.

Ricky was never far from my sight when he was at home unless he was sleeping. I was preparing the state-mandated policies and procedures, such as documentation describing how we were going to care for each of our clients and how we would implement the standards. I had written similar documentation before at the Center, but state approval for the physical changes I wanted to make and the adaptations required for a small home in the community were problematic. The state continued to insist on commercial sprinklers, automatic shut-offs in the air conditioning system, and seven exits, and the costs kept increasing. I began to think that maybe I had made a mistake and that this whole idea was more than Stan and I could handle. I kept my doubts to myself because Stan was already uncertain, and I did not want to add to his doubts.

I didn't want to back down but the continuous stream of difficulties was weakening my resolve. I needed to succeed and I was afraid that I would lose my nerve. If I jumped in and bought a home, however, I would force myself to continue since I did not want to be a landlord. I called a realtor friend and told her what I needed. We looked at single homes but did not find one big enough for six people, each to have a room. I thought that a duplex might work best, but it also needed to be in an area with multiple family homes to reduce objections to a group home. Soon my realtor friend and I were traveling all over the city looking at duplexes. The home I found was on a street with many duplexes but the street behind it had lovely, single-family homes. The duplex had a front home with two bedrooms, 1 ½ baths, living room, dining area, kitchen and an attached garage, which joined the two homes. The back home had three bedrooms, two baths, a kitchen with eating area, and a large living room. The garage was not attached but at the end of the driveway, right next to the back door.

At the next table talk I told Stan in an upbeat tone, "I found a home I think might work. When can you see it?"

"I can't believe you're actually buying a house." Stan managed to look both incredulous and doubtful. "We really are going to do this. I have to go to New York tomorrow but how about Saturday?"

"Great, I will call Audrey and set it up for 2:00 in the afternoon. That will give you time to go to services at the synagogue. Is that OK? I responded.

"I guess," said Stan. "Where is the home?"

"It's on the west side of town near Interstate 59 and Gessner on Beechnut," I said.

"Near Sharpstown---isn't that a busy street?" Stan asked.

"Yes, but if we try to buy on an inside street, we're going to deal with many nervous, angry homeowners who are afraid of group homes for people with mental retardation, and think that a group home in the neighborhood will lower property values. People are often afraid of what they don't know or understand. I don't have the time or the inclination to deal with that now. We'll build a fence and have plenty of staff to watch the clients. They aren't going to be roaming the streets, I assure you," I responded confidently.

On Saturday Stan and I met the realtor and walked through the house. I pointed out that we needed to convert the connector garage to a family room and open it up to the back house. We could convert the living room in the back unit into a bedroom and hall off of which the other three bedrooms opened. There was no way we could break up the master bedroom in the back house so we had to have two people share a room. This actually gave us an extra room that I thought might make a game room. It was getting exciting.

In the front house, we could reduce the size of the master bedroom to create a hall, so we could have another exit. There were two half baths that shared a tub and shower. I could convert the dining room to my office and use the kitchen for storage. It looked like the perfect house.

We did not have near enough money yet to start renovation, so we had to become landlords to two families. Stan let me know that I was the one taking care of the property, and we closed on the house that we called Beechnut House in 1983. This was right before the bottom fell out of the economy in Houston and the prices had begun to drop but not near what they would. The mortgage holder had a GI loan that was transferable, so I got the mortgage at a very good rate for the times.

At the next table talk we had a lot to discuss. We had learned that my father had just been diagnosed with lung cancer. My Dad, a widower since 1972 and a practicing attorney, carried his 84 years in a stately manner. He had many friends but had lived alone in Cleveland, Ohio since my mother died. I was devastated. It was important that I be there for him.

"I need to go to Cleveland as soon as possible," I said anxiously.

"I know and I'll make arrangements for you to fly this weekend." said my wonderful husband.

"Can you take care of Ricky?" I asked.

"I'll do it. Don't worry. We'll be fine, he said." Oh by the way, I met a fellow who used to work at my company, Panhandle Eastern, today, and he's gone out on his own as a contractor. I told him about what we were doing, and he's interested in possibly bidding on the job. When you get back from Cleveland you can meet him, if you want." Stan spoke in a very positive manner.

"That's great, but first I must see what I need to do for my Dad," I said. For the next year I traveled every other week from Friday through

Monday to Cleveland to be with my Dad. His doctor advised him that if he underwent radiation therapy, he might have a year to live, but if he did nothing, he would die within the next two months. Dad chose to live one more year, and it was wonderful being with him every other weekend. He had given up driving so I became his chauffeur, and we went wherever he wanted so he could enjoy his remaining time.

Finally in November of 1984, during one of my hundred calls to the Texas Department of Health, the office that dispensed licenses for ICF/MR homes, I finally heard what I had been dreaming of during the past three years. "O.K., Renée, We'll approve the use of the residential sprinkling system and you won't have to have an automatic shut off in the ventilation system. Let us know when you have completed everything and are ready to be licensed."

We had climbed three more rungs of the ladder. We still had a lot to do to get ready for licensure, and the last two months of 1984 and the first two months of 1985 were busy getting ready. In addition to purchasing all of the furniture and linens, outfitting the kitchen, meeting with the contractor to have the beds made like the one Ricky was using, and reviewing all of the adaptations that we needed to make to the duplex, I was completing the policy and procedure manual.

While traveling back and forth to Cleveland, my head was full of all of the things that needed to be done back in Houston. As I left the plane in Cleveland the first weekend in January 1985, I was wondering to myself how long I could continue to make these trips, and that weekend my Dad passed away. It was as if he had read my thoughts and was ready to move on. Dealing with the loss of my last parent was traumatic, and although I expected to lose my parents at some time, the loss of the moral support I had always received from them was frightening. I knew that if I was in trouble, I could always talk to either my mother or father and receive help and advice, rarely anger or disappointment. The knowledge that they were there for me even after all of these years had given me the courage to move forward when everything had looked impossible.

Because I was an only child, my father's brother and my mother's brother were all the family I had left. Both of them were in their 90s, and I felt some responsibility for them since they were both bachelors. One was living in Cleveland, Ohio, in a government housing project and the other was living in Buffalo, New York in his own apartment. Weekly calls and occasional visits were our means of connecting.

After my father's funeral, I shipped much of the living room, dining room, and kitchen furniture to Beechnut House. My folks definitely had a presence in Vita-Living's first home.

The state required that all residents take their own medication. Since most of the residents would be taking many different medications at different times of the day, figuring out how to meet this requirement seemed insurmountable. If Ricky was the model, it was unlikely that anyone coming to the Beechnut House could read or write. The residents not only had to take the correct medication, they had to put their initials in the correct place on a medication sheet indicating they had taken their medication as prescribed. How was I going to solve this problem? I talked to many people who had small community homes, but their residents all had moderate or mild mental retardation and, with training, they were able to initial the medication sheets and take their own meds from the medication bottles. At Beechnut House, I figured I would have to hire nurses to give the medications and this would be impossible on the money we would receive.

I heard about a pharmacist who worked with many nursing homes and met with him. Mr. Morgan became our savior. He had used blister packs in nursing homes before and thought they would work for Beechnut House. The blister packs were cards with 30 indentations covered with plastic (blisters), each of which held the medication for a single dose. He said he could put all of the medications a resident required for a specific time of day into one blister unit, no matter how many different medications the doctor had prescribed. All the resident would have to do is push the medication through the plastic blister into a cup or container. I really thought this made sense. I gave him a hug and told him if this worked, he was our hero.

I asked him to give me a sample blister pack with candies instead of pills so I could try it out on Ricky. I rushed home to see if Ricky could or would push through a blister. First I gave Ricky some small candies and then showed him the blister with its candy "pills" and how I could push the candies through the blister into a little cup. Then I asked him to eat the "candy pills." I told him there were more candies in the blister pack. Ricky was highly motivated to get to the candies, so after many trials he pushed the candies through the blister into the cup. It worked!

The next hurdle was devising a method for each resident to mark the medication sheet for each medication he or she took, complicated by the fact that there might be many different medications in each blister. At the top of the blister pack on the cardboard I placed stickers of common items such as baseball cap, car, butterfly and so on and then put the same stickers on the medication sheet. I observed whether Ricky could match the stickers and he could. I also placed a photo of Ricky on the medication box to see if he was able to identify his box by his photo. He could. I now knew that I had a strategy to train residents to take their medication. Although nobody had used this approach to self- medication before in these small community group homes, I was hopeful the state would approve it. I hoped they would allow our un-licensed staff, at least in the beginning, to assist a resident, by placing their hands over the resident's hand and guiding him or her in pop-ping the pills out of the blister packs. Another hurdle overcome if--and this was a big "if"--the State approved.

We would have to make many changes to turn the duplex into a sin-gle home for the six residents. Carlos, the contractor who had worked at Panhandle Eastern came back with the lowest bid. He had some good references, including one from Panhandle, and Stan knew he had a good reputation. Little did we know that this was the start of a 20-year-relationship. Carlos introduced me to two friends of his, a plumber and electrician who also became good friends to Vita-Living over the years. Holidays or not, we were always taken care of if there were electrical, construction, or plumbing problems. It was comforting to know that we were in good hands if an emergency arose.

The leases for the duplex were up the end of 1984, so I wrote to my renters of two years to advise them that we would not be renewing their leases and expected them to be out of their flats by the end of the year. Immediately after the holidays, we started making over the two units into one home. After the workmen had reconfigured the build-ings, they had to paint the walls and place doors outfitted with chimes in the new areas. There were seven exit doors out of the building, and each door chimed if someone tried to leave the building. We built a fence around the yard with a heavy gate that was locked except when cars were expected. We only needed one garage as the other had been converted to a family room. My folk's furniture fit neatly in the living room and made a warm friendly space for visitors.

I had converted the front dining room into my office and placed my computer there. Nutrition was an area of particular interest to me because of my background as a dietitian. I was certain that if we ate healthy foods and exercised we would be healthier. Since sugar was definitely a stimulant, it was especially important to limit the amount of sugar in our diet given the hyperactivity of many of our residents. We served fresh fruit and vegetables as often as possible. I was the chief cook and food-buyer for the first few years, so I had complete control of the menu and diet of the residents of Beechnut House.

We received a fixed, daily, per-person rate from the state. It was up to us to provide all of the services required for whatever the rate was. My staff cost was high so I needed to save in other ways. The cost of food was one way I thought we could save. My goal was to feed our residents well on $3.00/day per person. It was not a problem for me to develop a menu that helped the heavy residents lose weight and the skinny ones gain. We made all of our own mixes using minimal amounts of sugar. I prepared a four-week cycle menu. For three years I met my goal of keeping the cost of the food down to $3.00/day per person by using a lot of beans, cheese and eggs as well as whole grains and fresh fruits and vegetables purchased at local outdoor markets. At least one day each week we had chicken, fish, and red meat. One of our more difficult recipes was cheese soufflé. so I ended up being the souf-flé chef as well as the bread baker.

Being on the road so much the past year had given me plenty of time to think about the client/staff relationship. Many of the residents were going to be aggressive, probably spitters, hitters, kickers, biters, and pinchers. Most would have little or no speech and could be easily frustrated. I was constantly thinking of how I wanted staff to treat the residents. The people I hired were only human, and I knew I needed the help of a good psychologist, but, more important, I needed to be able to impart my particular philosophy of care and concern to the staff. The residents would be prone to tantrums and had to be talked to firmly when they were not successful in getting what they wanted from their tantrums. We could not let them succeed with their tantrums. That is easy to do with a two-or-three year old but not so easy in someone like Ricky, who was 5'8" and 170 pounds strong. I was planning the specific training I needed to do. I would need:

- to teach staff how to move into the resident's space and not be afraid that they might be hurt.

- to not take verbal or physical aggression personally.

- to be patient and avoid a battle of wills in dealing with an angry, aggressive person.

- to respect residents for who they were and treat them as much as possible like the adults they were while recognizing their limitations and their childlike manners.

I knew training would not be easy for either staff or residents, but I had learned that, with time and interest, we could find distinct likes and dislikes for each resident that we could use to change behaviors. It is the humanity that is common to all of us that I wanted the staff to recognize. I was obsessed with figuring out a training plan.

As we got closer to the opening of Beechnut House, I had to look for staff. I wanted to recruit young people who were willing to learn and not afraid to face challenges. All of the residents would be gone from our program during the day Monday through Friday. Since I needed staff particularly during the afternoons, midnights, and weekends, I thought college students would be ideal. I preferred someone who had experience working with people with mental retardation, but if a candidate didn't, I was willing to train him or her. It was important that my staff members have an open mind in dealing with the negative behaviors they were going to see. The staffing pattern I designed called for three staff in the afternoon when all of the residents returned to the house, one awake and one asleep staff during the midnight hours, and three staff in the mornings until the residents left for their day program. The midnight staff cooked the entrée and deserts and cleaned the public part of the home as well as assisted with wake-ups. The asleep staff was available if there was a behavior problem and to assist in the morning with wake-ups.

The most important and first person I needed was what the state called the QMRP or a Qualified Mental Retardation Professional, who served as the program director and was a state required position. I hoped that Kathy, the social worker from Cullen and a good friend, would take that position since she and I were in total agreement about the care of people with severe mental retardation who presented behaviors that were difficult to handle. I had seen her work at Cullen and felt she would be perfect for this experiment. She agreed, but since I was still waiting for some money from the state, I had to ask her to work for two weeks without a salary. We had spent all of the money we had to start the program and would receive no further funds until we started caring for residents. Kathy's husband and she agreed they would give up her pay for the "cause". In response to newspaper ads, we found a mature woman who had experience supervising a small group home in New York and a young woman who had worked in a group home in another state and had two years of college. We were lucky to find a woman to cook and clean during the midnight shift. We hired the remainder of the staff once we had all of the residents living in the house.

I paid $1.50 an hour more for direct care staff than most other agencies because I knew that the people we were going to serve were going to be difficult. I needed stability in the staff, and I was willing to pay more to achieve it. In addition to finding staff, I had to obtain contracts with a local hospital, medical doctor to serve as primary physician, dentist, a registered nurse, occupational, physical, and speech therapists, and a PhD psychologist. Fortunately I had contacts with many of the therapists and with the doctor we used when I was at Cullen. The doctor helped me get a contract with a local hospital. I served as the dietary consultant so saved the cost of another consultant.

One of the most important therapists was the psychologist because of the type of people I would be serving. I had met Dr. Jesse David Wood (David) when I was at Cullen and he was working on his doctorate in psychology. I heard he had just completed his doctorate and was opening an office, so I invited him to lunch and described what I was doing and how important a psychologist would be in changing the behaviors of the residents at Beechnut House, the first home of Vita-Living. I was elated when he agreed to work with me. Although his rate ($60.00) an hour was $15.00/hour more than the other providers were paying, it was so critical to have someone willing to work closely with me to help our residents that I was ready to pay whatever it cost.

A consistent schedule of activities for the residents was essential. They needed to know what to expect every day. I decided to create a 24-hour schedule similar to the successful one I had created when I was consulting in New York.

By 6:00 A.M. in the morning staff had awakened each person and assisted with their personal care and dressing. Residents had breakfast and morning medications by 7:00 A.M. They brushed their teeth and prepared to leave for the day program by 8:00 A.M. All the residents attended the workshop at the Center from 9:00 A.M. until 3:00 P.M. when they were picked up to return to Beechnut House. On arrival, they took their lunch boxes to the spare kitchen to be emptied and cleaned for the next day and got assistance washing their hands in preparation for their snack. A one-mile walk followed the snack, and then it was time to prepare for supper. Each resident had chores ranging from setting the table to making salad and simple food preparation. After dinner the residents took their plates to the sink, and helped wash pots and pans and swept the floor.

After supper clean up, each resident participated in training programs that had been determined at the group meeting (staffing) held within 30 days of their admittance. The staff assisted the residents with their programs such as money management, sex education, safety sign recognition, and so on. There was always some leisure time before bed when the residents could do what they wanted. The staff helped them prepare their lunch for the next day and placed it in the refrigerator. All the residents and staff had to play a group table game such as Monopoly or a card game such as Fish before retiring. Most of the residents did not interact well with others, so I wanted them to have the experience of interacting with the other residents and the staff in a fun situation. Showering and personal hygiene activities before sleep took at least an hour so it was 10:00 P.M. before each was in his or her room ready for the night. Within this schedule, we factored in the individual likes and dislikes of each resident to include activities such as going to the movies, reading simple books, rug hooking, or doing puzzles.

It was three years from the time Stan and I decided to start Vita-Living before we called the state to advise them we were ready to apply for licensing. We received permission to start bringing residents into the program in March of 1985. I wanted to high-five everyone who had helped.

Since we were willing to take people no one else served, it was easy to fill all of our beds. Of course, one was reserved for Ricky. We did no marketing but let it be known to all my previous associates and at the Mental Health and Mental Retardation Authority of Harris County that we were open for business. We made the decision to serve both men and women because that seemed more normal than having only one gender in the home. I learned that it was also much more expensive, because we always had to have a female staff on the premises and at least two large males to help our clients who were aggressive and self injurious.

Getting ready to open was an exhilarating time. I remember having a meeting with the nurse, psychologist, and the QMRP, about a week before we opened. The electricity was off and we sat around a table in candlelight reviewing folders and planning activities for the first two residents. Everyone around the table was high on hope and optimism that this program would work well and all would do well. Most of the people outside of our little group did not hold out much hope that we could succeed working with residents others had not been able or willing to help. The residents coming to Beechnut House were people who could not find a place in any other small group home in Harris County.

Many had been asked to leave or refused admission to other homes or had lived in a state institution and been removed by their families.

We brought the residents into the program slowly, about one a month. I wanted to allow us the time to give each one the attention required to develop the most effective program possible.

One of my biggest commitments was that I would never ask anyone to leave our program simply because he or she was too difficult or too expensive to serve. I remembered the night I was forced to take Terri home from the Center and the vow I made that I would never repeat it if I had a program. This commitment was expensive. I had to have extra staff. There was many a night when three staff was not enough, and Kathy and I worked as direct care staff. Everyone who worked for Beechnut House had to agree to our philosophy of acceptance no matter how unpleasantly the resident acted. I was not going to listen to a staff person tell me someone was too hard to serve or did not fit into our program. It was up to us to come up with a successful plan for each person.

The residents needed an attractive home but also a home that they were not successful at destroying. A few of the physical adaptations included:

- A "punching pillow:" Nailed to the hall wall was a board covered with foam and upholstery material that clients could use when they were frustrated and felt like hitting something.

- Windows that did not break: I investigated many types of windows and finally found bulletproof glass, Lexan. This was an expensive option, but we had no choice if we were concerned with the safety of the residents.

- Inexpensive décor: The rooms were decorated with baskets I purchased at flea markets and Target and posters given to me by many of the galleries I frequented.

- Furniture that could not be tossed: The tables and chairs were the heaviest we could find so that they would be difficult to throw. The beds were made with attached nightstands and four drawers that couldn't be removed attached under the frame.

- We purchased plain vinyl placemats, and using indelible markers mapped out the placement of the plates, glasses, and eating utensils on each placemat to give the residents a template for setting the table.

The staff all wore carpenter aprons filled with freshly popped pop-corn, which they gave to the residents all day long whenever the residents did something requested of them. If we asked a resident to sit down and he/she did so, he/she got popcorn. If we were going on a walk and they all came when called, they received popcorn. If we asked them to participate in their training activities, they received popcorn.

The bedrooms were outfitted like Ricky's room at home. The lighting was in the ceiling and there was nothing else in the rooms except personal items from the clients. The only decorations were posters, if that. In Ricky's bedroom one wall was painted with an abstract pattern made from dipping sponges into a variety of different colors and making a swirling pattern on the wall. He tore off any posters or papers on his walls.

We had to have a vehicle to transport the residents and as luck would have it, Stan won a station wagon at a convention he attended in February of 1985. I took this as a good omen.

We had overcome all of the obstacles placed before us. *We did it and were ready to go.*

Chapter VIII

IT WAS A 'GO'

Iᴛ ᴡᴀs 1985. The CD-ROM was developed, Bob Ballard found the wreckage of the RMS *Titanic*, the bottom fell out of the Houston economy, and Ricky, who was now 29 years old, had two favorite movies, *Back To The Future* and *Rocky IV*.

One of Stan's responsibilities was to find people for our board. On the promise that we would not ask them to donate, he found 12 mid- and-top level executives to serve with us. Looking at the spreadsheet, any businessman would question how we were going to pay our expenses. Since serving people with severe and profound mental retardation in a small community home had never been attempted before, there was no history. I felt certain that eventually the State would have to increase the funding, but I was not sure when. The price of oil dropped and the industry---the mainstay of the Houston economy--was beginning to show signs of distress. In addition, Mexico's economy was changing with a new President, and many of the wealthy Mexicans who came to Houston to spend big dollars on personal items could no linger do so. Within four months the Houston economy had worsened so much that most of our board members had lost their jobs or been transferred out of the city. The remaining members of the board were Stan, our friend Page Anderson, and myself, which was actually easier for me since I had more freedom with the smaller board. Stan and Page never questioned me about the programs.

Before we brought any of the residents into our program, Kathy, the program director, David, the psychologist, and I developed a way to change the behaviors that were keeping those we wanted to serve out of the community. Some of these behaviors were so unpleasant and distasteful that I had to remind myself of a poem written by Terence, the Roman poet and dramatist and onetime slave, "Homo seum humani nihil a me alienum puto" ("I am human; to me nothing human is alien"). As we moved forward, this small phrase became my motto.

It was very important to me that everyone working with our residents understood what we were trying to accomplish.

First we defined "challenging behavior" either as behavior that results in self-injury, injury to others, damages to the physical environment, isolation or as a behavior that interferes with learning new skills and isolates the person.

Second, we stressed that such behaviors are a means of communication. Most of the people we were serving had limited communication skills. They let everyone know they did not want to do something by hitting, kicking, biting or spitting. To further complicate things, they might use the same modes of communication to tell us that they were hurting someplace or that they wanted attention. The challenge for us was to discover which message the behavior was communicating.

Third, we recognized that the planning and monitoring of the program was a team effort. The team consisted of the resident, if possible, the guardian, the people working hands-on with the resident, the nurse with a report from the physician, the program director, the psychologist and representatives of whatever other therapies the resident needed. I was involved in all of the meetings because I wanted to be a part of the dynamic that would nourish the changes. We met as often as necessary but at least monthly about each resident, but during the first year, I was in touch daily with our program director and psychologist, either in person or by phone, to talk about the progress or lack of progress of our residents.

Fourth, we recognized that an assessment of the resident had to be performed by the psychologist using his testing materials and by the staff through direct observation. The resident's staff person collected data to show when a behavior occurred, what happened immediately before the behavior occurred, where it occurred, and what happened immediately after it occurred.

Fifth, the psychologist had to develop the program plan and present it to the team. The team prioritized the goals and objectives, with the ultimate goal being for the resident to be able to control his own behavior so he could be as independent as possible. The programs were not carved in stone. Included in the plan were the individual likes (rewards) and dislikes (consequences) for each person and the alternative

communication skill or replacement behavior staff were to teach him/
her.

Sixth, we recognized that mental retardation cannot be cured, but
with adequate supports its effect on the person can be limited and
modified.

Since this approach in dealing with persons with severe mental retardation was not common, it was essential that our staff training be successful. These six principles were the basis of our training
program.

The state required that each resident have a written program plan
called an Individual Plan of Care developed at a meeting, called a
staffing, to be held 30 days after the resident entered the program. The
plans were recommendations based on assessments performed by con-
sultants and staff prior to the staffing.

The state also required that a Human Rights Committee be formed
to review all behavior programs that used negative consequences and/
or psychoactive drugs to change behavior. Since most of the residents
served in Beechnut House required behavior plans and were on psychoactive drugs, this was an important committee. The Human Rights
Committee was composed of representatives from the community who
had no obligation to the agency and had to include at least one family member of any client being served by the agency. Our committee
consisted of me (as the family member), the Director of Research at the
Texas Research Institute, a PhD. in family counseling who had worked
with me at the Center, a retiree who had worked with people with mental retardation in New York, and a man who investigated allegations
of abuse at another agency. The committee met at least quarterly or
as needed and reviewed any programs where the resident received
psychoactive drugs or had a behavior program using negative consequences (aversives).

Finally, after more than three years of preparation, we were really
ready to bring in the residents. The day after we celebrated our opening, I received a call from Dr. Frank Borreca, the Executive Director of
the Center. He had an aggressive resident at Cullen who broke furniture and windows, and had to leave Cullen so he wondered if I would
accept him at Beechnut House. " Sounds like our kind of resident," I
said with enthusiasm. Send me his records, and we'll plan on him moving in as our first resident."

Dressed in jeans and a freshly ironed white shirt, Paul was brought
to Beechnut House by his sister on the afternoon of March 15th around

4 o'clock. Karen, the direct care worker, Agnes, the supervisor, Kathy, the program director and I greeted him. His sister pulled a shiny black suitcase into the house and helped him put his clothes into the drawers under the bed or into the closet behind sliding doors. "Paul, this is a lovely room," she said.

Paul did not answer but nodded his head up and down. He was 5' 7" and about 150 pounds, in his 30s and had lived in a state school for 20 years until he moved to his sister's home. He had no relationship with his parents and thought of his sister as his mother. He called her "Becky Mom."

Paul's diagnosis was severe mental retardation, poor impulse control, and a history of seizures. The only medication he took was for seizure control. While sitting or standing, Paul performed isometric exercises with his arms and hands all day long. Consequently his arms were like steel wire, and if he became aggressive he could do serious damage to property and people.

His sister kissed him good-by and promised to see him the next week. Karen showed Paul the rest of the house. He really basked in the attention from the three staff and was so easy to get along with that we thought the stories about his aggression and property destruction must have been wrong. There is usually a short "honeymoon period" when a new client does not show his true behaviors, but in Paul's case, even after the arrival of the second resident in April, Paul remained even-tempered and a pleasure to be around.

During the thirty days prior to Paul's staffing, the psychologist, the speech therapist, the occupational therapist and the nurse performed a series of assessments to determine his needs and offer recommendations for his program. Paul also saw the doctor and dentist. His sister, Kathy, Agnes, the Supervisor, David, the psychologist, and I attended the staffing. We began talking about programs to deal with his self-help needs, such as shaving, tooth brushing, mixing hot and cold water, and showering. Paul particularly enjoyed preparing his own sandwich for the next day. These activities kept him and the staff occupied when he was at the house.

David had developed a behavior program for Paul before his arrival based on the records we received indicating he destroyed property and showed aggression when he became angry or frustrated. We waited two months before we had to use the program, only implementing it when the third resident, Derek, arrived. There was no obvious reason why Derek and Paul did not get along, but whenever the two were near each other, one or the other would strike out. Paul was much stronger but easily frustrated when teased, and Derek, who was much smaller, loved to tease Paul. He pretended he was going to touch Paul and Paul screamed and attacked, or he would sidle up to Paul as if he were going to sit or stand next to him and Paul screamed and attacked. We decided to keep the two apart as much as possible, so we assigned staff one to each to keep them separate when they were in the same room or eating together. This was impossible to do all of the time, but we were able to reduce the fights considerably.

Shortly after Derek moved in everyone was relaxing in the family room after dinner. Derek stepped in front of Paul while Paul was sitting watching television. Paul jumped up like a flash and raised his arm to strike Derek. Staff moved in immediately and directed Derek out of the way. Screaming in frustration, Paul pulled a shelf down and kicked a hole in the wall.

Paul was directed to his room where he proceeded to tear his closet doors off the hinges and use them as battering rams to destroy his walls and open up live wires. He pushed the windows out of their frames; smashed his television set onto the floor, tore all of his magazines and posters into little pieces and spread them over the floor. Fortunately there was nothing else in his room other than the specially designed bed. When Paul was calm, he picked up all of the pieces he had torn and helped staff clean up the dry wall that was on the floor. He could not stand a messy room, so he took whatever time necessary to clean up his room after nearly destroying it.

We knew that we had to move rapidly to implement his behavior program. The program called for the staff to throw his clothes on the floor and mess his room right after he had straightened it. He then had to straighten his room again, which he did screaming in anger. This strategy is called overcorrection, and the idea was to replicate what he did but exaggerate the process and take control away from him.

We made an emergency call to David advising him that we were implementing the behavior program he had written. Then we made another emergency call to Carlos, our contractor, asking for immediate repairs to Paul's room. Paul could not sleep there unless repairs were completed. Carlos came within the hour and covered the wires and put the windows back in their frames. He also removed the closet doors and Paul had no closet doors for many years.

The next day David met with all of the staff to be sure they knew how to implement the overcorrection program. The program involved

staff helping Paul throw his clothing and papers on the floor to simu-
late the property destruction of the house and then requiring him to
pick up everything and put it away. The staff explained to Paul why
they were messing his room before it started but did not talk to him
while they were helping him toss his room. The messing of his room
occurred three consecutive nights in a row after each episode regardless of how he behaved for those three days. Repetition helped Paul
associate his behavior with the consequence. This plan produced positive results so quickly that we used it no more than four times the first
year.

The staff made it clear to me that they did not like following this
program, but when they saw how effective it was they changed their
minds. I knew we needed to do something extreme if we were to
change Paul's behavior, so I was more open to David's ideas than the
other staff. I was elated that this plan worked so well and so quickly.

One afternoon Paul was finishing his snack in the kitchen and
started to whine about something that the staff could not understand.
A staff person immediately directed him to his room, sat with him on
his bed, and talked about what was bothering him. Since he did not
seem to be calming down, staff directed him to the punching area on
the wall in his room. The punching area was a 24" square wood base,
covered with foam and cotton cloth stapled to the back, hung at a level
that he could comfortably punch. As far as I knew, a punching mat had
not been used in a group home before. Paul punched the cushion with
great force and gradually the tone of his voice quieted and he stopped
whining. After he stopped punching, he and the staff person came into
the family room to talk through hand puppets. Paul picked a lion for
himself, sat in one of the chairs and gave a rabbit to the staff. Through
the puppet he was able to explain that he was tired and hot and wanted
to be left alone. He went to his room and we avoided an explosive incident. Puppet talk, which is modeling language so to better express
feelings, worked well with Paul and we used it throughout the year.

The records also indicated that Paul picked at his skin to such a
degree that he was in danger of causing serious damage to himself.
Actually he had created a basal cell carcinoma behind his ear that required a skin graft to heal it. David suggested a program he called
"Reinforcement of Incompatible Behavior", which meant finding an activity for Paul that was incompatible with his picking at his skin.

One night a staff member noticed Paul picking at his arms while
he was watching television. We had a stash of crafts for the residents

to try, and she found a package of rug hooking. She sat next to Paul and started hooking. When he appeared interested, she offered to teach him and he started to hook rugs. Hooking required the use of both of his hands, so he stopped picking while he was working on crafts. He eventually hung some beautiful mats that he had hooked in his room.

We encouraged all staff members to brainstorm ideas that might work with our residents. There was no idea too far-fetched or "bad" as long as it was not illegal or abusive. We kept David busy sorting out all of the ideas that we threw at him. I believe we were able to keep our staff even with the difficult behaviors they had to deal with because we encouraged them to participate in the plans for the residents and we supported their efforts.

Paul had many strengths, and we wanted to build on those strengths, a key element in changing behaviors. He did not like staff to be angry with him. He liked attention and affection. He could entertain himself with television and arts and crafts. But he needed to learn how to express his anger, frustration, and unhappiness verbally to reduce the need to damage property or people. If he was unable to talk about his feelings, we needed to find a way for him to act out his anger in a socially acceptable manner.

Paul had learned to use aggression and property destruction to get what he wanted, and it had been effective in the past. He wanted to leave where he had been living and had been asked to leave other placements such as the Center. I refused to accept this option at Vita-Living, so we were motivated to find a way to wean him from using aggression and property destruction to get his way. Staff used the talks and mat punching almost daily. Since Paul had such low verbal skills, a staff person assisted him in expressing himself by asking him questions and listening to him as long as it took. That is why the puppet talking worked so well with him. Though developing this behavior change program sounds easy, it took years to see a change in his behavior. Now no one would recognize Paul as the angry man he once was.

During the residents' daily walks we noticed that Paul fell frequently, so we purchased knee guards used by hockey players to protect him. In addition, a staff person always walked next to him to support him if he tripped. Paul liked his day program so there was no problem for him during the day. It was when he returned home and interacted with the other residents that his temper flared. We spent much time sitting next to him on his bed helping him control his temper. Gradually over the years, the incidences reduced from three or four a day to three or four a week and then three or four a month. Today Paul has lived at Beechnut House for 22 years. He is much calmer, and we use the over-correction program only once every few years. It continues to remain important to talk with Paul when he starts to whine and allow him to talk about and honor his feelings. Treating him with the respect he deserves is an important part of his program plan. He removed the punching cushion from the wall in his bedroom three years ago and has not needed it since. He continues to see his sister regularly and visits her on holidays and at least once a month. She gave testimony at one of our fundraisers stating how grateful she was for our program and how lucky she felt that Paul lives at Beechnut House.

Watching the slow but steady improvement in Paul's behaviors reinforced my philosophy of never giving up on the residents served by Vita-Living. I never saw them as too difficult, difficult, yes, but never too difficult.

Tony became the second resident of Beechnut House. I first met Tony when I was the director at Cullen and I was familiar with his many difficult behaviors. He was a handsome 21-year-old, with hair neatly trimmed and even features, about 5'10" tall and 130 pounds. His mother brought him with one suitcase by bus to Beechnut House. She carried a stick to protect herself from him because he struck out at her frequently. After seeing his room and the rest of the house, she attempted to kiss him goodbye but he dodged her and ran from one end of the house to the other, ending his run by butting his head into the wall.

On psychoactive medication, Tony had a diagnosis of severe autism and moderate mental retardation. He struck at anyone in his space and was a master at making holes. Our walls were covered with place-mats that I stapled over the holes until someone came to repair them. It became obvious that he never went back to the same spot to head bang if it was covered with a placemat. I thought we might be able to use this information, but I wasn't certain how. Tony did not appear to understand what we said to him, and he did not speak or sign to others. He used his aggression and self-abuse to test limits and irritate other people around him. Attention from others---negative or positive---frequently reinforced these behaviors. He wanted no one in his space, could not tolerate loud noises, and seemed to be overwhelmed by what he saw and heard during ordinary activities of daily living. He had practiced head banging since he was born and also attacked others by raising his arm, making a tight fist, and slamming the fist into the shoulder or back of the other person. A precursor to Tony's self-injurious or aggressive behavior usually started with him humming while moving his fist up and down next to his ear.

On a Sunday, shortly after Derek, the third resident, arrived, a significant incident occurred. Tony hit one of the staff members, who was bent over playing a game with Derek, so hard on her back that she lost her breath and almost fainted. I sent her and Derek to the backyard and told her to stay outside while I remained with Tony to implement his behavior program. The behavior program had one component dealing with his running. When Tony ran, a staff person was supposed to put up a hand with the palm facing out, much like a traffic cop, and say, "Stop". When I held out my hand, Tony bent down and took a bite out of my wrist. So much for that plan. I was wearing a carpenter apron filled with dry popcorn. I tried to reward Tony with the popcorn, one of his favorite foods, whenever he sat or complied with a request, but he continued to strike out. In between his attacks he ran to the walls to head-butt, making holes in all of the walls in the public areas of the house. Kathy had taken Paul to the emergency room because of an earache, and when she returned she noticed all of the bruises and bite marks and exclaimed, "What in the world happened to you?"

"Tony happened to me. I am worried about his head, look at all of the holes. He really needs to go to the emergency room, but I am not taking him. We need a Mr. T," I said.

"I know a Mr. T. without the gold jewelry," Kathy said. "He was a friend of my brother's and still visits my father regularly. I'll call him if you want."

"You've got to be kidding," I responded.

"No, really. He's an engineer, but I bet he would come if I called him and we could take Tony to the emergency room," Kathy assured me.

"Call him. I want to meet this man," I said. Kathy called Bob and we were lucky that he was home that Sunday. He was willing to come to Beechnut House and help take Tony to the emergency room. I called the doctor to tell him we were bringing Tony to the hospital, and he asked who was bringing him. I saw Bob get out of his car and responded, "A *very big* man." Bob was 6'5" tall and had a body that was so large he had to have his shirts and suits custom-made. When Tony met Bob, he put out his hand to shake Bob's and acted like a perfect gentleman. Obviously he knew better than to tackle a man of Bob's size, so he could control himself when he wanted to, I realized. On their return from the hospital, Bob reported that the doctor saw no damage to Tony's skull. Apparently Tony's skull had become calcified from years of head banging. Bob stayed to talk with us for a while, and I asked him if he knew anyone his size who needed a job. He mentioned that he had a truck-driver friend just out of a job who was not as big as he but was strong. He needed work badly and could learn if we were willing to teach him. His name was Wren. We needed a strong man desperately, and Kathy and I were willing to train someone if he was willing to learn.

I was concerned abut hiring someone without the education or experience I thought necessary, but Kathy assured me that Bob would not refer someone to us who was not a good person. I knew that Kathy and/or I would be there when he was on duty and could continually train him and monitor his work. Initially, Wren had difficulty writing the contact notes required, but he wanted the job badly and he wrote the notes with a dictionary next to him until he learned how to document what was necessary. Wren wound up being a good investment. He stayed with us for 15 years.

We tried many different behavior programs to change or reduce Tony's aggressive and self-injurious behaviors. One morning Tony hit a staff member on her back with his fist and then ran and hit his head into the wall in the kitchen. Immediately the staff person placed a knit cap on Tony's head and had him paint the hole with a dry brush for a few minutes. He complied and laughed. We tried this technique for a few weeks, but there was no indication that this plan would be successful.

One afternoon, on returning from the day program, Tony made a tight fist and with a grimace on his face struck the staff person who was giving him his snack. The staff member immediately covered Tony's head with a covering resembling a pillowcase for a few seconds. We tried this for a few weeks, but Tony liked the isolation and hit the staff person and then handed him/her the covering so he could have it placed over his head.

I had read about a school in Japan that used exercise to effectively help people with autism. I thought we should try it and suggested this to David. He liked it too, so we purchased a stationary exercise bike, a basketball and basket, and used a running track that was about a block away. These activities were incorporated into Tony's behavior program.

One Sunday everyone was sitting in the family room, and I looked at Tony and noticed him moving his hands obsessively next to his ears and humming. This was the signal that he was about to become aggressive or run and butt his head into the wall. I asked a staff person to quickly escort Tony to one of the exercise spots and stay with him until his agitation left him. With a staff person on either side, Tony was led to the exercise bike. They stayed with him for 30 minutes or until he calmed down. When his exercise session was over, he sat on a chair in the family room and played with building blocks. I was so excited that I ran around the room giving everyone high fives including Tony. This was the beginning of a slow but dramatic reduction in the instances of Tony's aggression and self-abuse.

I noticed that Tony never butted his head into a wall when there was a covering on the wall so we had the idea of painting the wall with a picture to see if that would protect the wall. One weekend when Tony went home, a Girl Scout troop painted a seaside scene on the wall in his room. For over a year he never touched that wall, and then about a year and half later he made holes with his feet and head. I guess he decided that he no longer liked that picture.

In addition to Tony's exercise plan, we invaded his space as often as we could so that he could learn to tolerate sharing the house with five other people. His room was private and he could go there whenever he wished, but in the public areas he had to share space at the dining table, and in the family room and participate in the group game every night. There was a different person inside the shell around Tony. I wanted to release that other person. That other person had an infectious sense of humor and often led the laughter when something funny occurred in the house.

Gradually Tony tolerated the other residents and the staff to the point that he formed an attachment with Kathy. She allowed him to touch her eyelashes and he allowed her to touch his. I watched this with great trepidation, but he never hurt her, and it was a big step forward for him to trust someone and have someone trust him.

David prescribed what he called "Sensory Integration Training and Intervention" activities. Staff were instructed to help Tony in activities that involved rocking or spinning, simple puzzles, primary reader, play dough and looking at newspapers or catalogues. He loved to have his hands in water so he earned the task of washing pots and pans. He loved to rinse the dishes before they were placed in the dishwasher. Gradually Tony's head butting and aggression continued to decrease. Today, 20 years later, Tony has stopped making holes with his head and has not been aggressive to others for the last 5 years.

When I reflect back on the work we did with Tony, I realize again how important the principles of acceptance, consistency, and the program itself were to his success. At this time, autism is not curable but the behaviors that develop around it are just that—behaviors. They are a means of communication, and it is up to the caretakers to discover what the behaviors are communicating. We intervened and released that other person within Tony.

About this time I realized that we needed more help than I could afford, so I called the Volunteer Center, thinking it might be a source of helping hands not so much with the residents as with filing and cooking. I talked to a Mr. Brown and was told that the Volunteer Center always sent someone out to interview a new applicant. After I hung up, I was so busy that I forgot about the request.

A few weeks later I answered a knock on the door from two young men from the Volunteer Center, who introduced themselves and said they wanted to check out our program. The smell of freshly baked bread drew the two men to the kitchen where I was making dinner. They eagerly accepted my offer of a bowl of vegetarian stew and fresh bread. After eating, they met the residents who were playing ball in the back yard and toured the house. I made two good friends for Vita-Living that day that have referred wonderful people to us over the years.

Volunteers have been critical to our success. A few notable ones stand out. In June the first volunteer referred from the Volunteer Center came to Beechnut House. Louise offered to come one night a week to file for us. We had a small office, so as I was writing checks she was filing. I commented that I hoped I wouldn't go to jail since I wasn't sure that I was doing everything for payroll correctly. She looked up at me and asked, "Do you need some help? I'm a payroll expert. That's what I do for a living. Have you sent in your quarterly report?"

I admitted that I had no idea what she was talking about. She offered to write a letter requesting forgiveness from the IRS and to help me with payroll. She did this for two years and then found the man, Richard, who has been our Chief Financial Officer for over twenty years.

A registered nurse, who came from Australia and could not yet work legally in this country, offered to cook for us and did so for a year until she could work in her career. She was one of few who could prepare the cheese soufflé that was on the menu.

A wonderful woman, who now serves on our board, Sue Sheridan,

Ed.D. volunteered to help us create table games that were age appropriate and doable for our residents. She modified the games such as UNO, checkers, Dominos, and card games such as Fish and then trained the staff and residents how to play them. In addition, she developed and videotaped training programs for residents about making sandwiches, setting the table, and other ordinary daily activities.

Diedra, a secretary who worked all day in a law office, came at 9:00 P.M. to type for us and stayed until she finished, often as late as 2:00 or 3:00 in the morning two or three nights a week. She did most of our typing that first year

Our third resident, Derek, was brought to Beechnut House by his father at10:00 A.M. one morning in May. Kathy and Agnes greeted him, and immediately he took Kathy's hand as she led him to his bedroom. In his 20s, Derek lived with his father who felt he could no longer handle him. Derek was under 5' tall and weighed less than 100 pounds. He was verbal but spoke in two word sentences (telegraphic speech) such as "cool morrow?" which meant "Is there school tomorrow?" In addition, he repeated over and over again what was said to him (perseverative speech). His diagnosis was severe mental retardation with hyperactivity and poor impulse control. He was on psychoactive medication, and many years before, had undergone an operation for a bleeding ulcer that left him with only about a fourth of his stomach.

The 30-day staffing team--his father, Kathy, Agnes, David and I---determined that he needed programs to help him shower, brush teeth, shave, and mix hot and cold water. In addition, the team recognized that they needed to address Derek's many problem behaviors.

He had a history of uncontrolled psychotic-like behavior that occurred about once a year and lasted from three to six weeks. His face broke out in a large rash with sores on his lips and he hallucinated. He feared the images he saw and the voices he heard and woke up screaming and terrified. Staff comforted him until he fell asleep again. Despite many tests, doctor's found no definitive cause for this condition, and the cycle of psychotic behavior continues until this day.

There was a period of time in the beginning when Derek screamed for 24 hours straight. Staff told me they would rather he hit them than have to listen to him scream but scream he did. He might stop for a few days and then he started up again. We directed Derek to his room when he screamed for any length of time, and gradually he stopped. No one spoke to him as they led him to his room. If he stopped screaming, a staff member immediately invited him to join the other residents again. He hasn't had a screaming session in over 10 years.

Derek's aggressive behavior towards others included slapping, scratching and pulling hair. One day upon returning from his day program Derek visited me in my office. I was writing at my desk and he was looking out of the window when I heard him say, "Pull Hair." Before I could stop him, he had grabbed a hank of my hair and was seriously pulling it. Tears ran down my cheeks from the sharp pain but I covered his hand with mine and, speaking very calmly, loosened his grip. That same day he slapped Wren in the face when he was being bathed.

The behavior plan proposed to reduce his aggression involved using Derek's love of papers and magazines. He always carried some paper with him, so for a week, staff members removed the papers from him randomly, at different times and regardless of his behavior, placed them on a shelf within his sight, and said nothing to him. The idea behind this program was that it might confuse him, so he might control his behavior in an effort to keep his papers. After a few weeks staff reported a small decrease in Derek's aggressive behavior.

When Derek was aggressive, staff members also guided him to a table to do a task such as counting cards or putting a puzzle together. He received praise and backrubs when he stayed on task and no praise when he was aggressive. Staff labeled the scratching, pulling hair or slapping and said, "No pinching," "No pulling hair," and so on.

Derek put anything and everything into his mouth. One evening Derek saw a piece of apple on the floor and quickly put it into his mouth. Kathy saw this and said, "Oh, no. You put that dirty thing in your mouth," and took him to the bathroom to brush his teeth for about two minutes. We repeated this plan every time Derek put food from the floor into his mouth.

For many months Derek masturbated in the closet and fell asleep on the floor. One morning about a month after he arrived, the midnight staff person informed me that she had found Derek asleep on the floor of the closet. I called David, and he suggested that we provide Derek with a large pillow for his bed. When a staff person discovered Derek in the closet, that person should direct him to his bed and the pillow, label what he was doing, and say that it was private touching and should be done in his bed. This worked well for Derek, and he returned to his bed during the night.

As soon as we found a more socially acceptable alternative for one of Derek's behaviors another socially unacceptable one popped up. I remember well the day I heard him coughing and gagging and ran into his room to see how he was. He looked straight at me and projected vomit all over my clothes. I was not happy. I cleaned myself as best I could. Later that day I heard the coughing and gagging again and went to him, but this time I directed him to the bathroom with one hand behind his neck and one hand on his arm. I held his head over the toilet until he finished his vomiting. I said nothing, gave him a glass of water and took him back to his previous activity. I told staff that when they heard him forcing himself to vomit to move quickly and follow the procedure I followed. As soon as he was involved in the previous activity, he was to receive praise. When Derek did not get what he wanted, the vomiting stopped after two episodes.

Three months after Derek's staffing, we met again and after reviewing all of Derek's behaviors and all of the plans to change them, the team decided to concentrate on one or two of the behaviors and leave the others for later. The team determined that aggression and screaming were Derek's most disruptive behaviors, so the plan would concentrate on decreasing these behaviors. Derek seemed to like the sensation he received when he screamed (self stimulation), and he tried aggression when he was asked to do something he didn't want to do. In addition, staff monitored closely his putting of foreign objects into his mouth.

Over the next two years Derek showed slight improvement. He could sit at the table during mealtimes without putting his hands into other's foods. He also signed if he wanted seconds. The staff continued behavior programs that involved staying on task and ignoring the screaming. Gradually over 20 years the screaming stopped, and his aggression dropped to one instance a month or less. I attributed our success with Derek to the consistency of his daily routine and our total acceptance of him as a human being no matter how he acted.

Elsie, our fourth resident, was a woman in her 20s admitted in May around the same time as Derek. She was living with her mother and came from a large extended family. Every week many of her nieces and nephews visited with their grandmother, and Elsie struck out at them, apparently jealous of the attention her mother gave to the young children when they were in her home. She showed none of this aggression when she lived at Beechnut House and so was an easy person to serve. Her diagnosis was severe mental retardation but there was no sign of psychosis and she was on no medication.

During the period when we admitted the first four residents, Ricky continued to live at home, but I was eager to help him transition to the house. Stan drove him to work, and when our station wagon picked up the Beechnut House residents, it also brought Ricky back to Beechnut House. He had a snack and spent time with the residents until I was ready to leave for home. He seemed happy with this schedule until one day in June when he indicated that he wanted to stay at Beechnut House because it looked as if the residents really were having a good time. I decided that Ricky had picked the time for his move.

The next day I brought his clothing and personal items to his room. When he returned to Beechnut House that afternoon, I told him he would stay at Beechnut House. I was not sure that he understood what I was saying, but when I left and he stayed that night, he got the message and was not happy at all. He ran after the car when I left until my car turned the corner.

Frequently he ran into the street, followed by the staff trying to bring him back to the curb. I knew that if I did not force myself to leave, he would never accept living away from us. I talked to Stan and we both agreed that this was a quality of life issue. We stayed up all night talking because we knew how important it was for Ricky to realize he could not be with us every minute of every day and night. If Ricky did not learn to live without us, when we were no longer around, he would have to be either controlled chemically with drugs or physically with restraints. Neither of us wanted that for him, so we decided to take a calculated risk that he would stop running into the street once he realized that I was leaving everyday but returning the next day. I was frightened of the possible consequences of our decision. How could we live with ourselves if he or a staff member was hurt while running into the street? I tried to leave when he was involved in an activity that he liked. After about a week of him being upset every time I left, he accepted my departures and seemed to settle down when I told him goodnight. Staff also rushed to close the gate quickly after the car left so that Ricky could not run out. Most nights I stayed until it was time for bed and he was engrossed in television. Finally he became the fifth resident.

In July Kathy handed me a pile of papers dealing with injuries inflicted on the staff. Tony pinched and hit so hard that Agnes had to see a physician. Ricky threw a chair that hit Wren. Derek tripped Karen and she complained of back injury. I had to come up with strategies both to protect the staff and to continue the work with our residents. One Sunday I was passing the television set when a football game was on. I noticed that the players were wearing something bulky on their arms and shoulders, which Stan said were guards. I went to a sporting goods store and asked to see the guards that football players used. I purchased enough arm guards, shoulder guards, and shin guards so that every staff member could wear them. From then on all staff members were required to wear guards during the entire time they worked with the residents. This practice dramatically reduced injuries, and everyone was grateful to me for offering them the protection. The best result of the guards was that they allowed staff to move toward the residents instead of pulling away. Picture the six residents with three or four staff wearing the arm, shoulder, and shin guards as well as carpenter aprons filled with popcorn, walking their mile everyday in the neighborhood. I can only imagine what the neighbors were thinking.

Shortly after opening, we received many calls from people who wanted to see what we had done and how we did it. It was not unusual to have 5 to 10 visitors per week in the first few months of operation. We had an open house about two months after we started and welcomed many people who did not believe that we could successfully serve the type of people we did. Some of these people were so impressed with what they saw that they wound up serving on our board for many years.

In June our sixth and final resident, Julia, a 30-year-old woman with Down Syndrome, moved into Beechnut house from Austin State School. She was the first person to come into Harris County as a result of a significant lawsuit(the Lelsz lawsuit) that required that the state pay for people living in state schools to move into the community. She shared a room with Elsie and neither showed any difficult behaviors. We were all very grateful for that.

Elsie and Ricky became good friends. I observed them holding hands while watching television and communicating with each other although Ricky had no language and what little Elsie had was difficult to understand. This was the only time I noticed Ricky developing a reciprocal relationship with a person other than a family member. It was wonderful to see, and I thought it helped Ricky feel more comfortable in his new home. When he acted out, which he did frequently in those days, Elsie would shake her finger at him and say something that would cause him to lower his head and use a sign for sorry. I had trouble understanding her words but apparently Ricky had no difficulty with her speech. Before they retired for the night they would meet in the family room and hug each other and say good night in their fashion. As a parent I was thrilled that Ricky could experience a close relationship with a real friend. This "romantic" relationship lasted until Elsie returned to her family home in 1993.

The state required that every resident be trained to take his or her own medication. Kathy came up with the idea of role-playing to train the residents. Every evening we brought out the bottles of over-the-counter medication our residents used. One of the staff held up the bottle and acted out the illness that would cause you to take that medication. For instance, if you had a stomachache, the staff person showed the pink bottle of Pepto-Bismol, pointed to her or his stomach and doubled over as if with a stomachache, and then said the name of the medication. Each resident copied the staff as best they could. The medications that served as props in the role-play were Pepto Bismol, Tylenol, Milk of Magnesia, cough medicine, and an antihistamine. We were not sure if role-playing would work with the mental level of the people living at Beechnut House, but gradually they learned what medications to take for stomach trouble, diarrhea, constipation, colds, fevers, and coughs. I think that acting out the illness and the color of the bottles helped them learn. As long as the bottles did not change, after practicing once a day every day of the week for years, they could determine what to take when ill. One day Ricky pointed to his head, indicated a headache and then went directly to the shelf where the medications were stored and pointed to the bottle of Tylenol. I was elated.

During the role-playing activity we dealt with how to recognize a wide range of human emotions like anger, sadness, and happiness. This is difficult for anyone but particularly confusing for someone who cannot verbalize feelings. We used hand drawn pictures to help. A staff member would draw pictures of faces showing these emotions. Then they would tell a story about a person who was sad, angry, or happy while pointing to the picture. A resident would be asked to point to the picture describing that specific feeling. Dealing with anger was the most difficult. In an attempt to model appropriate behavior for anger we had a set of pictures showing the different ways a person could behave when they were angry. For example, they could talk to a staff member, they could go to their bedroom to cool off, or they could try hitting the anger mat. The last picture was of a person smiling. We did this over many years and it certainly seemed to help our residents at Beechnut House recognize their feelings and act appropriately.

The first week of August we were surprised to see a team of three state reviewers at our front door. I knew it was inevitable, but I dreaded their visit. I was nervous that they would find fault with the unusual approaches we were taking. The people being served in other local group homes did not have the behaviors that our residents showed. I knew they did not have to deal with the level of aggression and self-abuse that we faced everyday.

The team arrived from Austin around 3:00 P.M. and stayed until the dinner meal was served; documenting everything they saw on pads of yellow paper. They left after observing dinner being served, saying they would be back to watch the breakfast meal. It was obvious that the staff was nervous, and I worried that they might forget the basics, such as having the clients wash their hands before and after dinner or helping the residents to the food instead of having the residents serve themselves. Since this was the first small group home in the community with such severely handicapped residents trained to self medicate, the state reviewers observed the medication pass at 5:00 P.M. A resident dropped a pill and fortunately the staff knew to pick it up, throw it away, and document the medication error. This was tricky and I did not know if they would approve. The review team said nothing during their observation but returned to the kitchen tables that they had turned into their desks and made notes, always closing the door for privacy. They returned in the morning, and one of the team followed the residents to their day program. The other two looked through the resident books to check out the programs and observe whether the programs we said we were implementing were actually being carried out. In the afternoon they observed our walk with the guards, carpenter aprons filled with the popped corn, our group game, and our medication distribution. The third day they returned for our exit meeting. I held my breath until I heard they were happy with the way we were handling our residents and the program. This was a huge relief. There were a few documentation errors, but there was no doubt that we would continue to be licensed. This was surprising to many outsiders but not to those of us who believed in our approach. Everyone was relieved and excited about our success.

In September of that year Mrs. Dempsey, a mother of a 21- year old daughter who had many diagnoses: autism, deafness, severe mental retardation, and mental illness, visited us. Mrs. Dempsey had heard about us and wondered when we might have an opening for her daughter. Because of her daughter's complicated situation, many providers from all over the country had refused her service. I told her that I did not think we would have an opening for a long time because our phi-

losophy was not to ask anyone to leave, and most of my residents had
been in the same situation as her daughter. Listening to her talk gave
me an opening I had been waiting for. I thought that this might be an
opportunity to get someone else involved in Vita-Living, so I suggested
she might want to do what I did. "How about buying a house and outfitting it to meet the state standards. If you agree we would run the
program and bring in other residents." She left after saying she would
talk to her husband and be back in touch. I did not hear from her again
for the rest of that year, but often wondered what she had done.

A few weeks later another couple came to see me about opening a
house for their daughter who had Down Syndrome without any severe
behavior problems. They did not like where she was currently living
and wanted to start a program for her. I outlined the same process for
them. They agreed to see if they could raise the money and said they
would get back to me.

Around this time a friend recommended that I join a group of
other providers in Texas in a professional organization called Texas
Association of Private Providers (TAPPR). I was not sure how I would
fit into the group, but I found it worthwhile and eventually served two
terms on the board. The fate of Vita-Living was closely intertwined
with the fate of the other providers since we were all paid for services
at a specific rate determined by the State Department of Mental Health
Mental Retardation Services. TAPPR's influence on the state's decision
makers gradually increased over the years since Vita-Living opened
its doors.

As the year ended, Stan and I believed that Vita-Living might indeed make it. I felt strongly our long-term health depended on bringing more families into the agency as soon as possible. Stan was not at
all sure that he wanted us to expand so rapidly. We disagreed about
this often and loudly, but Stan deferred to me as far as Vita-Living was
concerned. If Vita-Living was going to be around long after Stan and
I were, then we simply had to have more people invested in its future
success.

CHAPTER IX

TO BE OR NOT TO BE—
THE RICKY WALLACE PROGRAM

I KNEW I had to help Ricky, now 29 and 165 pounds, change from a man nobody wanted to be around to a man welcomed or at least tolerated by his peers. The question of how kept me up at night imagining different scenarios. My experience allowed me to believe there was a way to change his behavior, but I relied on my friend and professional associate, David, to help me grapple with the problem both as a professional and as a parent.

Ricky moved into Beechnut House in May 1985 with all of his challenging behaviors on display: hyperactivity, distractibility, and temper tantrums, as well as his refusal to do anything but eat and watch television.

One example stands out. On a typical June night around 10 o'clock, Ricky, in his pajamas and robe, was sitting comfortably in an upholstered chair in the family room watching TV when a staff member in a calm tone said, " Ricky, it's time to go to bed. Please turn off the television."

Ricky threw himself down on the floor and started crying, screaming, and kicking. Ricky did not want to stop what he was doing and go to bed. His behavior was worse when I was around so I tried to stay out of his space while the staff dealt with him. That night he looked at me to "save" him. I forced myself to turn away, swallowing my sadness and disappointment. His typical negative and childlike response to any request was embarrassing and frustrating to me. Until we figured out how to change Ricky's behavior, he would be stuck at the two-to-three year old stage.

The following day at 6:00 A.M. a staff person said, "Ricky, it's time to get up. You need to brush your teeth, wash, and get ready to go to work."

Ricky shook his head to signal "No" and flailed his arms at anyone approaching him while he remained in his bed with the covers over his head.

My heart ached that I could not make things right for him but I knew that although I was able to be firm with him at our home, in the Beechnut environment he had to listen to the staff hired to carry out his program. It would take time, as it did when he moved back to our home, for him to accept that he had to do what a staff person asked him to do. Every day I reluctantly reviewed his behaviors from the previous day and called David and Kathy to share my thoughts with them as well as to pick their brains. They were kind enough to talk to me about the previous day's activities and kept reassuring me that eventually Ricky would change.

Ricky's program had him return from his day program in the afternoon, deposit his lunch box in the kitchen, wash his hands, and sit down for a snack. He was to bring his dish and glass to the sink and then he and his housemates were to leave for the mile walk. Every day, once he was out the door, Ricky changed his mind and refused to walk. In spite of coaxing and prodding, he shook his head "No" and ran back to his favorite chair in the family room next to the television. The set was unplugged. There was nothing to watch so he ran from one staff person to the next to get attention, but all ignored him until his housemates returned from their walk.

On their arrival, Ricky broke into a big smile and welcomed all of them as if he was the host and they were the visitors. The staff pulled out the games and puzzles the residents liked from the storage cupboard. Ricky loved puzzles but could not concentrate on anything for more than a few moments. He started to fit the pieces together and then jumped up and ran to one of the staff people to get him or her to see what he had done. If that person could not stop what he or she was doing at that moment, he ran to another and another until he got what he wanted. He repeated the same attention-seeking pattern with any other activity, such as looking through a magazine. He craved constant attention the way Stan craved cigarettes---and was driving everybody crazy.

David had an idea for rewarding Ricky by showing him attention when he sat down or performed any activity that was incompatible with his constantly moving around. The goal was for Ricky to sit at any one activity for up to 20 minutes. I knew I had to try it with him. One evening Ricky ran to me with a magazine, and I asked him to sit down on the couch with me. When he did I looked at the magazine with him. If he didn't sit down, I turned away from him and refused to look at him. He then ran to another staff person who repeated the procedure. I forced myself to follow the program, but it was hard. I wanted to hug him and coax him to sit with me, but that would mean giving into him and causing him to fail. He did sit for as long as 15 minutes but was not able to reach the 20-minute goal until many years later.

Finally, I had an opportunity to do what I had requested Vineland to do for years: teach Ricky to communicate through signing. One thing that we could do together was "talk" with our hands. I read about the sign for love in one of the signing books I studied and showed Ricky the sign. I hugged him and then crossed my arms over my chest with my hands to my shoulders. He enjoyed making the sign and started using it instead of running up to people for hugs and kisses, which had been overwhelming and unpleasant to anyone unfamiliar with him. All of the staff used this sign as well as shaking his hand. Because Ricky often bit when he pretended to kiss, we allowed him to kiss his family but no one else. I could feel his teeth against my cheek and reminded him "No biting" when he kissed me. "Let's talk," I suggested verbally and with signs.

We sat on the couch in the family room and practiced signing "help," "talk," "quiet," "want," "please," "thank you," "more," "sit," "yes," "stop," "work," and "slow". I was excited to see how quickly Ricky picked up the signs for these words. His eye-hand coordination was poor, but anyone familiar with the signs could make them out. Ricky was finally able to communicate in a meaningful way. I loved to see the look in his eyes when I signed something he understood and he could respond and I understood. We both laughed out loud when we successfully communicated.

We placed a chart depicting the signs on the wall at the staff desk. Everyone practiced the signing along with oral speech when communicating with Ricky as well as other clients. None of the residents were good at oral speech, and both Derek and Tony also were on programs to use signs for communication.

We posted a rotating chore schedule in the kitchen for the residents. The day it was Ricky's turn to set the table, a staff person told him, "Ricky, please help set the table." Ricky ran out of the room to hide, lowering and shaking his head to indicate refusal---his immediate response to any request. It happened when he first arrived at our home, but over time he learned that Stan and I required him to comply. I was waiting for him to realize he had to comply at Beechnut House. He was still refusing to take the walk, and it was a struggle to get him to take a bath, brush his teeth, shave, or any of the other personal care activities. .

David recommended trying something called "paradox intervention," where the staff requested Ricky to do the opposite of what they really desired so that Ricky felt he had some say so and control. For example, if Ricky refused to enter a room, staff did not coax, beg or threaten but instead commented that the activities were with another resident and Ricky should *not* come in. I didn't think this strategy would work because I thought that Ricky was smart enough to figure quickly what we were trying to do. After two weeks we eliminated paradox intervention because it was not effective.

Ricky liked food, watching TV, going to movies, social praise, and attention from others. We offered these activities to Ricky as rewards whenever he did what was requested, but his behavior did not improve. In fact, it seemed as though there was an increase in his refusals in the two months he had lived at Beechnut House. I was aware that behaviors always became worse before they got better, but this was ridiculous. Stan looked at me with such disappointment when I told him about Ricky that I stopped describing all of the failures, and we talked about other things when I arrived home at night.

The problems came to a head in August when the state review team came to Beechnut House. They left for the day right after the evening meal was served, and as soon as they left Ricky indicated he wanted more food. He had already had seconds. "You have had seconds and that is enough to eat," I said in a matter of fact tone. He came toward me and I thought he wanted a hug. He raised his hand and I noticed the fork in his hand just as he jabbed the fork into my scalp. With blood cascading down my forehead I turned and walked rapidly out of the room. I heard him tossing what sounded like chairs, tables, and dishes at the other residents and staff. He was impossible to be around in a normal environment.

I was washing away the blood in Ricky's bathroom when I looked in the mirror and saw a pale hollow-eyed woman staring at me. Where was the self-confident person who had started Vita-Living? I straightened my shoulders and decided to go to Target to replenish our kitchen items and keep busy, as was my habit when things became difficult. Shopping was also a way to help me stop thinking about what happened with Ricky. As I walked past the family room, I noticed that Wren had finally restrained Ricky and he was seated in his favorite chair watching TV. I was not happy having him look at television since it appeared to be rewarding him for his behavior, but we had no choice at that time since the review team was returning in the morning.

While I went to Target, staff moved to put the kitchen back in order. I called David and said, "It looks as though I will have to ask my own son to leave our program if we cannot come up with a plan to help control his aggression and refusal to do anything asked. I know we will have to do something drastic in order to get Ricky under control."

David offered: "We can try 'compliance training'."

"What's that?" I asked with hope in my voice.

"It's an intensive period of one-on-one training with an immediate repercussion if Ricky did not comply with a simple request," David said. "I can do it over Labor Day if we can find another person to help. I'll ask Ricky to comply with simple requests such as 'sit down,' 'hands up,' 'hands down.' When he complies he can leave the room, so we must lock the door." David explained.

I did not think that I could be at Beechnut House and hear the crying and yelling from Ricky during the training, so I asked Andy to come home from San Diego where he was working on his doctoral program. I wanted someone from the family to help. In addition, I contacted Kip, a masters-level psychologist, who had worked with me at Cullen, and asked her if she would be interested in joining David. Thank goodness she was excited about participating in this attempt to help Ricky and me.

I also called the contractor, Carlos, and asked him for help in redefining our environment to reduce the possibility of Ricky throwing chairs and tables. He bought chairs with straight backs and legs and between the legs he built a box that held 75 pounds of sand. He put the legs on castors so they could be moved in and out of the table. I called them "sandbox chairs." The first time Ricky tried to throw a chair and failed he looked perplexed, tried again, and then shrugged and was redirected to another activity with little trouble. I could not believe it was that easy. In addition, Carlos weighted down tables to make them impossible to throw.

Easy did not apply to our compliance-training program. I explained the program to Stan, and he shook his head as if it was more than he wanted to know. "Do you think that this is what we need to do?" he asked.

"I'm at my wits end. If this doesn't work, I don't know what we'll do," was my exhausted reply. I spent most of my life burying my deepest emotions and using physical activities to release the pent-up feelings. When Ricky was home before he went away to school and immediately after he left, I had become the neighborhood's Mrs., Clean, scrubbing, ironing, and cooking into the wee hours of the night.

During this period, while we struggled to find the right training program for Ricky, I worked compulsively in my office and at home. I also worked with the clients and trained staff to become the Mr. and Mrs. Clean of the group homes. Beechnut House was spotless. All of this frenzied activity was a release for the emotions I felt seeing the staff handle my son with force.

Sometimes my feelings were so powerful I couldn't escape them. A few days after the kitchen incident as I was working in my office in the front of the duplex, I heard Ricky screaming and throwing things in the family room. Moving rapidly into the family room I saw holes in the wall where a shelf had been removed, magazines and baskets on the floor, and Ricky wild- eyed with his shirt torn at the sleeve, swinging one of the wooden shelf supports at Wren and anyone in his space. I had an out-of-body experience-- as if I were watching myself running over to Ricky where he had dropped the wooden beam and thrown himself down near the TV set screaming, crying, and kicking. All of the staff was in the room with mouths agape staring at me as I approached Ricky. I picked up the beam and with a force and strength increased by my adrenalin, I struck him again and again while screaming at him: " I've had it with you hurting others. You have to listen to the staff who are trying to help you." After a few moments--maybe a few seconds—I looked at Ricky and saw terror in his eyes and then straightened up to see the staff lined up at the other end of the room staring at me. I said, " I am his mother. Don't think that any of you can strike the clients. I will have you in jail if you do."

With that I dropped the beam, turned, and walked into my office where I picked up my purse and went to my car. I drove to the nearest parking lot and burst into tears. I don't know how long I cried, but when I was finished I felt totally depleted. I did not go back to the office but went home to tell Stan what I had done. That action could have closed the program had anyone reported it to the state.

Stan said, "I know how you feel. Remember when I got so frustrated that I struck Ricky? It tears at your heart. If the program does close, we will bring him home and care for him as long as we can."

"What happens when we can't do it anymore?" I asked.

"We'll leave it up to a force greater than ours. Maybe the kids will step up." Stan reassured me.

"Please call Beechnut House to see how Ricky is and if I hurt him," I pleaded. Stan spoke to Kathy and was told that Ricky had a small bruise on his shoulder but he seemed fine otherwise. She said they would monitor him closely the rest of the evening. I remembered that Ricky tolerated a high degree of pain before he indicated discomfort.

I fell into bed exhausted and drained. My sleep was filled with nightmares of being chased into a deep hole. The next day I returned to work and never spoke about the incident again. The fact that I did not speak of it didn't mean that it was out of my mind. I was acutely aware that, if provoked enough, anyone could lose control. I always told all of the staff to tell me or Kathy if they felt that they could not control themselves with any of the clients. We would give them some time alone to regain their composure, and if that did not work, they needed to leave for the rest of that shift.

Choosing the "compliance training program" and choosing to leave Ricky running after the car, when he first moved into Beechnut House, were two of the many excruciatingly difficult choices Stan and I felt we had to make. We were sure that if we didn't do something drastic now, then after we were gone, Ricky would have a life of either chemical or physical restraint in a locked ward somewhere in one of the state schools.

The compliance training, held in a special re-fitted room, proved extremely difficult. The room in which the training occurred was called the "training room." The word used when Ricky refused to do something was for him to "mind". We used the word "mind" because Ricky was familiar with it.

It was important that Ricky not be distracted from the training so the room was totally bare except for one sandboxed chair, the window had been boarded up, and the walls had plastic sheeting over wood over the dry wall. The door to the training room had a two-way mirror installed so that Ricky could not see out but a staff member could see into the room.

David brought Ricky into the room with Kip and Andy and requested that he sit in the chair. He refused to cooperate, he screamed, cried, lay on the floor and put his hands over his ears. As much as 30 minutes passed before David asked Ricky to sit in the chair again. David reminded Ricky in a calm voice that he needed to "mind" and that he could not leave the training room until he did. David's tone of voice became sterner as Ricky continued to resist by lying on the floor or turning his body and face toward the wall. If he struck out he was reminded in the same tone, "No hitting" or "No biting".

For 2 1/2 hours Ricky refused to comply. He tried unsuccessfully to turn over the chair and to hit someone, and he lay on the floor, shook his head "No," slammed his fist against the wall, kicked at the wall, and covered his face and ears with his hands. When he finally did comply, he did so only for a few seconds and then jumped up again. David requested that Ricky sit in the chair again—and after he got up and complied, he requested again...and again. David praised Ricky when he sat in the chair. Gradually Ricky sat in the chair for longer periods and over the course of 15 minutes complied with two or three requests, such as "touch nose," "clap hands," "show me your shirt," and again he complied. Finally after four hours, David told Ricky he could leave the training room but must "mind" the staff.

When Ricky left the training room, David requested that he sit in a chair in the family room. When he did not comply a staff person immediately directed him back to the training room. If he refused to walk the staff carried him in. In all, the staff escorted Ricky to the training room five times that night, but gradually Ricky complied quicker and there was a decrease in the amount of time Ricky spent striking out. The next two days were a repeat of the first with a great deal of resistance by Ricky early in the day and a gradual reduction in his refusal to comply by the end of each day.

I was thrilled to see Ricky smiling and happy Monday evening after the compliance training. I thought that if David asked him to jump off the roof, he would have done it. He "minded" whatever David asked him to do. The trick now was to have him "mind" the staff when they asked him to do something, a process called "generalization", which is a difficult concept for many people with mental retardation.

David set up a training period Tuesday evening to teach the staff how to handle Ricky when he refused to do something he was asked to do. They all practiced on each other. We stopped all the previous behavior techniques and only used the compliance training.

The first few nights after the Labor Day weekend, Ricky went into the training room at least 12 times a night. Kathy and I worked with the other residents so that staff people were available to work with Ricky. Gradually Ricky understood that he was going to have to do what was asked, and the trips to the training room dropped in half, to 6 to 8 times a night. My thinking during this period was constantly jumping from believing what we were doing was right and necessary to despairing that if compliance training didn't work, I would have put my son through this trauma for nothing. In Ricky's situation, using positive consequences alone just didn't work. If I was sure that Stan and I would live long enough and be healthy enough to care for Ricky all of his life, I don't believe I would have put him or us through this trauma.

I was especially encouraged when Ricky began agreeing to the mile walk everyday with his housemates. The first day after the training, Ricky refused as always to walk. He was escorted into the training room and stayed there for one hour. At the end of the hour, a staff member walked with him alone for the full mile. Gradually Ricky's compliance time decreased until by January he was following the program and walking with the group after their snack. He had finally gotten the message that he was going to take that walk either with the group or by himself. This took three months, but we had turned a corner.

On October 1st 1985 we held a staffing to review Ricky's programs. The psychologist, the nurse, the program director, one of the direct care staff, and I all attended. The compliance training was working, although slowly, and we decided that it should continue. Ricky refused to walk into the training room without assistance, so we reviewed and approved the holds the staff could use to move Ricky into the room. David came every two weeks or more frequently as needed to work with all of the staff. They practiced how staff members should help Ricky end an interaction with another person by using verbal reminders. The sign for love had worked well so he rarely ran up to people for hugs.

We also continued Ricky's communication training. Although his eye-hand coordination was poor, he loved using signs. We spent many hours "talking" to each other. Kathy was facile with manual communication and continually trained the staff.

Three months later in December, we approved a new way of moving Ricky. If Ricky refused to comply with a staff person's request, the staff person counted to three, reissued the directive in a stern but soft voice, and again counted to three. If Ricky still did not comply, he was immediately escorted forcibly into the training room. We used this technique for many years.

Stan or I had been driving Ricky to his work place everyday because he refused to get into a group van and ride with the rest of the residents. This had to stop, so we decided that if Ricky refused to ride with the other residents, he stayed at Beechnut with no television, no interaction with staff, and nothing to do but sit. He disliked staying home and being ignored so it only took two days for him to agree to ride with the other residents.

By 1986, a year into the program, I was feeling proud of Ricky's improvements in handling his aggression and oppositional behavior although he still had a long way to go. His trips to the training room now had dropped to between 5 and 7 per night as compared with 10 to 15 a year before. The compliance training was definitely working.

Until now the team did not think that Ricky could control his behavior well enough to go on recreational outings with the group. His only excursions into the community for recreation were with Stan and me. At this time the staff thought Ricky had earned the opportunity to join the rest of the Beechnut residents in recreational outings. I felt as though he had graduated from school. I was anxious for him to try learning more self-help skills, such as differentiating hot and cold water, washing his clothes, and learning to dress himself, including fastening his belt and putting his shoes on the correct feet.

I loved that I was now hearing the staff say to Ricky, "Good job I like the way you minded" or "I am proud of you. Good working." I walked around with a big smile on my face when he did well and when he didn't I walked into my office and started working furiously so I didn't have to think about what was happening.

Ricky's program incorporated attendance at the movies for him as a reward on Wednesday evening and Saturday, if he received a note with a star from his day program indicating he had done well. He understood this cause and effect very well and checked the wall calendar to see if staff had placed a star on the correct date. He knew that if he did not see a star he could not go to the movie that day, and he had learned to accept this consequence well. Stan and I brought him home every weekend and continued the reward of a movie, if he earned it by being compliant.

I remember one Saturday when Ricky had not earned his star, and I reminded him that meant he could not go to the movie. Stan immediately interrupted me and said, "Please let him go. I am not up to a tantrum today."

In front of Ricky I said in a firm voice, "Ricky understands that he did not earn his movie because he did not get a star yesterday from work. Isn't that right, Ricky?"

Ricky smiled and made the sign for "yes." He was so proud and so was I. Stan was pleasantly surprised. Instead of going to the movie, Ricky watched television.

We picked him up every Saturday morning and returned him to his work site Monday morning. When the van picked up all of his house-mates from the workshop in the afternoon, Ricky returned with them to Beechnut House. This worked well since he refused to return to Beechnut House directly from our home.

One weekend Stan and I tried forcing Ricky to return to Beechnut House on Sunday night instead of waiting until Monday. We got into the car, Ricky sat next to Stan, and I sat in the back seat. Ricky was happy to be in the car, but the minute the car turned in the direction of Beechnut House, he started screaming and kicking at the windows with both of his feet and his hands. "Ricky, we are going to Beechnut House and you have to stop kicking and screaming because you are going back tonight," I said. He continued fighting and became even more difficult when we drove into the driveway of Beechnut House. He shook his head and fought so hard that it took three staff people to pull him out of the car. When he was safely in the house, Stan and I faced each other and said, "Let's not do that again. We'll take him back on Monday to his work place." A lesson learned the hard way.

We continued using the training room until October of 1996 when Ricky only needed one or two trips a month. Then the team decided to eliminate the training room portion of the program. Instead we pur-chased a recliner for his bedroom. If he refused to "mind", the staff directed him to the chair in his bedroom where he stayed until he was willing to "mind." This program continues to this day, but Ricky sel-dom requires the use of his chair.

We know that Ricky's success depends a great deal on the mainte-nance of the structured program. Mental retardation cannot be cured but it can certainly be modified by support and care. Stan and I were as proud of him as we were of Melanie, Andy, or Lee. I believe that Ricky's success justifies my philosophy and the hard, hard work of the staff that were willing to stick with us through the difficult times using patience, consistency, structure, and respect for the humanity in all of us. Leonard Cohen in "Anthem" writes:

"Ring the bells that still can ring

Forget your perfect offering

There is a crack, a crack in everything

That's how the light gets in"

For Ricky the light was definitely shining through and he was light-ing up our hearts

CHAPTER X

BUILD IT AND THEY WILL COME

IT WAS 1986, the year that Space Shuttle Challenger disintegrated, killing seven; Elie Wiesel received the Nobel Peace Prize; President Reagan denied involvement in the Iran/Contra affair; and the New York Mets won World Series against Boston. Ricky's favorite television shows were *Head of the Class* and *Designing Women*. We needed more families to join us in the Vita-Living experiment, and I needed to find a way to bring more money into the Agency.

In January of 1986, Mrs. Dempsey called to set up a meeting with Stan, her husband, her daughter, and me to talk about starting a home for their other daughter, Kristine. Kristine was born in December of 1964 and had lived for 11 years at the Institute of Logopedics. In December of 1985 she was sent to the Stewart School in Kentucky for residential services, but three weeks later the school flew Kristine back to Houston saying they could not serve her. The diagnosis made by previous evaluators at the Institute was severe mental retardation, autism, schizophrenia, bi-polar, depression, and profound bilateral sensor-neural hearing loss (total deafness). Mrs. Dempsey was devastated when Kristine returned from the Stewart school and remembered that back in 1985 when she visited Beechnut House, I had told her that she could buy a house, and we would prepare it for licensing.

At our meeting, I talked about what I wanted for Vita-Living and why I was interested in expanding. I stressed that we never asked anyone to leave, and the Dempseys could feel comfortable that they would not receive a call one day informing them that they had to find another place for Kristine. When they left I did not know if they were interested or not. When the phone rang the next day, I worried that Mrs.

133

Dempsey would say they would pass. What a surprise when she said, "John would feel more comfortable talking to Stan."

"That's fine with me, but I assure you that Stan will tell John he can keep his money and his daughter. Stan is not thrilled about my plans for expansion and worries that I will be too busy and never be home," I told her.

"Then I won't do that," was Mrs. Dempsey's immediate response. The Dempsey family made the great (for us) decision to join Stan and me in the Vita-Living adventure. While they found and equipped a home on Campbell Street in the Spring Branch area, I met Kristine. One of the first things I noticed about Kristine was her striking face with her high cheekbones and her angular features. Her stiff walk was the result of a fall years earlier that injured both knees. Kristine knew sign language and when she did not get the response she wanted from a signed request, she continued signing moving closer and closer to the other person until she was in that person's face. It appeared that her fingers were screaming for attention.

At the same time we kept Beechnut House moving along with some improvement in most of the residents: Ricky was slowly increasing his compliance, Paul had fewer instances of property damage, Derek was still aggressive, but we could see a glimmer of success, Tony showed no improvement, but we were trying new behavior programs and I had faith that we would identify one that would work for him, Elsie and Ricky continued their attachment, and I was thrilled that Ricky actually had a friend all his own. Her roommate Julia was helpful to all of the residents but had a special attachment to Derek. When one of the men started acting out, Julia took Elsie's hand and walked quickly into their room where they turned on their television. Every once in a while she peeked out the door to see if it was safe to return to the public areas.

In addition to my concerns about the residents came concerns about finding enough money to cover payroll every two weeks. If it looked as though we could not make salaries for the staff, I called Stan, and he came to our rescue. I never asked where the money came from, but I was pretty sure that it came from us. "Thanks" did not seem strong enough to show my gratitude for his help and support.

While the Dempsey's home reconstruction was in process, neighbors anxiously came by and asked questions about who was moving in and what was being done. Carlos, the contractor, only told them that this was a home owned by the Dempsey family. When moving into any neighborhood, I felt strongly that there was no need for any special preparation for dealing with neighbors. I thought that we should move into a home the same way everyone else moved into a home, so we continued the reconstruction with no advance notice that we were planning to open a group home. There was always the possibility that the neighbors might use legal means to force us out.

Before Campbell House, (named after the street it was on) opened, the neighborhood homeowners association heard that the home was going to house five people with mental retardation and called an emergency meeting. Mrs. Dempsey, Stan, Kathy, and I all attended the meeting. After saying a prayer and a pledge of allegiance to the flag, the neighbors talked about the loss in property values and the danger to their children if we moved into their neighborhood.

Stan spoke for Vita-Living. He took off his jacket and walked up and down the room speaking in his authoritative voice. "Campbell House will be opened to serve five people who need assistance to care for them. The Dempsey's have donated the house because they have a daughter who needs the type of help Vita-Living offers. Campbell House will be a good neighbor. You are good people, you pledged allegiance to the flag, and said a prayer. How can you not open your arms to these people who have done you no harm and are in need of a helping hand?"

The room was silent. It was as if no one heard what Stan said. The group of homeowners took a vote and decided to ask the city of Houston to sue Vita-Living because the deed restrictions mandated that only a single family might live on that property.

The homeowners association succeeded in obtaining the help of the city of Houston to sue Vita-Living for breaking the deed restrictions for family use. It was hard to believe that our tax dollars were being used to interfere with our hopes and dreams. I was determined to stop the city. At no cost to Vita-Living, I obtained the legal services of Advocacy Inc., a non-profit agency that works to protect legal rights of Texans with disabilities. We prevailed because of a precedent set in 1985 in the "Cleburne Case" when the United States Supreme Court ruled that as many as six people living together in a home with staff assistance can be considered a family. Thus, residents living at Campbell House legally were considered a family. The city lost their case before it ever went to court.

Once we opened Campbell House, the neighbors demonstrated their anger every evening. Cars zoomed by the house and into our driveway honking their horns, throwing beer cans and other detritus, and hurl-ing epithets at the residents. Fortunately the only resident in Campbell House at that time was Kristine, and she was deaf. One night the ha-rassing became so loud and offensive that the staff cowered in the cor-ner of the kitchen and called Kathy. She drove over to the house and stayed there throughout the night to comfort the staff. I'd had it and called the homeowners association and told them that if the harassing didn't stop, Vita-Living was going to bring suit against the homeown-ers. I never received a call back from the homeowners, but the harass-ment stopped and we are still there. We contacted the neighbors and invited them to meet our Campbell family. In addition, we stopped to talk to neighbors while on our daily walks. Soon the residents of Campbell House enjoyed freshly picked grapefruit, oranges, lemons, and even bananas given by neighbors who had no problems with us.

In February David began developing a behavior program for Kristine. He made a diagnosis of moderate mental retardation with behavioral manifestations and profound bilateral sensor-neural hear-ing loss (ABL-III severe), in other words, Kristine was totally deaf, had moderate mental retardation, and some problematic behaviors. I ar-ranged for Kristine to come to Beechnut House during the day to par-ticipate in a program David had developed to reduce her aggressive and self-destructive behaviors. Programming for Kristine was easier than for many of our other residents because she worked for rewards, could tell time, and was fluent in sign language. Kip, the psychologist who had worked with Ricky, and Kathy, the Program Director, worked with Kristine during the day and she returned home in the evening.

All staff that worked at Campbell House had to learn sign language to communicate with Kristine. We bought books on manual signing, and I hired an instructor to teach the Supervisor who was then re-sponsible for teaching the rest of the staff. Everyone hired to work at Campbell House had 30 days to acquire the skills to communicate with Kristine.

The first day Kristine spent at Campbell House, she banged her head on the table so hard that we rushed her to the emergency room. She had opened an area on her forehead near the hairline so many times that the doctors thought they might have to graft skin to cover the opening. Fortunately they were able to stitch it closed this time.

David suggested that staff sign to her that head banging was "bad" and that she would receive a reward after a specific amount of time had passed without any "bad" behaviors. Staff wore the carpenter aprons filled with low calorie snacks such as pretzels, popcorn, and dry cereal to give to her after a period of time in which she showed no aggression or self abuse. Staff extended the period required for a reward for no self-injurious or aggressive behaviors from every five minutes to ten, fifteen, thirty minutes and finally an hour. Kristine responded to the rewards, and although it took many years her aggression and self-abuse gradually subsided. She never did need the skin graft.

The other residents we eventually served at Campbell House all had challenging behaviors, and we were able to help all of them except one. Eloise, a young woman who was still attending school, came to us in September because her family had been unable to help her diminish her self-abuse. She had bruises all over her body from hitting herself and throwing herself against walls and floors. We covered her with padding and she wore a football helmet with clear contact paper covering the opening. She spit continually, so staff people needed a certain amount of distance when working with her unless she wore the helmet. She also hit anyone who entered her space.

She went home every weekend and always returned with more bruises because she did not wear the padding at her home. Although I had many meetings with Eloise's family and the staff, I wasn't able to help the family feel comfortable about Eloise living with us and with the techniques we were using to help her learn self-control to reduce her self-abuse and aggression. Finally in December, after only two months at Campbell House the family took her back home.

I felt sad that we could not help her, but I had worked long enough in my career to know that there were no quick fixes. It took years for changes to occur in residents. I didn't become discouraged and tried to communicate that to Eloise's parents. We would have tried many techniques and I felt confident that eventually we would have identified a successful method of helping Eloise.

On the other hand, Rudy, who had a dual diagnosis of psychosis and mental retardation, did well because of a medication prescribed by a local psychiatrist and a behavior plan developed by David.

I remember the first day he moved into Campbell in August of 1986. He, his mother, and Kathy went shopping for food at the local grocery store and after they checked out, he and Kathy each carried bags of groceries. He suddenly stopped moving. As much as Kathy and his mother talked to him he appeared not to hear and refused or was unable to move at all. Kathy took the bags of groceries to the car and then drove the car to the supermarket door, got out, and Rudi's mother and

Kathy physically pushed and pulled him into the car. He kept repeating the words "Houston Astros" but made no sense.

The new medication prescribed by his psychiatrist, took care of the psychosis and the behavior program developed by David helped Rudi live with others and be responsible for his actions. He learned to perform his chores in the home and joined the other residents in the daily group game and group walk. At the end of five years he was able to join his mother when she moved to California.

After Eloise left, Kathy and I visited Austin State School—one of the state's oldest and largest--to find the other residents for Campbell House. We were fortunate to find two women and one man whom other agencies chose not to serve but whom I thought we could help.

Campbell House was modeled after Beechnut House in terms of its schedule of activities. For example, the residents took the mile walk, played the group games, and practiced role-play to learn self-medication. The home itself was a one-family home with a very large yard and large garage area that we converted to a family room, office, and storage area. There were five bedrooms and two residents shared one of them. The beds were made exactly like the ones at Beechnut, but in addition Carlos made two extra strong coffee tables for the family room. Sandboxed chairs were placed around the weighted dining room tables. We decorated all of the rooms with baskets and posters as well as the residents' pictures and personal items. At the end of the bedroom hall was a large punching mat like the one Paul used at Beechnut House.

One of our staff painted a beautiful mural of a garden on the wall as you entered the front door. She and her family lived less than a block away from Campbell House, and the entire family adopted Vita-Living as their special project. Their son worked at Beechnut House directly with the residents while attending the University of St. Thomas.

In June of 1986 Stan decided that we needed a brochure describing the programs at Beechnut House. He sent one of his staff to take photographs, Stan wrote the copy, and Panhandle Eastern donated the production. The cover was tan, with the words "Creative Caring" printed large in green across the top half of the page. Below were the words "the Vita-Living story, Community Residences for People Who Are Mentally Retarded. ", with a picture of our logo, an outline of a house with an inverted V as the roof and walls formed by the L and I. Today we still use the same logo, and I always refer to what we do as "creative caring". It is important to note that by 1990 advocates and professionals in the field discouraged the use of the words "mentally retarded". If we had printed the brochure in 1990, we would have said "Community Residences for People who have Mental Retardation." In 2007 professionals in the field and advocacy organizations replaced the words "mental retardation" with "intellectual disability".

I am grateful to the Panhandle Eastern Corporation for their help during the first 15 years of our existence. They printed two versions of our brochure and provided many in-kind services to us such as investigating the trashing of one of our homes and the destruction of all of the tires on our vehicles one weekend. Long after Stan died the organization that he spent 30 years serving remembered him by helping Vita-Living.

The year 1986 brought a gift of recognition for me. In November the *Houston Post* brought together an organization of professional women called Texas Executive Women (TEW), who searched for 10 women annually who were nominated by the readers of the paper for the title of "Woman on the Move". TEW looked for women who were leaders in their professions or businesses. One day the phone rang, and I was informed that my name had been sent into the nominating committee. They wanted to interview me. I was totally surprised and nervous about talking about what I was doing because I was not taking a salary. I didn't believe that anyone would think that someone who was unable to take a salary was doing a good job of running a business.

I learned that a woman, I did not know, who had a child with mental retardation, heard about me and thought I should be nominated. I met the members of the committee who were making the decisions and told them about Vita-Living and what I did. They came out to Beechnut House to interview me again and see all of the adaptations I had made to the house. What a surprise when I received the call that I was one of the 10 women chosen to receive the title of "Woman on the Move." The paper printed a big story about the luncheon honoring the 10 women and Stan attended the luncheon with Mrs. Dempsey and Kathy. This was great publicity for Vita-Living. People mailed donations to the Beechnut House, and we received numerous calls congratulating me and asking for more information. I was thrilled that the community recognized my work and Vita-Living.

In addition, in 1986, we were approached by June and Max Kelly, who also wanted a home for their daughter and other women with mild mental retardation. Their daughter had Down Syndrome and moderate mental retardation. I told them that they would have to raise the money to buy the house and that Vita-Living would have to charge them a monthly fee for my work to get the home licensed. It was impossible for me to spend the time to start another home without some remuneration for Vita-Living. Our agency was running very close to the edge financially. Stan knew the Kelly's and advised me against working with them. He said they were nice people but difficult to work with. I didn't listen to him and again made a mistake. When would I learn? The Kelly's agreed to pay Vita-Living a monthly fee, and I started the process of finding a home, outfitting it, and applying for the license.

With the possibility of heavy debt hanging over my head, I was constantly looking for other ways to bring in money. I read about our legislature approving bingo. Bingo purveyors had to tie into a nonprofit before they could qualify for a license. Non- profit agencies were looking for connections so that they could have access to the funds that bingo games generated each night. Although I knew very little about bingo, I was able to connect with one bingo game close to Campbell House. I had to go to Austin for orientation and, as luck would have it, on that very day, Kathy also, was called to Austin for training.

I received a call from Stan (whose name was on the Vita-Living call list) while I was at the Bingo training, that the state review team was at Campbell and demanded entrance. He informed Ms Short, who was in charge of licensing, that there would be someone there by 3:00 P.M. but that he had no idea where anything was and could be of no help. I immediately excused myself and called Ms Short to explain that both Kathy and I were in Austin and there was no way that I could get someone to Campbell before 3:00.P.M. She informed me that she would close us down and was directing her staff to return to Austin. I said, "You do what you have to do and I will do what I have to do, but Campbell House will not be closed."

"We will see about that," she replied.

My heart skipped a beat and I wondered if this was going to be the end of our second home. I felt as though I was on a constant merry-go-round. The worry about finances and the worry about licensing never let up. I felt secure that Stan would fix everything, so I called to tell him what had happened and then returned to learning how to make bingo work for us. I thought about my predicament during the 2 1/2 hour drive from Austin to Houston but felt confident that Stan had already handled everything.

On my return to Houston, Stan told me he had talked to a business associate who knew someone in the Governor's office and Campbell was not going to be closed. Sometimes you can beat city hall, but it is not always smart to do so, since now Vita-Living, and particularly Renée Wallace, were on Ms. Short's short list. We had a home about to be licensed in December, and it was within her power to put off the licensing if she wanted to do that. She did! When our third home, Kelly's House, was ready, I called the licensing office to advise them that we were waiting for them. Ms Short told me that she did not think that they could get to Kelly's House for at least six months. I knew this was payback for my going over her head, but I had an ace in the hole. Corinne, one of the women ready to enter the program, was the daughter of the Administrative Assistant to Congressman Mickey Leland. I immediately called her. "I'm afraid that we will not be able to open for about 6 months," I reported.

"What do you mean?" challenged the assistant. "It's taken me months to get my daughter to the point of moving to Kelly's House, and now I have to tell her she is not moving. That's not acceptable. Give me a little time. I'll call you back within the hour," she told me.

Before she could call me back, I received a call from Ms. Short. "All right, Renée. We'll be at the Kelly's House in two days." "Thank you," was all I said. It was obvious that a call from a United States Representative had some power behind it. I knew that I had made a serious enemy in Ms. Short and was certain I'd hear more from her.

In December our third home, Kelly 's House was licensed and five young women moved in. Mr. Kelly had an assignment in Ohio and left with his wife for one year while we ran the home. The women were all doing well adjusting to living together.

The five women living at Kelley's House were very different from those at Beechnut and Campbell. They had mild and moderate mental retardation and their behaviors were similar to those of pre teens and teenagers. They were not about to be told either what snack foods--- such as cokes, cookies, and candies---to eat or what to do.

Lorraine moved to Kelly's House from her family home. She had a boyfriend who did not have mental retardation, and later they married. We assisted her in learning how to care for a home, shop, cook, do laundry, and clean. We also helped her to understand about the relationship between a man and a woman.

Agnes, who was street smart and had mild mental retardation and mild cerebral palsy, had no family and had been living by herself and monitored by MHMRA of Harris County. She had gotten into trouble and so was directed to Kelly's House. She had friends she had made when living by herself and continued to see them but got along well with the other housemates. She knew the bus system and traveled all over the city. She later left the home and was enticed to move in with a woman who stole her money from the government as well as her clothes and the few pieces of furniture she owned. We tried to advise her against moving in with this woman but she refused to listen. Finally a counselor from MHMRA convinced her to move out and into her own apartment. MHMRA helped her outfit her apartment and she lived there until her death two years later.

The Kelly's daughter, Prissy, had moderate mental retardation and Down Syndrome. Her family had unsuccessfully placed her in another small group home but they were not happy with that placement and moved her back to their home. People with Down Syndrome are frequently stubborn. Her way of responding to something she did not want to do was to slow down. Sometimes it looked as though she was not moving at all but in reality she was moving very slowly. She was easy to work with and got along well with all of her housemates.

Corinne, diagnosed with mild mental retardation, came to Kelly's House from her family home after spending many years at a private school out of town but had been home for a few years, She had severe seizures, was aggressive to her mother when she lived at home, and aggressive to others in the group home as well as inflicting injuries upon herself when she did not like something that was asked of her.

One day she threw a brick at the program director, barely missing her. When a staff person asked her why she had lobbed the brick, she said that she wanted to live at home rather than Kelly's House. I asked for a meeting with her parents, her, and the program director. I asked her parents in front of her if she could go home to live. Both of them said that she could not come home to live but she could visit every weekend. I asked her if she had heard what her folks said and she said she heard and understood. I had a plan that I asked everyone to sign off on, that if she hurt herself or anyone else during the week, she could not go home that weekend. Both she and her parents agreed to the plan. The next week Corinne struck out at another housemate. She did not go home. That was the last time she missed going home on a weekend. She did so well that five years later she was able to live in her own apartment with assistance from our staff a few days a week.

Cindy had lived with her mother and sister before moving to Kelly's House, had just graduated from high school and had had an active social life. She had mild mental retardation, was very attractive, and had many boy friends. She was a typical teenager but more vulnerable, loved going to malls, shopping, out on dates etc. She eventually left the house, married and has lived successfully in the community with support from her family.

Fortunately the bingo game proved a new source of income. After the training I found a bingo game near Campbell House that was willing to have us as a sponsor one evening a week. Someone from the charity had to attend the bingo game on the night that the proceeds went to that charity. The Bingo game ran from 6:00-10 P.M., Monday through Thursday and from 10:00 P.M. to midnight Friday and Saturday. Since there was no one working for me I could ask to do this chore, it became one more thing for me to do. Stan was not happy about my being at a bingo game until 11:00 P.M. But we had to stay until the money was counted and sign the appropriate papers indicating that we were present during the game. I asked Mrs. Dempsey if she would come with me or go in my place sometimes. She agreed and so between us we were present one night a week for about a year. We dropped out because we just ran out of steam and could not do it anymore. I wanted to continue but Stan insisted that it was too dangerous and pressured me to quit.

The year ended with two new homes and 10 new residents and their families connected to Vita-Living. The money from bingo and the monthly payments from the Kelly family definitely helped our bottom line.

CHAPTER XI

TRIAL BY FIRE

1987 WAS a very busy year. President Reagan stood at the Berlin wall and shouted to Mr. Gorbachev "Open this gate, Mr. Gorbachev, tear down this wall." The Supreme Court ruled that Rotary must admit women. Andy Warhol died after gall bladder surgery, and Ricky's favorite movies were *The Last Emperor* and *Raising Arizona*.

Ms Short made another entrance into my life at the time of the second state review of Campbell House. The review team criticized everything we did. They said we were "not providing active treatment" although the behavior programs required that we provide constant attention to the residents. They said we had the residents eating off, "dirty, filthy" placemats although they were talking about the condition of the placemats after the residents had finished eating their snack. There were 14 deficiencies, including the fact that the physician had used a signature stamp, the program director's signature had been left off of one note, and so on. When they left Kathy asked them, "Don't you have anything good to say about our program?" "The only thing good they can say is "Good By." I said in a disgusted tone. They accused me of being rude to them. I later learned that Ms. Short had told the head of the review team to really hurt us with their report. In addition, she reported us for Medicaid fraud because we had accepted a side of beef donated by Mr. Dempsey from the rodeo. Actually nothing came of either the review or the accusation of Medicaid fraud, but we had to jump through all the hoops to clear the phantom deficiencies and the phantom fraud.

I thought I was paranoid because it appeared that the entire state was against me. I had no feeling at all and moved as though I were a zombie, which may have been the reason I was not as aware as I should have been that Stan was having some serious health problems. He was short of breath and frequently too tired to do much after he returned home from work. I worked late most nights so I was unaware of the extent of his fatigue.

Finally Stan saw our family doctor and was referred to an oncologist for tests. Together we went to hear the results. The doctor told Stan that he had lung cancer. We left his office holding hands. Before we returned to our respective offices, we stopped for coffee and a talk. I told Stan I would do whatever I could to support him through this ordeal. He said he understood but he did not know what he would do. The oncologist referred him to a surgeon and Stan agreed to have the operation to remove the tumors. I was scared that I would be left alone with a new business and a very handicapped son to care for. After the surgery the children and I met with the doctor who informed us that the cancer had spread to Stan's lymph glands. He predicted that Stan would heal from the operation but the cancer would return. Despair enveloped me. On leaving the doctor's office, I visited Stan in the Intensive Care Unit but he was out of it, and the nurse advised me to go home and visit first thing in the morning. I asked Melanie to drive and while she was attending to the traffic I was shouting at Stan, "Why didn't you stop smoking? What am I going to do now? How can I take care of Ricky and Vita-Living all alone?"

Then I started crying and could not stop until Melanie drove into the garage. I felt anesthetized. My head was splitting with all of the terrible things that could happen now. What would I do if Stan died? Actually I knew it was *when* Stan died because in 1987 lung cancer was certain death within two years. I played Scarlet O'Hara and said, "I will worry about that tomorrow"

At 2:00 A.M. that morning the phone rang. I immediately thought that something had happened to Stan. It was Kathy informing me there was a problem at Kelly's House. "Renée I hate to bother you tonight but the Kelly's House had a burglary," Kathy said. "The computer and some of the residents' jewelry and money were stolen. The residents are fine. What should I do?" "Please stay with the staff at the house," I said. "Call a meeting of the parents at my office around 1:00 P.M. I have to be at the hospital in the morning, but I will meet with them for about an hour before I return to the hospital." In the morning I saw Stan who was under heavy pain medication and could not talk. He was in the ICU so there were specific visiting hours. All of the children were present so I felt comfortable returning to the office to get ready for the meeting. Actually I was grateful to have something else to dominate my thoughts for a few hours.

I looked into the cost of installing a burglary alarm and additional outdoor lighting. Three of the fathers came to the meeting, and I informed them of the costs involved for the additional safety precautions. "Vita-Living doesn't have the money to cover these costs so can any of you help?" I asked.

The silence was penetrating. "Do you know anyone who would help us? I asked again. There were no replies. They all just looked at me as if I were asking for the moon. Finally, one of the fathers said, "Renée go ahead, I guarantee that we will get you the money."

We did and when I went to that father to ask for the money, he looked at me as though he had no memory of our discussion. Vita-Living paid. We could not demand it from the families because we were Medicaid-funded, and it would be considered double dipping, if we did. They could donate because we were nonprofit, but we could not require them to do it. I felt such a loss about my husband that I just shrugged and figured we would find a way, we always did. I thought I must have been walking around with a sign on my back that said "HIT ME." Trouble was sticking to me like spackle.

Taking care of Vita-Living and taking care of Stan kept me so busy, I had no time to feel sorry for myself. On the up side, all the homes were running smoothly. After the operation Stan did improve rapidly. We talked about whether he should go to M. D. Anderson, one of the best centers serving patients with cancer, and undergo both chemo and radiation. He chose to go to an oncologist from Methodist Hospital who recommended only radiation at this point. Stan did not have the patience to sit all day or a large part of a day at M.D. Anderson, so he wanted to go where the staff would take him at his appointed time. He continued to work all through the radiation process. I was good at putting all thoughts about the return of the cancer out of my mind. Stan returned to what appeared to be his good health after the radiation regime was over, and we returned to our usual routines.

Melanie told me that she wanted us to meet Andre, the man she thought she wanted to marry. She was going to base her decision on how he felt about her obligation to Ricky. She wanted him to know that she felt a deep responsibility for her brother, and anyone she married would have to understand that. They visited us over a weekend when Ricky was home. The weekend went as usual: Ricky went to the movies both Saturday and Sunday, and the remainder of the time we watched Ricky watch television. There was the usual argument with him over where he would eat and finally he sat for a short time at the family dinner table only to jump up to watch his shows. Apparently Andre passed the test because after he and Melanie returned to Boston, she informed us that they were engaged to marry. She wanted to be sure her Dad could walk her down the aisle, and so the wedding was set for November of 1988.

As Vita-Living expanded, I realized I needed some help. Rudi's mother, Christi, was looking for work as a secretary and asked if she could work in our office. We had no copy and no fax machine, just one computer and one manual typewriter--that was the extent of our high tech tools. After a few months she said she was going to find a copy machine because she was tired of going to Kinko's all of the time. I told her we had no money, so she said she would get a donation. I didn't believe her but she did indeed find a merchant to donate a copy machine to us when he got a new one. We still didn't have a fax machine, and it was another year before we got that as a donation. After six months she left for a job that paid more money.

I felt I could not run the office without help so I put an ad in the paper and hired another woman who actually walked out in the middle of the day leaving me a note, "Hasta La Vista." Mrs. Dempsey came into the office to help me at least three days a week, and I hired a temporary worker until I could find a full-time administrative assistant.

On their return from Ohio, the Kelly's were not happy with the way we were running the home. They did not like the menu, the activities the residents participated in, and the staff. They wanted to run the home without the responsibilities, particularly those required by the state. We held phone call after phone call and meeting after meeting, but to no avail. Nothing I did pleased them.

In August the Mental Health Mental Retardation Authority of Harris County (MHMRA) approached me to subcontract with them for the grant they received for a Home and Community Based Services (HCS) waiver program designed by the State to serve people with mental retardation at a lower cost. This program was the first to be opened in Harris County.

Until this time all of our consumers were served in the ICF/MR programs, which required that the consumers live in our homes and that we pay all costs except their clothing, because we owned the beds. Each resident received $30.00/month spending money. The state was always looking for better and less expensive ways of serving people. They thought that offering various models of residential care, such as in our homes, in their own homes, in foster families, or in their family homes would be more cost- effective. The participants in the HCS program received their regular SSI (Supplemental Security Income) or if applicable Social Security income. They were responsible to pay their own room and board plus any of their other personal expenses with that money. The HCS program paid for the cost of the staff who provided the services but nothing else. The homes run by Vita-Living served some of the people, but Vita-Living staff sent into their homes whether they lived with their family or in their own apartment would serve others. The state paid one daily rate for everyone served in the HCS program, regardless of where they lived.

Because I always wanted to bring additional money into Vita-Living and because of my excitement in facing new challenges, I accepted their proposal. The program called for 30 people to be admitted on a first-come, first-served basis in what was called a no reject program. That meant that we had to accept everyone who applied, regardless of what services they needed. All 30 applicants went through assessment at a unit called the core house, and thereafter, a meeting was held to determine their needs and develop a program for each client.

I asked Kathy to become the program director for the Vita-Living HCS program. She agreed, and we were faced with finding a new program director for the ICF/MR homes. We asked a young man, Kennedy, who had a degree in education from New York and was working for us as direct care staff, if he was interested in moving up at Vita-Living. I talked to him about the position as program director, and we both agreed to try it out. He is still with us today, now as a quality assurance monitor.

To serve as the core house, we rented a house that previously had been occupied by a band of gypsies and was in terrible disrepair. We had to refinish the floors, paint the walls, and purchase new window coverings and new fixtures for the bathrooms and kitchen. We found volunteers to help with the painting and received donations for the equipment needed. Once we got the core ready, we had to worry about residences for the people referred. We found apartments in one project and rented the number of units we needed.

The HCS people who lived in the apartments or who required 24 hour nursing care seven days a week and lived with their families were the most expensive to serve. Twenty-seven of the people referred by MHMRA needed residences, and only three lived in their family homes. All of them had behaviors no one else in Houston would serve and many had been asked to leave other programs.

I was intimately involved in bringing in all of the clients in the first HCS program, but two that stand out in my mind are Peter and Richard. They both were very needy and had no family or anyone else to care for them. Peter, about 5'8" tall and close to 300 pounds, was diagnosed with mild mental retardation and intermittent explosive behavior. He was in good health except for severe hemorrhoids. He spoke as though his tongue was swollen, and he had difficulty maneuvering it, so his speech was hard to understand. If he had to repeat himself he became angry, so I asked his close friend Richard to translate for me.

When I first met Peter, he had been asked to leave every placement since he had moved a year before to Houston from Austin State School. While at the core, he exposed himself in the front window. Fortunately staff saw it before we had to deal with neighbors or the neighborhood. I talked to him to find out why and received no information that made sense except that it sure created a lot of attention for him. I thought if he received attention without taking such extreme measures, he might not have to resort to exposing himself. Once a day I set aside time to talk to Peter, not necessarily for more than five or ten minutes, but it was our time. Once a week we went out to lunch, which was a real treat for him since he loved to eat out. I felt that Peter needed someone he could rely on and so he became a special friend to me. I cared about all of our clients but someone who had no family or anyone that cared about him or her needed someone who thought he or she was special. I was that someone for Peter. "I really like you," I told him. "I consider you a friend so I am talking to you as I would to a good friend. I don't like to hear that you ran off or exposed yourself to the neighbors. If we are to continue being friends and going out to lunch, you have to stop," I said in a serious tone.

"I unnerhan. Are oo oing oo ick me ou? (Translated) I understand. Are you going to kick me out?" he asked.

"No, you won't be asked to leave no matter what you do," I assured him. At that time there was no other agency willing to have Peter as a client. He had his own bank account, received an SSI check monthly, and in the past, had held a variety of jobs for as long as a month or two until he walked off. Every few months he went to the bank, withdrew most of his money, took a bus downtown, lived under the bridges until he hurt and then called us to pick him up. Peter knew how to take a bus anywhere in the city. I finally told him that if he continued to leave his home and live under a bridge, he would have to get himself home. Since he did not eat or rest properly, and there was no way to keep him clean, these trips were dangerous to his health.

Later I talked Peter into having a co-signer on his bank account. One of my staff agreed to be the co-signer, so when he chose to remove money from his account he had to get her signature. In fact, since the bank would give him his money without her signature, he didn't need her signature, but he believed me, and his belief certainly reduced the number of times he ran away to the bridges. When he felt secure and received enough attention to alleviate his need for other means of recognition, he stopped exposing himself. Peter's hemorrhoid condition became more serious, and we had to find a way to help him keep himself clean. In a catalogue I saw an ad for a bidet that could be attached to the regular toilet. We purchased the bidet, and his condition greatly improved with its use and the sitz baths prescribed by his physician.

Richard had been Peter's roommate at Austin Sate School and acted like a brother to him. Both of them had been placed at the state school when they were young boys around eight or nine years old. They were in their early 20's when I met them.

Richard also had no family. At 6'3" tall and 180 pounds, he was a good-looking man until he smiled. His teeth were black, because he was afraid of the dentist, refused to care for his teeth, and was a heavy smoker. His size was intimidating and usually no one could force him to do something he chose not to do. Richard had mild mental retardation with a diagnosis of severe schizophrenia. He heard voices and those voices told him not to work and to stay in bed covered with his coat most of the day. He had been asked to leave the same places Peter had and was referred to us because of our reputation in dealing successfully with difficult behaviors and our commitment to keeping our residents, no matter what.

Shortly after Richard moved into the core, I received a call from one of the staff that Richard had all of them cornered in the office. Whenever someone opened the office door, he threw one of his metal trophy awards from Special Olympics. "Call the police," I yelled. I drove over to the office at the core and as I was arriving, I saw the police enter the house. As soon as Richard saw them he put his hands behind his back, got up, and started to walk out with them. I followed to the police station and talked to the officers, describing Richard's condition and asked them if they would talk to him. He appeared to be in awe of the police and I thought it might help. They did talk to him and I believe it helped for a while. The next day I held a meeting to decide how to help Richard handle his refusal to get out of bed in the morning. Present were David, Kathy, the nurse, and I. "What does Richard like?" I asked.

"Richard is fixated on money. He must have it, but when he has it he becomes agitated until he spends it. He also likes cigarettes and coffee," Kathy told me.

"What about paying him to get out of bed every morning?" I suggested.

"We cannot use his money. It would have to be our money. I don't believe this has been done before. I don't know, it might work," Kathy responded.

"We have to have someone sit with him while he lies in bed with his coat over his head every day," I reasoned. "We would save money if we paid him to get out of bed. He would have enough money to buy cigarettes and maybe we could get him to go to a day program or even work," I said hopefully. "I think it is a win, win situation. What do you think?" I asked David

"I think it's worth a try," he said.

We met with Richard and told him that if he got out of bed in the morning we would pay him $1.00 every day. His eyes lit up and he nodded in agreement. Getting him out of bed was helpful, but we still had to get him out of the house to a day program. We then decided that Richard would receive his 1.00/day only if he went to a day program, preferably one that was geared toward job training. His psychiatrist, with whom he had a good relationship, had received a grant to open such a job-training program called DADD (Day Alternatives for Dually Diagnosed). Trying to convince Richard he needed to attend was another matter since he heard voices telling him not to work. David worked with him on how to handle his voices, and the psychiatrist tried a variety of different medications. One day the director of the job training program and three of our staff literally picked Richard up, forced him into the car, and drove him to the training program. We dropped him off in front of the building and then drove a short distance. Staff got out of the car and watched him to see what he would do. He sat on the grass for about 15 minutes and then entered the building and remained there until he was picked up. He did not do much work but he drank coffee and smoked cigarettes and every once in a while attempted a project. This was the beginning of Richard's getting up and out of the house to attend some day programming. Every day the program director had to talk to Richard in the morning and coax him to go to work. He was still getting his dollar a day if he went to a day program out of his residence. It worked most days.

Richard always said he wanted to work because he wanted to earn money. We found him a job as a pot and pan washer in a Holiday Inn. The day program sent staff to train him and then gradually faded out until Richard was there alone. We drove him there and picked him up. It was only a four-hour job during the dinner hour. A few days after he started working alone we were told that the cooks could not find their pots and pans. Richard hid them under the sink rather than wash them. That was the end of that job.

Ricky was going into the training room less and was much more compliant. Stan and I continued to live as if everything was normal. It was the end of the year. I was dreading what the next year might bring, but no matter what, January 1988 came and we were forced to face it. I was worried about Stan's health, worried about the financial situation of Vita-Living, and worried whether I was up to managing it all.

CHAPTER XII

IT WAS THE WORST OF TIMES

THE YEAR 1988 was upon us before we knew it. Moscow withdrew from Afghanistan, Vice President George H.W. Bush was elected President, Prozac was introduced, the Wall Street Dow Jones closed at 2168.57 up 11.8% from its 1987 close, and Ricky's favorite movies were *Big* and *Rain Man*.

The year was a busy one with our managing the three homes, Beechnut House, Campbell House, and Kelly's House, as well as our HCS program of 30 people. Finally in March, I realized that Stan had been correct, and the Kellys were too difficult to work with, so I told them that there could only be one person in charge, and if they wanted to be in charge, they could have the house. At first they hesitated, but within a week I received a call from Mr. Kelly telling me that they wanted to take over the home. I felt relief to be done with all the bickering and aggravation. I said nothing to Stan. I knew that Stan would never bring up to me his admonition concerning the Kellys, but I was embarrassed that I had failed with them.

I offered to return everything except my policy and procedure manual, that detailed all of the policies and procedures developed to meet the state standards and that reflected my philosophy. It was that philosophy that the Kellys apparently objected to. I told them the manual was important for licensing and that they should hire someone who knew the state rules and regulations and had experience working with the state. They paid no attention to my words and thought I was exaggerating the importance of the paper. Finally in April we let the state know that we were no longer the owner of the five beds at Kelly's House. The Kellys hired a nice woman to run the program, but she knew nothing about state licensing or the requirements. The review team from Austin never came to Kelly's House because their program manager did not know what was needed, so Kelly's House could not obtain a license. Eventually the home was donated to the Mental Health Mental Retardation Authority of Harris County. When the house broke up, two of the women returned to their respective homes, and the other three came into our HCS program.

In March I finally found an administrative assistant: Mae Keener. She was worth waiting for. She became a wonderful friend to both me and to our residents. We had converted the living room of the front unit of Beechnut House into another office and that is where Mae worked. Her desk was a favorite stopping place for the residents after they returned from their day program.

One incident stands out in my memory. I parked my car in the driveway when I came to work. One day shortly after Mae started with us, I heard a crash as the residents were walking to the van that took them to their day program. I ran outside to discover that Tony had banged his head so hard into my rear side window that he had shattered it. We examined Tony's head and found only a small cut that we treated and sent him on to his day program. My car was another matter. I returned to the house to get a broom and cloth to clean up the mess. Mae asked if she could help, and I told her not to bother---I would take care of it. She ignored me and came to my assistance. She asked, "Is this a common occurrence here?"

"Well, Tony does bang his head into hard objects," I told her. "The walls are usually his targets. He has never banged his head into a car window before."

"Oh, I see" she said quietly. She told me later that when she returned home after the broken-window incident she told her husband, "This job is very peculiar. I don't know if I will stay with it, but it's interesting."

I felt I needed to explain to Mae more about our residents' behaviors. I did not want her to be frightened so I spent some time every day talking about the residents' different problems, why they behaved as they did, and what we were doing to change their behaviors. She learned some signing so she could "talk" to Ricky. She purchased handicrafts that required the use of both hands for Paul, and had a conversation with Derek when he returned from work. She gave Julia a permanent and helped Elsie with her personal hygiene care. "Do you want to be the supervisor of Beechnut House or my administrative assistant? " I asked.

She laughed and said, "I care so much about the residents that I forget I have other duties. I know what I need to do for you." I could not be angry with her because she cared so much about the residents.

The state required that all of the clients in both ICF/MR and HCS had to be out of the home during the day. The people living in the three group homes went to day programming at the Center. None of the day programs operating at that time welcomed the people served in the HCS program, because frequently they displayed behaviors that were difficult to manage, such as running away, aggression to others, and hallucinating. I asked the day programs to work with us since I was certain that these behaviors could and would be changed over time, but the day programs were not inclined to give us the time to create such change.

We had no choice but to start something ourselves. The cost of establishing and running a workshop or day program was not something I had in my budget. Using my personal money, we rented a building and developed a program of age-appropriate activities. Some of these activities were board games, shopping experience that included handling of money, personal hygiene activities like nail and hair care, and job preparation activities, such as interviewing, proper dress, and completing applications. It was not what I hoped it would be because of financial limitations, but we kept the clients busy and hoped they gained something from this experience. The state paid $18.00 per individual for a day of training, which was totally insufficient to cover the costs of running the program. Stan and Renée had to cover the deficits again. Money was tight and even the extra money that MHMRA had agreed to pay for the HCS program barely covered the operating costs.

More and more people came to visit and observe what was happening in our programs. As a result of the Lelsz lawsuit, which forced the state to move people out of the state schools into the community, the first people released from the state schools were those with mild and moderate mental retardation and no interfering behaviors. Now some of the people with severe and profound mental retardation were being referred to the community. Most of the providers who had opened programs after the lawsuit settlement still were not accepting those with severe and profound mental retardation, or were not keeping those with more severe needs, particularly behaviors that required extra staff. We remained one of the very few agencies serving people who were more expensive to serve.

All of the residents in Beechnut and Campbell Houses continued to improve but very slowly. We looked for even a bit of improvement to indicate we were on the right track and then carefully and consistently followed the behavior programs as written, constantly reevaluating progress or lack of progress.

Stan was following a normal work and social schedule. He was approaching his 65th birthday at which point retirement was mandatory in his company. He was experiencing heavy sweats after waking, showering, and having breakfast. He returned to shower and dress in clean clothes almost every morning. He gained 60 pounds, and I was surprised that the doctor never mentioned the danger of that weight to his heart, but now I know that the doctor probably wanted him to have extra weight since he knew the cancer would return.

We went to Boston for Melanie's wedding in November. She wanted both her mother and father to walk her down the aisle, and as we started to walk Stan doubled over in pain. The procession stopped until the intensity of the pain decreased. Finally we reached our seats and for the rest of the evening Stan moved very little. I brought the food to him and watched him closely throughout the evening. I forced myself to admit that the cancer had probably returned. We said nothing to our children at this time.

The next morning we returned to Houston and to the doctor. As soon as Stan described the pain and the sweats, the doctor told us that he thought the cancer had probably metastasized to his liver. The x-rays proved the doctor was correct, but the cancer had also spread to his bones. This was devastating news to both of us and forced me to eventually face the truth that I was going to lose my partner.

At first I refused to face Stan's impending death and pretended that nothing had changed, but finally, as Stan started on a regime of chemotherapy that required that he go into the hospital for overnight treatment, I realized that I had to make some important decisions. I stayed with Stan at the hospital and then brought him home the following morning. He was sick for the next few days. When he began to feel better, it was time to return to the hospital for another chemotherapy treatment.

My second in command, Kathy, informed me that she was leaving to get married and her fiancé was pressuring her to leave immediately. I did not want to hear that, but she did leave. I spent as much time as possible with Stan, but I had no idea how to do that and run Vita-Living, particularly now that Kathy was leaving. I was talking to a consultant who had helped us with the HCS billing requirements and who had started the first HCS program in south Texas. I proposed that he take over Vita-Living while I quit to care for Stan. He eagerly accepted. The next day as I was driving to the airport to fly to Austin to give a talk, I realized that I could not turn Vita-Living over to anyone, let alone someone I barely knew.

As soon as I reached the airport I called him and advised him that I changed my mind and could not give up the management of my agency. I offered him the position of Director of the HCS program. He accepted and took over right after Kathy resigned. I then met with all of my administrative staff and told them that I would be working out of my home. I brought my computer, a copy machine and a fax machine home and turned our family room into my office. There were no cell phones at that time so I had a new line put into the family room so I could have a phone access while I was at my desk. I came to the Beechnut office a few times a week when I had someone to help Stan, but for the most part I did all of the work out of my home. I conducted the staff meetings held at 10 P.M. every other week at each of the homes because I was still training the staff my philosophy of acceptance and strict adherence to the program plans.

Each house and the HCS program were billed separately and the payments arrived at different times in the month. Mae deposited the checks when they arrived in any account that needed bills paid--a full time job in itself. I was not as aware of the financial predicament we were in because I was so distracted and had such a wonderful friend and employee as Mae.

Hearing his moans and seeing the pain my husband was enduring was very difficult. One of his happier activities was playing poker with his friends. He was in a wheelchair now so every two weeks I helped him get to his game at one of the players' homes. This meant that I had to haul the wheelchair in and out of the trunk twice on each trip. I was always happy when the game was at our house so I did not have to deal with the wheelchair. I read or watched television while the "boys" played poker.

Ricky continued to come home every weekend, but I have to admit that we no longer argued with him over eating at the table. It was easier to serve Ricky his meals in front of the television then go through the hassle of forcing him to eat at the dinner table. Stan and I tried to continue eating at the kitchen table, but often I served him his meals in the bedroom and ate mine when I could. I don't remember eating that much, but I gained 40 pounds while Stan was so very ill. I must have eaten everything he didn't. Ready or not both of us faced the next year not knowing what to expect.

CHAPTER XIII

IT WAS A VERY BAD YEAR

1989 was one of the worst years of my life. It was the year of a magnitude 7.1 earthquake in San Francisco, the year United States invaded Panama, the year of the Tiananmen Square uprising, and finally the year the Berlin Wall fell. Ricky's favorite movies were *Driving Miss Daisy* and *Parenthood*.

I worked out of my home and took Stan to his treatments as well as his poker games. Page Anderson was a good friend to both Stan and me and volunteered to help Stan anyway we needed throughout that year, frequently taking Stan to his appointments. The chemotherapy put Stan in remission for a month or six weeks and during the remissions we traveled to Las Vegas, his favorite place but unfortunately not mine, for many weekends. He invited his brothers, sisters-in-law, and our children to meet us there, and many of them came. During the day they gambled, and I rented a car and traveled to an art gallery in Kanab, Utah, that was about two hours away. I returned in time to go out to dinner and the shows. We also traveled to Stan's family home in Detroit. It was comforting to be with the family even if only for a few days. The remissions were not long, but they did allow for some relief from the pain for him and the sorrow for me.

In May, the doctor tried an old chemo cocktail that only worked 20 percent of the time and told me to advise the family to be ready for the end. Stan had his chemo on a Tuesday and came home Wednesday morning. Around noon I heard Stan calling to me, "Reno (his nickname for me), I have no pain. I can walk."

I ran to the bedroom and saw him standing next to the bed. We both started to laugh as I ran to him for a bear hug. We were ecstatic as we

161

called all of the family to tell that we really thought this might be the turnaround. By Friday he took back the wheelchair and talked again about returning to Las Vegas. I was so happy about his good health that I was actually looking forward to our time together wherever he wanted. He played blackjack and poker, and I went to my favorite gallery. We enjoyed the shows and the food. In June he said he wanted to go back to Vegas. Ricky had just been diagnosed with hepatitis C and could not leave Beechnut House. I did not feel I could leave with Ricky so sick, so I asked Andy if he would leave San Diego, where he was completing his doctoral dissertation, and accompany his father. He agreed, and he and four of Stan's friends went with him to Vegas for four days. During that time, the cancer returned and Stan was in severe pain much of the time. When he could not tolerate the pain, he asked Andy to take him back to his room to rest and take some pain medication. After an hour or so he would return to the poker table. On his return to Houston, he was due back in the hospital for another chemo treatment.

Again he was in a wheelchair. When the plane landed a severe rainstorm hit Houston, and it was impossible for me to get to the airport to pick him up. After many hours, he and his friends were able to find a taxi and they dropped Stan off at the hospital where I met him. It was June 27th, my 64th birthday. When I arrived he said, "Happy birthday, Hon. Your present is in the top drawer of my chest."

"Thanks so much. I can't believe that you remembered and felt well enough to buy it," I exclaimed. At that moment his horrible disease faded from my mind, and I just felt blessed to have Stan for my husband. On arriving home, I rushed to Stan's chest of drawers and found my favorite perfume "White Shoulders" wrapped in strawberry red velvet with a large bubble gum pink bow. I forgot for the moment that my man was in the hospital fighting for his life.

The day after Stan returned to the hospital from his trip to Las Vegas, the doctor discovered that the cancer had severed his spine and he was paralyzed from his waist down. When Stan learned that his spine was severed he said, "I don't want any more treatments. I'm through trying to beat this monster. I'm ready for the end."

I said nothing, remembering my promise to him that I would support him with any decision he made. It was so hard to think of him gone, and it was harder to imagine how the end would come. I informed the doctor of his decision. The doctor totally ignored what I said and ordered further radiation treatments. When Stan was wheeled into the treatment room, he loudly informed them that he wanted no further treatment of any kind. I was furious that the doctor had paid no attention to what I had said. The hospital moved a cot into Stan's room for me and I stayed with him until August 1st when the hospital discharged him. While I was with him I said, "How lucky we are to have Vita-Living! I'd have to choose between caring for Ricky or being here with you if we had not been lucky enough to have a place for him." Stan smiled and nodded. Ricky still was confined to Beechnut House with Hepatitis C and did not receive a clean bill of health until the day Stan returned home.

As soon as Stan told me he wanted no more treatments, I contacted David, and asked him for help with Ricky. I did not know how to tell Ricky that his father was dying so he would understand that Stan would be gone from our family. When Stan was physically able, he called Ricky every night to ask him about his day. Although Ricky couldn't talk he laughed and tried to communicate to Stan. Frequently he held up different objects to the phone as if Stan could see them. Staff would tell Stan what he was showing him.

David picked out some movies that had scenes of dying and grave-side burials and sent them to Beechnut House for Ricky. Staff members sat with Ricky and talked about what was happening when they watched the dying and graveside scenes. Fortunately Ricky had a high level of understanding for someone with severe mental retardation and could relate to the scenes in the movies.

Stan was released from the hospital on August 1st. The doctor asked if we wanted hospice services in or out of the home. Neither of us knew anything about hospice services, so we refused hospice. The doctor helped me connect with a good home health agency and we had nursing care around the clock. I converted our bedroom to a hospital room, and I slept on the couch in the family room.

Andy came to Houston to help me and be with his Dad. After about a week Stan started to develop bedsores, so I bought an air mattress. I had to figure out how to move a 200-pound man so we could place the mattress on his bed. Help came from some of my big male staff people, some of the contractors we used, and Andrew. We had eight strong men; four on each side lift Stan up with the sheets while the nurse and I placed the air mattress on the bed. When Stan was awake and if he felt like it, Andy and I talked with him or just sat in his room with him.

Melanie gave birth to our second granddaughter, Samantha, on

August 7th, seven days after we returned home and received congrats by phone from her Dad. Stan received many cards and phone calls on his birthday (the 14th), but he spent most of the day sleeping. Melanie, Andre, her husband, and little Sammy were supposed to come to Houston on August 10th, but Samantha developed jaundice and could not leave the hospital. .

Stan died August 16th at noon and Melanie, Andre, and Samantha arrived at our home at 1:00 P.M., an hour later. We waited for Stan's brothers and their families to arrive before the funeral was held. Stan had served as president of Congregation Brith Shalom and so we held services in the sanctuary, as he had requested.

When Stan was laid out, David took Ricky to the funeral home and talked to him about what he was seeing. On the day of the burial, David and Kip took Ricky out to lunch and then to the gravesite. After the family had left the cemetery, it's staff kept the grave open until Ricky arrived so he could shovel some dirt into the grave. Ricky accepted Stan's disappearance from our lives better than I did.

After the funeral the family spent the week together following Jewish ritual, and then I spent a week with Melanie and her family in Boston.

I took Ricky home, but it was every other weekend instead of every weekend. The first time Ricky came home after Stan's death, he decided to test me when it was bedtime. I told him it was time to go to bed and asked him to take his medicine and turn off the television. He shook his head and threw himself down on the floor, screaming and kicking. I turned off the television and felt my face become warm and the palms of my hands perspiring. My heart was beating fast and my breath was coming in short bursts. I knew I would have to handle Ricky's temper tantrum correctly or it would be the last visit home for Ricky. I could not wrestle him and force him upstairs. I took a deep breath and said, "Ricky Wallace, you will take your medicine and go upstairs to bed or you will not come back home again. Not come back again," I repeated this warning at least five times, each time in a louder voice. I was watching Ricky out of the corner of my eye and noticed that he had stopped screaming and was looking at me as I was yelling at him. Suddenly he laughed, jumped up, took his medicine, went upstairs, took his shower, brushed his teeth and went to bed. Wow, how did that happen? I believe he really understood what I said and believed me when I told him he could not come home if he did not take his medicine and go to bed. What a relief. I had no more problems as far as going to bed was concerned.

One nice thing that happened to me and Vita-Living in October was that the American Association of Mental Retardation gave me a leadership award. The annual award recognizes an agency that portrays "courage and dedication resulting in an outstanding contribution in the field of mental retardation." I experienced the satisfaction that my peers recognized the work we did.

In spite of the recognition I felt as though I was a zombie. My feelings were frozen within my body and, if I let them defrost I felt I would float away. The song that Stan and I danced to when we were courting and first married kept going through my mind: "I walk alone because to tell you the truth I am lonely." I was frightened of the future but knew I could not let my fears interfere with my plans for Vita-Living. It wasn't only because of Ricky, but I felt a responsibility for Richard and Peter and Kristine and all of those who became my sons and daughters at Vita-Living. It was a heavy load, but I was determined and felt that I really had no choice but to succeed. I was ready for 1990.

CHAPTER XIV

WIN SOME, LOSE SOME

1990 was the year that the American Disabilities Act was signed into law, the country went into recession in June, gasoline prices soared to $1.33/gallon, nutrition labeling became mandatory, and the Dow Jones ended the year at 2633.66 down from 1989. Ricky's favorite movies were *Dances with Wolves* and *Pretty Woman*.

I was so busy trying to take care of what was left of my program that I had little time to feel sorry for myself. I worked from 7:00 A.M. until 11:00 P.M. every day and was too tired when I got home to think or feel anything. I fell into bed exhausted and set my alarm for 5:00 A.M. the next morning to get ready for the fight to survive. Many a day I would look up at the sky and talk to Stan, hoping and praying for him to take care of the situation for me as he had done for so many years.

As Stan had gown weaker, it appeared that I might be able to receive a small salary as finally the State had increased the rates they paid us per resident. The rates did not cover all of our expenses due to the large number of staff (three staff for six residents) we required to carry out the behavior programs, but with Stan so sick I had to have an income.

When I informed Stan that I might be able to get paid, he said, "Good. You'll need it. Please do not underwrite the Mental Health Mental Retardation Authority of Harris County (MHMRA)." I remembered his advice when I returned to work at the Beechnut office to find a serious financial deficit that was getting worse every day.

On my return from Stan's funeral, I realized that Vita-Living was facing financial ruin. My staff had not wanted to bother me while I was caring for Stan and preoccupied with his health. Throughout that year our cash flow situation had fallen into dire straights, mostly because of the HCS program that I had subcontracted from the local county agency. The residential cost of serving all these people was so high that the rate previously agreed upon was inadequate. At first I was not so worried because the fiscal year for MHMRA started September 1st, and I thought I could renegotiate our contract and our need for an additional $35,000/year. I heard, however, that MHMRA's new executive director refused to negotiate any contracts, so we were providing care for 30 people without any assurance of payment. While we did receive the amount specified in our original contract, MHMRA would not give us the additional money I had requested. I was terrified that Vita-Living was on the edge of financial collapse.

Since I was not sure how to handle the financial situation and my best friend and advisor was no longer there for me, I called my lawyer and asked what he thought I should do. We were six months beyond the time we should have signed a new contract, and there was no indication that MHMRA was interested in signing with us or even discussing it. My lawyer advised me to tell the local agency that we could no longer afford to underwrite their program and that they would either have to give us a new contract plus $35,000 or take back the program.

I asked the director of Mental Retardation services to meet with me. While he was sitting opposite me at my desk, I handed him a check that I had just written from my personal account to cover the costs of the HCS program. "I can't continue to underwrite MHMRA's program. What do you suggest I do about this?" I asked.

"I will talk to the executive director and let you know," he promised. I was so sure that MHMRA would not want to serve the difficult people we were serving that I really thought the agency would agree to give me what I asked. A few days later, he called to report that MHMRA had decided to take back the program. My heart sank because I was not sure if we could continue without the money from this program, but I knew we could not continue losing money every day either. I asked if he shared with the executive director how challenging the clients were to serve and how well all of the clients had done since they were with us. I also asked if they were willing to buy all of the furniture and household items we had bought that were necessary to establish homes for 27 people who were living in our apartments. He assured me that he had shared with the executive director all of that information and that she insisted that MHMRA would take back the entire program, but was unwilling to reimburse for anything we had purchased.

I was crushed by the news. I visualized losing my company, but with a shake of my head I decided that I was not going down without a very good fight. The day program closed first, and then all of the residential and at home clients returned to the MHMRA. We had 30 large notebooks holding the client's records, each costing $45.00, plus plastic sleeves for all the forms in the books. I offered to sell the agency the books, but again was told that they would not pay for anything. On my direction, the Vita-Living staff removed all the paper from the books and bound each client's records with large rubber bands. On the day that MHMRA was to pick up the paperwork, it was raining, so we placed all of the banded paper into plastic garbage bags to protect it. I was pleased to learn that this strategy really upset the executive director. By the end of March, 30 of my clients were no longer my clients. I did not have enough work for all of the staff so some were hired by MHMRA. The person that MHMRA assigned to run the program had no experience dealing with people with these challenging behaviors and chose not to listen to our staff who went to work for her. As a consequence, some of the clients suffered and regressed dramatically. The loss of these people who had improved so much under our care saddened me. I worried about them, but as usual for me, I was able to place my concerns on the back burner, and work harder to keep what I had.

My friend Peter and I had a long talk in his apartment the day before he left. "Peter, MHMRA is taking their HCS program back. You became a client of Vita-Living when we had an agreement with them to manage the HCS program. They paid us to manage the program for them. We can't continue to run the program because we need more money and they refuse to give us more. I don't want to lose all of my friends but I have no choice but to help you leave."

"I unersan. Can we sill ha unch?" he asked.

"Of course, but it will be once a month," I told him. "You will be in a day program that is a long way from here. You and I will still be friends. I will check on you, and we will have lunch. You can call me anytime you want. My telephone number is on this paper. Keep it where you can find it."

Peter nodded and said, "ee sure at u ake all a da ings in da armen." (Be sure that you take all of the things in the apartment.)

"Don't worry about that. Be sure that you pack all of your things to take with you. Do you have a suitcase and enough boxes?" I asked. Again Peter nodded and opened his door for me to leave.

We tried to meet with all of the families and clients to explain the move. We mailed a letter to each of them and held a meeting for those interested. My friend Kathy had to return to the workforce and was hired by MHMRA. She kept me informed about how the clients were doing. She told me that Peter had exposed himself to children at the apartment complex and was taken to a psychiatrist and a psychologist, who did not know him or his history and had no knowledge of what we did to help him with his problem. The doctor placed him on Depo-Provera, a drug often used for sex offenders, with blood clots as a potential side effect. Peter made three trips to the hospital because of blood clots, each one a life threatening experience. One day when I was visiting him in the hospital, I met one of my former staff members who now was working for MHMRA. He said, "I bet you think Peter wouldn't be here, if he had stayed with you."

I responded, "I know he wouldn't have been on Depo-Provera because there was no need. He wasn't exposing himself."

Richard reverted back to staying in bed all day with his coat over his head because the agency staff thought that our program of paying him a dollar a day to get out of bed and go to a day program was poor programming. They paid a staff member to sit with him while he lay in bed until the other residents came home. He then got up to smoke and socialize with his housemates. This plan for Richard continued for 10 months before the agency staff admitted that paying him might be worth a try and reinstituted our program.

Shortly after Stan died, I received two calls that were important to the future of Vita-Living. The first was from Jim Hart, who had replaced Stan at his company, Panhandle Eastern, and asked if he could help. I told him I needed people for a board since now the board consisted only of Page Anderson and me, and we needed at least three people to meet state requirements for a nonprofit agency. Jim Hart said he would help me, and soon after I received a "How to" book about boards from one of his staff people. The second call came from Mallory Robinson, a friend of ours, who also asked if I needed help. I replied to her in the same manner, but heard nothing for many months. I was too busy to read the book so I pushed it out of my mind, but I knew it was essential that I find board members.

Six months later Jim called again, and again I told him of my need for board members. He offered not only to serve on the board but also to serve as chair. Mallory also offered to serve on the board and she brought in a young lawyer who was a friend of her son's, Michael Rubenstein. I called Mr. Pozmantier, a friend of Stan 's and our insurance advisor, who I had been told by those who knew him, was too busy with his work and other philanthropic obligations to be on another board. He accepted membership to the board and has been very active and supportive ever since. Naomi Dempsey, Kristine's mother, Millie Cowen, who had two children in our program, and Ariel Smith, a guardian of one of our HCS clients, all agreed to serve on the board. We now had eight board members.

The challenge for me was to find a way to keep their interest and make all of them serve because they felt strongly about Vita-Living, not just out of loyalty to me or Stan. I accomplished this by maintaining Vita-Living in a positive cash flow position and by obtaining recognition for the work we were doing in the community. I received many awards from local and statewide community organizations for the work of Vita-Living. Maintaining a positive cash flow position forced me to continually search for new and different ways to create income. Starting new programs and expanding the programs we had brought more income to Vita-Living. It was a gamble to start a new program because you never knew if clients would come to you and if the state would continue to fund the program, but if you did nothing, nothing changed. I kept our precarious financial situation from the Board until 1991, when I was able to see a light at the end of the tunnel.

We applied for our own HCS program in 1989, right after I returned from Stan's funeral. We received notification from the state that we had been approved to open our own 30-person HCS program in April of 1990. I didn't want to repeat the high cost of establishing residences, so we decided to go to the schools and the children's clinics to see if we could serve children who still lived at home. We knew that parents needed help with these children when they came home from school and on weekends, so we started an after-school care program and a weekend recreational program. Most of the children we served were from families with working parents and many were one-parent households. The stress of dealing with a child with mental retardation can be difficult so there are a high percentage of divorces in these families and hence many single parents raising their children.

The HCS program offered a component that paid for a one-time remodeling of a home to make it more handicapped accessible. The most common remodeling requested was for the bathroom. The state required we obtain three bids and the cost be no more than $7,500. One of our new clients was Pat, a nine-year old girl, with profound mental retardation and cerebral palsy. She was totally helpless and had to be cared for in all aspects of her life. Her mother, a single parent, asked us to help by bathing her daughter everyday because she has not been able to do more than hose her down in the back yard. We tried to remodel her bathroom, but the way the home was constructed made it impossible to do for the money allowed. So instead, we bathed Pat everyday after school and on weekends when she came to the core. There were other families who took advantage of bathing at the core. We received a grant for a tub that opened on the side so we could bathe our wheelchair clients and we installed a handicap accessible shower.

The families were so grateful to have the after-school care, which included training in simple skills. School buses brought some of the children to the core house, and we transported others. At one time we had as many as 20 after-school children at the core that we served a snack of cereal and milk or fruit and milk. The snack offered the children training in feeding and socializing. Proper positioning of the children was important for eating and waiting for their return home. The parents picked up their children, if possible and, if not, we drove them home. The trips our drivers had to make to transport the children to their homes noticeably increased our transportation costs, but even so we came out ahead financially.

The applicants were accepted on a first-come, first-served basis, but because we visited schools and children's clinics to advertise our program, the majority of those in our program were children living at home. We gradually completed our 30 client limit and found working with the children challenging but easier on the budget because we received the same amount of money from the state regardless of whether we served the client in his or her own home or in one of our residences.

There were three children who were medically fragile and required nursing around the clock. With the introduction of new methods of maintaining life in newborn infants, there were many children with multiple handicapping conditions living into adulthood. Rita was just one example. Rita was ten years old with a diagnosis of profound mental retardation, cerebral palsy, with bilateral hip displasia, seizure disorder, estropia, microcephaly, spastic quadriplegia, gastrostomy, and a respiratory disorder. She lived with her parents and brother in a one-story home and both her parents worked outside of the home. Through HCS funding we had been able to remodel the bathroom to accommodate her handicaps and purchase a special wheelchair-outfitted van. After seeing the living situation, I was able to help the family purchase a special hospital bed for the living room so Rita could be included in the family activities. She was on a 24- hour ventilator and had a licensed nurse with her at all times, primarily to provide suctioning when necessary. Due to all of these adaptations and equipment, she was able to stay in her home and attend the local school. A handicapped equipped van from the school district transported her to and from school. When she reached her 22nd birthday, she was unable to be served with 24-hour nursing through the special Medicaid program serving school-age children. The HCS program limited the number of hours they would pay for nursing, so the state forced her parents to choose between placing her in a nursing home or Richmond State School. Her parents chose Richmond State School. The move was difficult for us and especially difficult for the family, but she was well served at Richmond and has done well.

I thought that opening another ICF/MR home would help our bottom line so I started to look for a home we could purchase. I realized I would have to pay for it myself, initially, but it seemed a wise move to do now because there were rumors that the state was going to stop licensing new ICF/MR homes. I thought that ICF/MR was a more cost-effective means of serving people with severe mental retardation residentially than the HCS model. My son Lee had married, had three children, and lived in a small community west of Houston called Katy. When he decided to move to Dallas, his home became vacant. Since the real estate market was slow and his home did not sell, I decided to use it for a group home. We opened our fourth group home, the Smithfield Crossing Home, named after the street of the same name in Katy, Texas. We maintained the ICF/MR homes within our budget, and with the new HCS program, our finances were beginning to look better.

We sought clients at Richmond State School, which was the state school closest to us. Again I went to the wards that were not frequented by most providers and found five men with profound mental retardation. The sixth man came from the community. His mother had visited me right after I opened Beechnut House and wanted us to care for her son. When she heard about our new home, she asked that her son be admitted.

Helping men who were in their 20's and had spent most of their lives in a large state school to adjust to a small home was challenging. Change is difficult for everyone, but for people who have lived in one place for ten or more years and have IQ's of less than 20, it's monumental. Within the first week, windows and toilets were broken, food was spilled, furniture scratched, and clothing torn. There were four bed-rooms in the home so four of the residents shared two rooms. I was not certain that our method of self -medication could work with these resi-dents, but if the state allowed staff members to use their hands to cover the hands of the clients and assist them in pushing the pills through the blisters in the blister packs, it might work. The state allowed such hand over hand assistance. The supervisor, Josie, was a woman who had worked in the first HCS program and had requested to return to us at the same time Smithfield Crossing Home opened. She was excited about working with these men and as of 2009 was still the supervisor.

The people in this home were not as aggressive or self-injurious as those in the other homes, but due to their very limited intellectual functioning, we had some difficult behaviors to deal with.

Oscar had profound mental retardation, was not toilet trained, and was put on toileting schedule where he was taken to the toilet at very specific times and rewarded with praise and pats when he performed, much like a little child. He had a self-stimulating behavior of swing-ing his head from side to side spraying spit all around him. When he was in a spitting mood, we isolated him by having him sit away from the group in the house or in another row of seats in the car. He now has few toileting accidents, and has stopped his head-swinging, spit-spraying behavior. This improvement was slow but gradual over the 17 years the home has been open.

Owen, 6'1" tall and 240 pounds, had profound mental retardation, autism, and pica, which means he ate inedible objects, such as string, and buttons, and shredded his socks and underwear to eat the thread. His program required that he have a bag of nuts, pretzels, and raisins with him to eat at all times during the day. The crunch of the snack food seemed to satisfy him and kept him away from the inedibles. At night we locked his closet where all of his clothes were stored. When he became agitated, he jumped so high that he almost reached the blades of the ceiling fan, so as soon as he became agitated a staff person ac-companied him to the fenced-in-back yard where he could jump all he wanted, or if the weather did not allow him to jump outside, he used the exercise bike.

Jim, who had been run over by a large truck and had undergone a craniotomy, had profound mental retardation and mental illness. He broke many toilets because of his heavy masturbation when he was in the bathroom. Since once we had found him on top of the air con-ditioner outside because he liked to feel the movement of the machine, we had to fence in the unit so he wouldn't hurt himself. We hired extra staff people for midnight shift to redirect Jim from bothering the other residents when he wandered about during the night. Medication to help him sleep had not been effective.

Larry had profound mental retardation plus "Angelman's Syndrome", so named after the pediatrician, Dr. Henry Angelman, who first described the syndrome in 1965. People with this syndrome are often known as "angels" both because of the syndrome's name and because of their youthful, happy appearance. Larry was always laughing and happy but gagged when he was at the table. When he started to gag, we removed him from the table and returned him to finish his meal when he stopped. He also poked his fingers into his eyes so his program directed that a staff person remind him to remove his fingers. If verbal redirection didn't work, a staff person guided his hands away from his face. Since he had endured physical abuse when he was at the state school, his family was anxious about the quality of care he received with us.

Dwayne had Down Syndrome and profound mental retardation. He liked to tear his clothing, so we locked his closet during the night and gave him newspaper and old magazines to tear instead. Today we no longer have to lock his closet and his need to tear everything has disappeared.

All of the families became more involved with their children once they moved out of the state school and into the community. I met with the men's families, before they moved into Smithfield Crossing. Some of them were anxious about the safety of their children in the community. I reassured them that we had three staff when they were awake and in the home and two staff at night compared to one staff to ten or more clients in the state school.

I visited this home at least weekly to observe the staff working with the residents.

I was also very involved in all of the residents' annual meetings and led the staff meetings that occurred every two weeks.

Josie has assisted and encouraged her residents to grow way beyond what anyone expected from them. Now some of the men clear the table and put the dishes and silverware into the dishwasher. Another pours the juice and helps set the table. Yet another sweeps and assists with the laundry. They all help cleaning their personal space and at this time only one still needs hand over-hand assistance with his self-medication. They have all lived at Smithfield Crossing House for 17 years and we hope will grow old together.

During this time, I brought Ricky home every other weekend. He took the absence of Stan in stride. He knew where his father was buried and often indicated he wanted to see the grave. We drove there and placed stones on the graves of his father and his grandparents who were buried next to Stan. Ricky's visits home included his going to movies Saturday and Sunday and watching television when he was not at the movies. After the first weekend following Stan's death there were no more serious problems going to bed or getting up to go to work. He never wanted to go to work but we stopped for a doughnut on the way to the workshop and he did want that doughnut.

I asked the staff with an artistic bent to help us paint shirts and make paper earrings for sale at church bazaars and fairs. We spent many an afternoon and weekend painting men's shirts and paper to make jewelry for sale. This brought in a small amount of money for a lot of volunteer work. Although the year started out to be a disaster financially, the new HCS program and the new ICF/MR home brought us back from the brink of financial ruin. The year ended with Vita-Living in a more favorable financial situation. In addition to the new programs, the state increased the rates paid to the providers and we no longer had the financial drain of the first HCS program. I was able to continue taking a salary and all of the staff received a first-time small Christmas bonus.

When the New Year arrived, I was looking forward to good things happening for Vita-Living in 1991.

CHAPTER XV

WHAT GOES AROUND, COMES AROUND

THE YEAR was 1991. A cease-fire ended the Persian Gulf War, the Soviet Union broke up, the cost of a first-class stamp rose to $.29, and Ricky's favorite movies were *Thelma & Louise* and *Dances with Wolves*.

Rumors came to us that the executive director of MHMRA was telling anyone who would listen that Vita-Living was a poor provider of services and had done a poor job with the clients. I was furious and again called the lawyer asking him if I could sue for defamation of character. He advised strongly that I forget it. He said that if I sued, it would make more of her remarks than they were worth. I remembered Winston Churchill's words, "Lies travel around the world while the truth is putting on its boots." Thank goodness I listened to the lawyer and Mr. Churchill.

The state approached Vita-Living about participating in a new program called Community Living Assistance and Support (CLASS), designed to serve people in the community with a primary diagnosis of a developmental disability other than mental retardation and mental illness that occurred before the 22nd birthday. Mental retardation could be a secondary diagnosis. For example, someone with cerebral palsy or autism could also have mental retardation as long as the physician stated that the cerebral palsy or autism was the primary disability.

Residential services were not available in the CLASS program since the participants were expected to have the mental capacity to handle their own residential needs. CLASS had a case-management as well as a provider component but the same agency could not provide both. The state thought that case management needed to be separate to remain impartial in advocating for the participant. I thought about the work connected with both and decided that we could not handle another provider component, but the case management should be easier. The only new staff I had to hire was two case managers who could use the front duplex of one of our new homes as their office. To save money, I handled all of the admissions and the director of the HCS program monitored the case managers. It was critical to have accurate information and timely admissions in order for Vita-Living to begin receiving payments from the state. We could serve no more than 30 people and were under a tight timeline to admit them. I thought about the advantages to Vita-Living in participating in this program. First there was the additional money; second there was the recognition we would receive as the first agency in Harris County to start this new state program; third CLASS could serve as a source for more clients for our HCS program. The HCS and CLASS programs were similar in that the recipients received only those services that the team determined they needed. The CLASS program did not offer the supervised living arrangements that many of the participants with mental retardation needed. Since the families were already familiar with us, there was a good chance that they would choose Vita-Living for their HCS agency when they were notified that they were eligible for those services. CLASS did become a source of new clients for the HCS program.

The disadvantages included having to work with many direct-care agencies and absorb large transportation costs because our clients were scattered throughout a multi-county area and the case managers had to travel to them.

In the CLASS program we served many people who were physically impaired to the point that they required 24-hour attendant assistance in all aspects of their life. Most of them lived independently in apartments designed for people with physical limitations. I was amazed at the wide variety of conditions we encountered including spina bifida, anoxic brain syndrome, quadraplegia and paraplegia, fragile X, muscular dystrophy, cri-du-chat, WalkerWarhburg Syndrome, Rett Syndrome, and tuberous sclerosis. I learned about many new medical conditions and how people were living with the limitations these diseases forced on them.

Beechnut, Campbell, and Smithfield Crossing Homes were functioning well and full all of the time. The Smithfield Crossing home was too small for all of the activities our residents liked, so we converted the garage to a family room. We did not want problems with the homeowners association, so we left the garage exterior unchanged and just remodeled the interior into a combo dining room, activity room. We placed two tables to seat four each on one side of the room with the sandboxed chairs similar to those at the other two homes. At the opposite end of the room were a rowing machine, a stationary bike, and book shelves holding group games and puzzles.

Kathy continued to report to me on Peter's situation and it was not good. The inability of the MHMRA to safely care for him caused the executive director to consider sending him back to the state school, but the Lelsz class-action lawsuit settlement barred anyone who was a part of the lawsuit from returning to a state school. Almost a year to the day that the original HCS program was returned to MHMRA, I received a call from the state office asking if I would consider taking back the program.

I was so elated that we had been vindicated that I didn't know what to do first. I wanted to shout from the rooftops. I told the state staff that I would have an answer by the next day and called a meeting of all of my administrative staff that afternoon. We talked about the pros and cons, and finally I had to admit that we could not afford to take the program back unless the state was willing to give us $100,000 start-up money. We had to start from scratch to furnish nine apartments and hire and train extra staff. I was certain that we also would have to start from scratch again as far as the behavior programs were concerned.

The next day I asked for the start-up money and was told that the state never gave start-up money. That was the end of that joy ride. On a personal level I felt vindicated, but that didn't help Vita-Living. Kathy told me that I would receive a call from the executive director's assistant. She thought it was about taking Peter back. The next morning around 7:00 A.M. as I was brushing my teeth, he called. "Heyyo I can't alk now. I have a mout full of toopase. Ca me a office ater," I muttered. I had trouble finishing brushing my teeth because I could not stop smiling.

When he called I informed him that we needed to meet to talk about the conditions under which I would agree to take Peter back. One condition was that I wanted to take back his two roommates, because they were good friends and had been together for many years. At lunch the next day I informed him that I wanted $200.00/day per person, and I would provide both day and residential services. He talked about the men using their Supplemental Security Income checks as part of the $200.

"Absolutely not. That is their money and they need it for personal spending. I want $200/day per person so that we can provide well for them and Vita-Living has no extra money to do that." I stated adamantly.

The assistant hesitated, so I said, "I don't care either way. I would like to serve Peter again but I'm doing fine, and if you can't give me what I need to serve him well, I certainly understand."

I didn't know if he knew of my relationship with Peter, but I did a bit of poker playing and hoped I could keep a poker face. I also told him I wanted a letter from the executive director stating that we were a viable agency performing well and that she was grateful that we continued to serve the clients of MHMRA. It was important that she admit that she had been wrong when she maligned us. "That's no problem," he claimed.

I received the letter thanking us for serving MHMRA's clients so well and stating that we were a valuable agency to work with. I never did know if the letter carried the actual signature of the executive director of MHMRA of Harris County. It didn't matter.

Obtaining the contract for $200/day each for the three clients was a wonderful break for Vita-Living. On a personal level, it allowed me to move outside of our comfort zone and spread our wings. I couldn't stop smiling. I had had the idea of creating two businesses for the three housemates. All three of them had been with us in the old program so we knew them well. For financial record keeping and program monitoring, we needed to separate this program from the others, so we named it Residential Alternatives for Individuals with a Dual Diagnosis (RAIDD). The three men had been diagnosed with both mental retardation and mental illness and that was known as a Dual Diagnosis.

To provide training and counseling when the men returned from their day programs, we hired two people to work with the three clients from 3:00 P.M to 11:00 P.M. The two businesses we started were a ceramics studio for Peter and a landscape business for the other two men. Two staff members worked from 7:00 A.M. to 3:00 P.M. and assisted with wake-ups in the morning. The other two daytime staff went directly to the businesses and worked from 8:00A.M. to 4:00 P.M.

Peter had to work in a safe environment because he could not afford to risk another blood clot. His doctor had prescribed Cumadin, a blood thinner, for him and I had to figure out a way for him to work with a minimum of exposure to bruising. Someone had donated a kiln to us, which led me to think about ceramics, but I had no idea how to use the kiln. While on a trip to San Diego to visit Andy, I was impressed by all of the beautiful Mexican tiles. Why couldn't we make tiles? I thought. Again, it was a challenge I couldn't resist. On the flight home, I developed a business plan that required finding a ceramist and a staff person who knew how to work with Peter and convincing Peter that he wanted to learn ceramics. We had the money; now I had to find someone with the know-how.

We found two apartments that opened into each other on Memorial, a prestigious street. This allowed each of the men to have a bedroom as well as a room for staff, a large living room, dining room, two kitchens, and an activity room.

During my visits to galleries--a favorite pastime of mine, I had become friendly with a masters-level ceramicist, Liz, who was between jobs. We went out to lunch and talked about her accepting the challenge of working with someone with mental retardation and mental illness. She agreed although she had never worked with someone with a handicap.

Liz was intimidated when she first met Peter. He was a large, often surly man who spoke with a severe speech impediment so she had to learn how to communicate with him and become familiar with his speech pattern. In one instance he came to her to ask for pennies for his collection, but she thought he was asking for her panties. She rushed to Pat, the other staff person, to tell her about the incident. "He collects pennies and was asking you if you had any," Pat said. Liz was embarrassed by her mistake and apologized to Peter. Gradually she became familiar with his speech pattern and was able to understand him most of the time.

Pat was a woman who had worked in direct care for me with people with mental retardation for more than ten years. She had two valuable qualities: she was experienced and patient with our clients, and she was talented in the crafts arena. She was anxious to learn how to create ceramics, and she loved working with only one client at a time since she was accustomed to working with 10 or more in a classroom setting.

We started with our one kiln in the garage of one of the homes we used for the core. Very quickly we realized that we needed more room so we found a space in a warehouse area where there was room for three more kilns as well as areas for painting, drying, and finishing. Mrs. Dempsey helped us find tables and workbenches, and after we

had worn out our welcome requesting donations, we purchased whatever was needed to outfit a ceramic studio.

David and Kip were available to counsel Liz if she had any concerns
working with Peter or any of the other clients who became employees
of the ceramics studio. We had warned Liz that Peter had a habit of
running off, but she was told that he knew the bus system better than
most and to let Dan, the program manager, know immediately if that
happened. One afternoon Peter just got up from his chair and walked
out of the door and down the path to the bus stop. She shadowed him
until he got on the bus and then she called for help. "I have only one
client and I lost him. This is so embarrassing," she said when she called
Dan.

"Don't worry, Peter does this but he will return soon. He doesn't get
lost. I'm sure he's all right." Dan said. Peter did return to the tile studio,
and after Liz told him how upset she was that he ran off, he said he
would not do it again and he did not.

Peter was well aware of the young woman who was his boss at the
tile studio and one day he exposed himself to her. He wanted her attention and he certainly got it. I received a call from a very frustrated Liz
describing what had happened. I went to the studio the following day.
"Why did you expose yourself to Liz?" I asked him. I don't like that behavior. You don't need to do that to get attention. You receive all of her
attention by coming to work and doing the best you can. We can't continue our lunch dates if you expose yourself again," I said with great
emphasis.

"I am thorry. I won do i again," he muttered in an embarrassed tone.
He never did again as long as he was with us.

David suggested that Liz develop a program that would keep both
of Peter's hands busy, making it impossible for him to masturbate. She
had him hold a tile with one hand while he painted with the brush
held in the other hand and kept him working steadily. Pat and Liz
worked well with Peter. He had poor eye-hand coordination, but they
were highly motivated.

One day Liz called to advise me that she didn't know how to make
the tile studio work because Peter's hands shook so much that he could
not handle the brushes well. We talked about different approaches to
decorating the tiles when she suddenly said, "I have an idea. I can cut
designs out of bumper sticker paper, place the designs on the tiles, and
Peter can roll the paint over the designs."

"What a great idea! Matisse cutouts would be great to use. I have the book "JAZZ"," I responded enthusiastically. "Would you like to use it? Pat and Peter might enjoy seeing what a famous artist did."

"I was thinking of Matisse when I thought of cut-outs. Please bring the book to the studio." She said.

Liz also learned about task analysis because she had to break down every job or task for the clients into workable sections that they could learn. Every design or pattern had to be looked at in that fashion. Since our clients could not read, Liz drew pictures of the tasks to be done. The ultimate goal was to make professional-looking tiles. In addition to cutting out designs and rolling paint, Liz used the slip trail and sponge methods of painting. Peter could perform both of these methods without Liz being right next to him.

The slip trail method involved Liz or Pat filling a plastic bottle with the paint and Peter squeezing the paint out of a bottle to make abstract designs. Frequently they used this technique to decorate around the rims of bowls and plates as well as covering tiles.

The sponge method involved Liz or Pat preparing a shallow bowl of paint and then cutting a sponge to a size that Peter could handle easily. He dipped the sponge into the paint and then pressed it against the tile. Once we had other clients in the studio, they were taught to roll out clay and use cookie cutters to make designs, to pour the silt into molds, and to trim the products when they were removed from the molds. We used the designs from the cookie cutters primarily to make tree decorations

While I was taking my walks through galleries I made a friend, Bruce, who sold me some prints. He liked our tiles and what we were trying to do and took it upon himself to search for places to sell them. One decorator he dealt with heard about us from him and gave us our first big order for decorating a large kitchen in the posh Memorial area of town. She visited the studio and was so impressed with the work we did that she commissioned us to make 500 tiles with Matisse-like designs. Each design had to be unique. What excitement in the studio and in my heart.

This was what I had dreamed about, a legitimate business where our clients could work and receive an hourly wage and we could pay taxes. As our ceramics business expanded, the clients did receive an hourly rate of pay equal at least to the minimum wage and enjoyed their work, but we never made enough income to pay taxes. After the kitchen was completed, the decorator invited Liz, Pat, and Peter to visit and see their handiwork. They took photos to show future customers.

Other clients began to show an interest in our business and came to work alongside Peter.

Word spread about our work, and a few architectural firms contacted us. One of our first big commissions was for making tiles for the hydrotherapy room at Southwest Memorial Hospital. Then we were hired to make custom-designed tiles for a fireplace in a large country club in San Antonio. Soon we placed our tiles in the Texas Children's Hospital as well as other businesses in Houston.

Liz stayed with us for two years and then Pat took over. She had learned well and was as successful as Liz in developing designs and products to sell. Because of her vast experience working with people with mental retardation, she was excellent with our employees. We eventually had 11 employees with disabilities and 4 staff members to help them.

I wrote many proposals for grants for additional funding for the tile studio and finally received a grant for a marketing person to help move our products. At a dinner party held in my home, I had covered my table with black and white tiles painted in abstract designs. One of my guests, Leila, admired them and mentioned she was looking for a job. After talking to her for a while, I said that I was looking for someone to help me market our ceramics. She wanted the job, and so another friend of Vita-Living was found.

We had gone from making only tiles to making tableware to include candlesticks, dinnerware, and bowls of many sizes. Through our new marketing services, we received orders for murals and tables as well. I was so excited when Leila told me she had found a home for our line of dishes and accessories in a ladies clothing store in the River Oaks shopping area, a choice retail space, for one month between Thanksgiving and Christmas. Three weeks before Christmas she called me to say that a man who had seen our products in that store wanted to help us rent a place in the Galleria. I could barely contain myself: The Galleria was one of the best retail locations in the city. The space was small but perfect for us. I visited it two weeks before Christmas. The sales representative offered it to us for $300.00/month. I told him I would think it over. Deciding to spend always made me hesitate.

When I reached my car and started the motor I hit the side of my head with my hand to knock stupid out of it. How could I not have jumped at the chance to have an outlet for our ceramics in the best location in the city? As soon as I reached home I called him to thank and accept his offer. The next person I called was Naomi Dempsey, and she helped furnish the space so we could start selling before Christmas. She found shelving, a beautiful desk, a few chairs, and a cash register. Mr. McCord, our chief financial officer, established a credit card connection and we were in business. We decorated the store for the holidays and the ceramics literally flew off the shelves. Unfortunately this level of activity did not continue after the first of the year, but we were able to keep the store open for eight years.

A number of volunteers were interested in helping at the tile studio and in the store. The most loyal was Naomi Dempsey who came at least once a week to clean tiles after the designs had been rolled onto them. She also cut designs and performed whatever other jobs were needed. There were three volunteers at the store, but one of the most steady and loyal was Mrs. Bishop. She came in to purchase something, fell in love with our products, and offered to volunteer one day a week. She continued until we closed the store. Then I asked her to serve on our board. She couldn't but referred me to her husband who was kind enough to accept and is still serving on our board.

We attended all of the craft fairs in the area we could. There was no extra staff so I took the ceramics to the fairs, set up the tables, and became a saleslady. Pat came up with the idea of making magnets in the shapes of dogs, cats, flowers, and houses. I thought they would not sell but at the first fair we showed them, people crowded our booth and we sold out. So much for my business savvy.

Our second business venture was a lawn-care business, which made sense to me because it was work our clients could perform under staff direction and because we had 10 properties we had to maintain. The lawns needed continuous care and we had to hire someone to do the job. It provided work for Richard and Jerome, the third housemate, and eventually eight other men became our gardeners. We were fortunate to find a staff person who had experience in gardening and caring for people with mental retardation. We started with just eight yards but eventually we had three employees working alongside ten residents tending eighteen homes and yards. We acquired two lawn mowers, a leaf blower, a trimmer, all the smaller garden tools and two trucks to carry the lawn-care teams to and from the houses. We were in business. Richard spent most of his time drinking coffee and smoking, but he did get out of bed and go to work everyday. The other residents were hard workers and did a good job.

I purchased a duplex to use as a core unit and an office for the CLASS and HCS programs. My plan was to convert it to a home if we needed the space, but to start with we used the front unit for after-school care and weekend recreation and the back unit as offices. We now had two offices, both in homes we owned.

1991 ended on a good note. Financially we were in better shape than we had ever been thanks to the RAIDD program. The residents in our homes were progressing in their respective behavior programs, and we were gaining a good reputation as a case-manager provider in the CLASS program.

Ricky was going into the training room less often, and we both found pleasure in his visits home with very few problems. He and I continued to enjoy going to movies and watching television together.

Ten years had passed since Stan and I sat at the kitchen table planning this new venture and I was looking forward to the next ten years. If Stan had known, he would have been surprised and pleased at how far we had come.

CHAPTER XVI

THE REST OF THE STORY

IT WAS August of 2002, a hot, steamy Southwest summer night. Vita-Living's 20- year celebration at the Westin Hotel was exploding with enthusiastic talk and laughter. People exclaimed over the rainbow of colors on our ceramics covering two tables in the outer room where the hors d'oeuvres and drinks were being passed. I could not stop my body from moving with the music of the quartet playing in the corner. Colored balloons pulled at the ties connecting them to the ceiling. Ladies in lace and chiffon floor-length gowns swished across the floor with men in ties and jackets accompanying them.

Andrew acted as master of ceremonies; Melanie had prepared a nine-minute video about Vita-Living, and Lee was busy photographing the event. The music played throughout dinner, and after dinner Andrew talked about my serving as an alchemist bringing forth the best from what others considered dross. I received the Giraffe award for "sticking my neck out" when I started Vita-Living. Kathy Doherty, my good friend, who helped me start Vita-Living, talked about the agency's start-up. I told the audience about the "angels on my shoulder" who helped me start and maintain Vita-Living. I remembered the people we lost to illness and accidents and applauded those who were present and continued to keep Vita-Living afloat.

At the end of the celebration many people talked about their involvement in the formation and maintenance of the agency. Laughter and chatter trailed those who wanted to spend more time talking about old times in my hotel room until after midnight. I fell into bed exhausted but exhilarated. My mind wouldn't stop revisiting the many events that had shaped Vita-Living over the past decade

I remembered the time I left some important work at the office on one of Ricky's weekends at home. I told Ricky I had to return to Beechnut to get some work I had forgotten. When Ricky and I were in the car on our way to Beechnut House he started to scream and kick at the windows. I pulled over to the curb and said, "Stop that immediately. I left some papers at the office and I need to drive there to get them. You can stay in the car while I run in and get the papers I need."

Ricky continued to scream and kick. I started to turn the car around and shouted, "I will turn around but you will not come home again. It is important that I get those papers and you must drive with me. You do not have to get out of the car. I must get those papers. You will not come home again."

He stopped screaming and put both hands in front of his face and waved them back and forth as if they were windshield wipers. "Are you willing to drive with me to Beechnut House?" I shouted. He nodded his head and smiled. We drove to my office in Beechnut House and while he waited in the car I ran in to get the papers I needed. I was reminded again how well Ricky understood consequences and how important it was to develop trust between us.

One of my biggest concerns had always been possible abuse by staff. I attempted to set up systems to provide as much protection as possible for the residents in my care. For instance, in Ricky's case, when he had to go into the training room, I insisted that two staff members accompany him, to provide witnesses to what occurred in the room.

One of my male staff, a former football player, who I thought was good with our clients, approached me saying that he was going to work at the Center day program and wanted to stay on at Beechnut House in the afternoon. He commented that he would be caring for the group where Ricky worked. I told him, "No one can work with Ricky Wallace all day and also all evening without losing control. You must pick one shift or the other."

His said that he preferred to work days. I understood and wished him well. His first day on the job at the Center was his last day with Beechnut House. That afternoon Ricky had to go into the training room many times and when I was leaving around 9:00 P.M. Ricky pointed to his head. I thought he was telling me he had a headache and asked one of the staff people why he was not helping Ricky get some Tylenol for his headache. The staff immediately helped Ricky get the Tylenol while I reminded everyone that they had to be sensitive to the residents' attempts at communication. Laughing, the former football player said to Ricky, "You know you don't have a headache, Ricky. You're just acting."

Again I reminded both of them that they had to respond to the attempts to communicate by our residents and got into my car to drive home. Around midnight I got a call from Kathy telling me that Ricky had been slapped many times in the face by the large man with hands the size of Texas. She said that the other staff member who had accompanied Ricky into the training room that evening was 5'8" and weighed about 145 pounds so he was afraid to talk about the "big guy" when they were together. He felt compelled to tell Kathy about the abuse when he arrived home from his shift. I was distressed that I had not been able to prevent my son from being hurt even though I was in the building.

The next morning I went to the Center's workshop and talked to the person in charge. His second-floor office provided a view of the shop area where the clients worked. I told him about the incident and said I did not want that man working with any of my clients. I watched as Ricky came into the area where the ex-football player worked and ran up to hug him. I could not believe that Ricky did not carry any hard feelings against this man who had slapped him in the face many times the night before. Fortunately the Center fired him so he was no longer around to hurt someone else.

Ricky continued to improve and was now out of the training room. He used his chair in the bedroom if he needed to be removed from the activities. I looked forward to his biweekly visits home. We had a good time going to the movies and watching television together. My other children lived so far away that I treasured the time I spent with the one child who lived near me.

Our ability to provide life-long care to our residents was always on my mind. Many people who worked with our clients left for a variety of reasons, so frequently we needed to reassure the residents that we were there for the long haul. I remember one of our clients asking who would care for him now that his staff member had died in a motorcycle accident. I tried to put him at ease by telling him that I, and all of the people who worked at Vita-Living, would care for him as long as he was with us.

All of our clients were slowly but surely improving, and more and more people in the state were aware of the work we were doing. I had been invited to serve on the Mental Retardation Planning Council

(MRPAC), a committee of the Mental Health Mental Retardation Authority of Harris County composed of advocates for people with mental retardation as well as representatives of the various school districts and hospital districts and two private providers. A new executive director and a new director of Mental Retardation Services welcomed me to participate with them. Apparently the difficulties connected with the return of the first HCS program were forgotten. The state organization (TAPPR) that I had joined in 1985 had undergone some changes and was now called Private Providers Association of Texas (PPAT). I attended more of the meetings and had the time to learn about the mechanics of rate setting in Texas. It took me many years to begin to understand that the state determined the rates they paid us by how much it cost us to provide services. That did not make sense to me but it seemed that the more we spent the more we would get. It did not encourage efficient administration of programs. I served on the board of PPAT twice for three-year terms in 1997 and 2001.

The state removed the cap of 30 people per HCS program and suddenly a flood of people wanted to come to our HCS program. We accepted them as fast as we could, but we were limited by our small infra structure. We had one person in our financial department, the chief financial officer, and my administrative assistant was doing all of the billing. To cope with the influx of clients we hired additional staff members who could serve in the financial area and in the front office as a receptionist.

I remember receiving a call from the state rate-setting department requesting that I serve on a committee formed to restructure the rate process. It was important to me personally because both the provider and advocacy sectors had recommended me. It was important to my agency because we needed a fairer distribution of state money, and I had the experience and knowledge to talk about the cost of caring for the difficult-to-serve population. My acceptance required that I be in Austin for meetings at least monthly. I had hired additional staff in accounting and administration, so I felt comfortable being away from Vita-Living when necessary to serve on this committee as well as the MHMRA committee that met monthly. It took two years of meetings before the state implemented the new rate structure of fee-for-service. If all went well, it meant that for the first time since we opened, Vita-Living should receive a fair rate to serve our clients.

My uncle Howard, who lived in Buffalo, New York, was the only member of my family still living. We talked every week and about four times a year I visited him. He had just turned 95 when he passed away after breaking his hip. One day I picked up the phone to hear a voice introduce himself as my uncle's lawyer from Buffalo who explained that Vita-Living had been mentioned in my uncle's will. We were left $100,000 but there were some problems with the settlement of the estate, so it might be a year or more before we received the check. I had no idea that my uncle would remember the organization I built and rushed to tell Kathy and Mae who were the only ones in the office at the time.

In 1994 we finally received the $100,000 from the estate. I was so elated that all the administrative staff and I celebrated at a lunch where they each received a $1000 check. As a result of the inheritance, we were able to hire a professional fundraiser and I called a headhunter to help us locate the right person. Joy was the first person interviewed and I chose her for the position. Beyond her years of experience as a development director, she had a sister with cerebral palsy. She did advocate successfully for Vita-Living through grant writing and organizing wonderful galas. We raised $75,000 and then $80,000 after expenses at the galas we held the following two years. It looked as if we might be able to put some money aside for our future. I thought about starting a not- for-profit foundation to accrue funds whose interest would go into operations for Vita-Living. I discussed this plan with the lawyer on our board, and he started the process to obtain the (non profit) 501 (c) (3) status for the foundation. We finally received nonprofit status in 1998, formed a board to oversee investments, and hoped we were on our way to a more stable financial position. All money raised through fundraising was to go into the foundation.

The most obvious way to increase our bottom line was to continue bringing more people into the HCS and CLASS programs. The state reviews of both programs continued to be outstanding, and both programs were growing. We now had 60 people in our HCS program and 50 people in our CLASS program.

In 1997 the new rates--based on level of need--came into effect. Vita-Living benefited greatly since we served people with great need. I was giddy with the monies that were being paid to us for the care we were giving. The extra money was subsidizing the tile studio and allowed us to keep the store open even though it was not making money.

1998 and 1999 were easier on the budget, but there were rumors that the state was going to start cutting our funding again, and that's exactly what happened. First the state reduced and then cancelled the recommended increase based on the cost-of-living index; in 2000 the state cut 24 percent from all residential rates. We were still able to maintain the quality in our services but were forced to consider closing the tile studio and the store. Desperately trying to hold the ceramics operation together, I requested help from a group of retired executives who assisted non-profit agencies. They determined that the cost of the ceramics was more than we could recover through our sales so in 2000 we sadly closed our ceramic operation and the store. This was a painful decision for me and for all of those who worked and volunteered with us.

One of the most successful activities our residents participated in was our "Give Back To the Community Program." Those residents who were not working but who were capable of performing useful tasks were asked to help others less fortunate and many volunteered. Staff people worked with the residents to deliver Meals on Wheels through the Jewish Community Center for five years. Annually they were recognized at the Volunteer Appreciation Banquets where they received little gifts for the work they did. For two years residents went to the Christian Community Service Center where they helped stock the shelves in the kitchen and sorted clothes for distribution to the homeless. Occasionally they helped at the Memorial Presbyterian Church on their Serving Others Saturday (SOS) performing whatever tasks were needed.

Families were referred to us when they had children who had been asked to leave other agencies or who had been refused services by other agencies. Two families who had sons difficult to place and who had been asked to leave the last two placements decided they wanted to start a program for them. One of the families owned property with two homes, one large and one small where they wanted the boys to live. They knew that they would have to hire staff to assist them. Both of the boys had mild mental retardation. One had autism and the other had a personality disorder and a chromosomal anomaly. I prepared a proposal outlining a program for them with approximate cost to the families since there was no government funding available to them at that time. After I prepared the proposal and contacted them, I didn't hear from them again that year. This was not that unusual. Many families came to me for help in finding care for their children, but most had no money and, if their children were not eligible for government funding, they could not place them in a program. I was willing to help any family who sincerely wanted to develop something for their child.

A few years later one of the families who had requested a proposal for a program for their son called for a meeting. They explained that the program they had tried to start had not been successful, and their son, Arthur, had just been asked to leave the fourth program he had attended. David knew this young man and explained that he had been sexually abused as a young child. As a result of that abuse, he showed interest in young children and needed to be closely supervised. I thought we could protect him and society from him. Both of Arthur's parents were physicians, and his mother, who had been fighting cancer for the last five years, was not well. We developed a program for Arthur.

He was eligible for HCS funding, so I suggested that his parents purchase and furnish a home for him and two other clients. I also recommended a realtor whom we had used successfully in the past and the name of a financial advisor to help them establish a "special needs trust" for their son. It took six months to purchase and set up the home and obtain the trust. At the end of that time the mother succumbed to cancer just as her son was entering his home.

We worked hard to maintain him in the community. On one of his weekend trips home, his father took him to a cafeteria and left him alone while he went back to the counter. Arthur went to the men's room and approached a young boy. The boy's father brought charges and for the next year Arthur could not go home with his father without one of our staff along. His father hired a lawyer and Arthur avoided jail, but it was three years before he was allowed to go with his father for one day without one of our staff people accompanying them.

In 1992 I had received a call from Kip asking that we serve a particular client, Lucy, who had literally been in—and been asked to leave--every public program and at last two private programs in the state. I told Kip that I would consider it. A few weeks later she called to tell me that Lucy had pulled a toy gun on two policemen who almost killed her thinking the gun was real. As a result she was quickly put into a state school. I forgot about it, but in 1995 we received a call from Lucy's mentor who was serving on the Board of the Texas Mental Health Mental Retardation Department and insisted that she come to Vita-Living. Lucy had been forced to leave the state school and no one in the state would serve her. I knew we could serve her well under certain conditions. " She must receive a level of care that will pay for one-on-one staffing during her awake hours," I said. "In addition she must have a guardian. Lucy has mild mental retardation with a severe personality disorder, so she can't have control of all of the decisions in her life. If she did not have a diagnosis of mental retardation she would most likely be in jail," I told her mentor.

"I understand," her mentor said. Within a week I heard from the state that Lucy had received the level of care that I requested and I heard from her mentor that she had found a guardian for her, Marlene Wood, who had a daughter in our program and was willing to help Lucy.

Dealing with Lucy became a daily problem for me and for my staff. At 5'11" tall and over 200 pounds, with short, cropped hair, Lucy could easily be mistaken for a large man in the dark. She ran away at night and threw rocks at neighbors' windows. She was jailed for shoplifting when she was at a local store with our staff. The jail called us to please pick her up because they could not handle her.

One day I received a call from a neighbor: "You had better do something with that girl or we'll take you to court," the neighbor warned. I was baffled by this situation since I didn't want to ask Lucy to leave, but I also didn't want to lose my program or go to court. I requested that the staff review their records and prepare a chart for me so I could see if there was a pattern in the times and days she ran off. I found that Lucy acted out primarily on the weekends when her schedule changed and she did not have to go to a day program. I called my favorite psychologist and asked if he knew of any program that would work with her on the weekends. He referred me to Birch Farm in the country about 1½ hours away. I called the farm and explained about Lucy, and they were willing to take her.

The director of the HCS program and I visited Birch Farm and were impressed with the surroundings. The residents lived in cottages with large living areas but had their meals in a dining hall and slept in bed-rooms set for four people.

Some of the residents went home on the weekends, and when that happened those beds became available. The grounds were beautiful, with farm animals and rare birds. The aviary was fascinating with songbirds that were not only beautiful to listen to but beautiful to look at. I left there with the desire to offer Lucy an opportunity to come to the farm on the weekends if we could afford it because we'd have to discharge her from our program (so we did not receive payment), but also I had to pay the farm. I thought it over and talked to our financial officer. We decided it was important for Lucy and for Vita-Living that we do what we needed to do to make Lucy realize that there were consequences for her acts. In my mind what we did was another example of creative caring. As nice as Birch Farm looked, they were strict and knew well how to handle difficult behaviors. I thought that taking control away from Lucy was important at this time, so we didn't tell her she was going until just before the time she was to leave. "You have bothered the neighbors by throwing stones at their windows and ringing their doorbells in the middle of the night, and that cannot continue," I told Lucy. "You need some time away from home so you are going to a farm on the weekends. You need to learn how to behave in the neighborhood where you live. The staff at the farm know about your past experiences, and I think they can help you. We will pick you up on Sunday. Kory will drive you. See you on Sunday," I said.

She looked puzzled but said nothing. When they came to a tollbooth Lucy jumped out of the car and sat on the road next to the booth blocking all traffic. Two state patrol officers arrived and told her to get up. She shook her head negatively but looked at their pistols with some anxiety. Finally, with one on each side they lifted her up and placed her in the car, admonishing her to stay there. She did until they reached the farm. On future trips, while Kory drove, Lucy sat in the back seat between two large staff members.

On Sunday I met her when she returned to her home. "How was your stay at the farm?" I asked.

"Do I have to go every weekend? For how long?" She responded.

"It depends on you. We will decide when you go, but I need to be sure that you won't annoy the neighbors before a decision is made that you are to stay home for the weekend. How you want to behave will be up to you, but for now the decision whether you are to go is up to me," I said firmly.

This was the beginning of a change in Lucy's behavior. It took about eight months to gradually reduce the amount of time Lucy spent at the farm on weekends. Finally she was able to stay at home without bothering the neighbors.

A few months later her mother called and thanked us for not giving up on her daughter as everyone else had. This made me feel that what we were doing was worth doing. I remembered that success is one step beyond failure if you stay in the game, and one thing we did well was stay in the game.

I remember receiving a call from the Children's Protective Services (CPS) requesting services for a brother and sister, ages nine and seven. Both of them were HIV positive in addition to having mild retardation. They had been asked to leave all of their foster family placements because of their behaviors. It was essential that a home be found for them. They could not return to their mother who was also HIV positive and found to be an unacceptable parent. The board met to discuss whether we should go out on a limb financially to serve these children. I presented the case that this is what Vita-Living is all about. We needed to provide the home for two children whom no one wanted. We rented a home, outfitted the home with donations, staffed it with trained staff, and saw tremendous improvement within the year. The rate the county paid us for the care of the children was the highest level paid by the agency. At the end of the year both children had improved to such a degree that they were acceptable to foster families and left us. Although the staff was sorry to see them go, we knew they would leave if we did our job well.

The community indicated its appreciation and recognition of Vita-Living through awards to me. I received a Commitment to Quality award from the Irwin Siegel Agency and Private Providers Association, the Houston Leadership Award for the work of Vita-Living for people with developmental disabilities and a "Woman of Influence" award from the National Council of Jewish Women based on the work of Vita-Living as well as the Giraffe award for "sticking my neck out".

I thought about the morning I arrived at the office to hear that our core had been vandalized, all of the tires on the vehicles parked there had been slashed and the computers and some food items had been stolen. All of our vehicles not in use were parked at the core behind a locked fence. In addition the perpetrators had spray painted anti-Semitic remarks on the fence in the backyard. I guessed those slurs were directed at me since I was the only Jewish employee. After calling the police, I contacted Mr. Hart, our board chair. The police took down the information but did nothing to find the culprit. Mr. Hart offered to use his corporation's security department to help us. With their help we found that an employee working at the core was guilty and were able to fire him.

In 1994, Chair of the Board Jim Hart met with me and suggested that I start thinking about a successor. "I'm not ready to even consider another person running Vita-Living," was my immediate response.

" I understand, but it will take time to train someone and it would be good planning for you to look around in your company and in other companies to see if you spot someone that you think might be trained to follow in your footsteps," He replied.

"I will do that but I plan on running Vita-Living as long as I am physically able," was my determined reply.

"When you find someone, I can arrange for one or two people to be tested by a competent psychologist to see if they have the personality to manage an organization such as yours. My company will pick up the cost," he offered.

I returned to my office with a lot to think about, but after thinking about it for a few days I decided to put finding a successor on the back burner. In 2000, the board again brought up the subject of a successor. They insisted that it would be best for Vita-Living to have a younger person in charge while I was still around to help if needed. I was not happy about their decision but agreed that it probably would be best for the agency. The woman who had been working as program director for HCS and CLASS programs was the person I thought might best fill that role. She was completing her doctoral work and had been working with us for the last seven years. We had increased the number of clients to 98 in the HCS program and to 225 in the CLASS program. She performed well in her positions and seemed to want the job so I recommended her to the board. The change over was to occur at the end of 2002, our 20-year anniversary.

I woke up the morning after our big party realizing that my job would disappear in a few months. I had mixed feelings about giving up my "baby" to someone else to care for. I wasn't sure that anyone could direct Vita-Living as well as I could. I suppose my feelings were no different from anyone who starts a project, nourishes and puts their money and energy into that project and then has to give it over to a younger person. I wanted to chair the board but the members of the board thought it best not to have me in that position. They wanted to see if the new Executive Director could run Vita-Living independent of me.

Joy, our development director, retired. Rather than hiring a new development director to write grants and organize fund raising activities, I decided that I would like the job.

So as of January of 2003, there was a new executive director for Vita-Living and a new job for me. I hired a part-time grant writer and advisor on fund raising activities and a part-time assistant for me. I took a course that helped me with ideas for raising money aside from just galas. I decided to try interesting people in Vita-Living by means of tours of the first small community residence licensed in Texas to serve people with severe mental retardation, the Beechnut House. The tours lasted only one hour always followed by a personal call to see if our story had affected the visitors. If they showed interest we asked them to bring other people to tours and also to host a table of 10 for the annual "ask" event. The event was a lunch or breakfast that lasted only one hour. Two families talked for three minutes each about how Vita-Living changed their lives, and we showed a five-minute video written and produced by Melanie. There were no charges for the meal and no asking for money until the end when we requested that if our stories moved them, they make a five year pledge or donation. We stressed how grateful we were for the gift of their time and, we hoped, their donations. At the breakfast during my first year as executive director of the foundation, we raised $270,000 in pledges and cash. "I can't believe that this really worked," I told Andy when I reported on the event. The new executive director of Vita-Living, Inc. was having difficulty finding time to complete her doctoral dissertation and run Vita-living so she decided to leave at the end of 2003 to complete her work toward her degree.

I moved back into the position of executive director of Vita-Living and continued as executive director of the foundation. We started a search for a new executive director and by October found David Leatham, who was offered and accepted the top position at Vita-Living, Inc. He had a masters in social work, over 20 years of experience working with people with mental retardation, and ran a program similar to ours in a neighboring county. I continued in my position at the foundation and was happy that David Leatham could handle the pressures of running the agency I birthed.

Larry Kryske wrote in *The Churchill Factors* that, "there is a special time in each person's life when all of his or her past preparations became perfectly aligned with some significant opportunity." I believe that happened to me the night Stan and I sat at the kitchen table and talked about starting something that had never been done in Texas. I was lucky that I had the time, energy, and resources to pursue this venture for over 20 years. I now feel comfortable that Vita-Living is in good hands and can continue our good work for the next 20 years to come.

GLOSSARY

Angelman syndrome is a neuro-genetic disorder characterized by intellectual and developmental delay, sleep disturbance, seizures, jerky movements––especially hand-flapping frequent laughter or smiling, and usually a happy demeanor.

Anoxic brain syndrome is caused by a lack of oxygen going to the brain There are two categories of brain injuries that deprive oxygen to the brain; *traumatic,* that which occurs outside of the body such as trauma to the head and *acquired,* that which occurs inside the body such as tumors.

Bilateral hip displasia describes unstable or dislocated hips and poorly developed acetabula (the sockets of the hip joints) in both hip joints.

Cerebral palsy describes a group of permanent movement and posture disorders that limit and that are attributed to non-progressive disturbances that occurred in the developing or infant brain.

Cri-du-chat syndrome (cry of the cat), named for the characteristic cry of affected infants that is similar to a mewing kitten, is a rare genetic disorder caused by a missing part of chromosome 5.

Down Syndrome, sometimes called trisomy 21, is a chromosomal disorder caused by presence of all or part of an extra 21st chromosome.

Esotropia: It is a form of strabismus or "squint" in which one or both eyes turn inward so the person looks cross-eyed.

Fragile X is a family of genetic conditions caused by changes in the FMR1 gene. Fragile X is a common cause of autism. Symptoms can range from learning disabilities to more severe cognitive or intellectual disabilities.

Gastrostomy refers to surgically creating an opening to the stomach for nutritional support or gastrointestinal compression.

Intellectual developmental disability or IDD: is the currently accepted term for what used to be termed mental retardation or MR.

Lelsz lawsuit was a class action lawsuit, Lelsz v. Kavanagh, filed against MHMR in Texas in federal district court in 1974, that addressed alleged abuse of those with mental retardation in Texas state schools. In 1983, the parties signed a resolution and settlement, which focused on services and conditions in three named schools (Austin, Denton, and Fort Worth state schools) and emphasized the least restrictive residential services for class members. In June 1985, the judge in the case ordered that 279 persons from the named state schools had to be moved to community residences by August 31, 1986.

Microcephaly describes a neuro-developmental disorder in which the circumference of the head is more than two standard deviations smaller than average for the person's age and sex.

Muscular dystrophy refers to a group of genetic, hereditary muscle diseases that are characterized by progressive skeletal muscle weakness, defective muscle proteins, and death of muscle cells and tissue.

Opisthotonus describes severe hypertension and spasticity in which an individual's head, neck, and spinal column arch backward toward the heels.

Paraplegia describes impairment of motor and sensory function of lower extremities, most typically paralysis from spinal injury.

Quadraplegia describes loss of sensation and mobility in both upper and lower body.

Respiratory disorder describes any disease affecting respiratory system.

Rett syndrome is a neuro-developmental disorder classified as an autism spectrum disorder that occurs almost exclusively in females. It was diagnosed by pediatrician Andreas Rett in 1966 and is characterized by small head, hands and feet and no verbal skills.

Seizure disorder refers to periodic disturbances in the brain's electrical activity, resulting in some degree of temporary brain dysfunction. Epilepsy is a recurrent seizure disorder.

Spastic quadraplegia occurs when all four limbs are affected with increased tone, decreased movements, and brisk reflexes. It is frequently associated with mental retardation, visual problems, and hearing impairment.

Spina bifida is a developmental birth defect caused by an incomplete closure of the embryonic neural tube (spinal column).

The Arc, founded in 1953, is the world's largest community based organization that promotes and improves supports and services for people with intellectual and developmental disabilities and their families. It includes over 140,000 members affiliated through more than 780 state and local chapters across the nation. Originally the National Association for Retarded Children, the organization's name changed in 1973 to the National Association of Retarded Citizens (ARC), in 1981 to the Association for Retarded Citizens of the United States, and in 1982 simply to the Arc.

Tuberous sclerosis is a rare, multi-system genetic disease that causes benign tumors to grow in the brain and on other vital organs such as the kidneys, heart, eyes, lungs and skin.

Walker Warhburg syndrome is a rare form of autosomal recessive congenital muscular dystrophy associated with brain (hydrocephalus) and eye abnormalities.